D0034675

CAN INTERVENTION WORK?

AMNESTY INTERNATIONAL GLOBAL ETHICS SERIES

General Editor: Kwame Anthony Appiah

In December 1948, the UN General Assembly adopted the United Nations Declaration of Human Rights and thereby created the fundamental framework within which the human rights movement operates. That declaration—and the various human rights treaties, declarations, and conventions that have followed—are given life by those citizens of all nations who struggle to make reality match those noble ideals.

The work of defending our human rights is carried on not only by formal national and international courts and commissions but also by the vibrant transnational community of human rights organizations, among which Amnesty International has a leading place. Fifty years on, Amnesty has more than two million members, supporters, and subscribers in 150 countries, committed to campaigning for the betterment of peoples across the globe.

Effective advocacy requires us to use our minds as well as our hearts; and both our minds and our hearts require a global discussion. We need thoughtful, cosmopolitan conversation about the many challenges facing our species, from climate control to corporate social responsibility. It is that conversation that the Amnesty International Global Ethics Series aims to advance. Written by distinguished scholars and writers, these short books distill some of the most vexing issues of our time down to their clearest and most compelling essences. Our hope is that this series will broaden the set of issues taken up by the human rights community while offering readers fresh new ways of thinking and problem-solving, leading ultimately to creative new forms of advocacy.

FORTHCOMING AUTHORS:
Richard Thompson Ford
Jonathan Wolff
John Broome
Sheila Jasanoff
Martha Minow
Philip Pettit
John Ruggie

CAN INTERVENTION WORK?

Rory Stewart
Gerald Knaus

W. W. NORTON & COMPANY

NEW YORK LONDON

Copyright © 2011 by Rory Stewart and Gerald Knaus

All rights reserved
Printed in the United States of America
First Edition

For information about permission to reproduce selections from this book,
write to Permissions, W. W. Norton & Company, Inc.,
500 Fifth Avenue, New York, NY 10110

For information about special discounts for bulk purchases, please contact
W. W. Norton Special Sales at specialsales@wwnorton.com or 800-233-4830

Manufacturing by Courier Westford
Book design by Iris Weinstein
Production manager: Devon Zahn

Library of Congress Cataloging-in-Publication Data

Stewart, Rory.
Can intervention work? / Rory Stewart, Gerald Knaus. — 1st ed.
p. cm. — (Amnesty international global ethics series)
Includes bibliographical references.
ISBN 978-0-393-08120-6 (hardcover)
1. Intervention (International law) 2. Intervention
(International law)—Case studies. I. Knaus, Gerald. II. Title.
JZ6368.S76 2011
327.1'17—dc23
                                            2011024887

W. W. Norton & Company, Inc.
500 Fifth Avenue, New York, N.Y. 10110
www.wwnorton.com

W. W. Norton & Company Ltd.
Castle House, 75/76 Wells Street, London W1T 3QT

1 2 3 4 5 6 7 8 9 0

CONTENTS

INTRODUCTION

INTERVENTION

For twenty years, intervention has been the most extravagant and noble, ambitious and dangerous element of Western foreign policy. The U.S. government has spent over three trillion dollars; more than a million soldiers have been deployed from over sixty countries. Many lives were saved in Bosnia through intervention; many lives were lost in Iraq through intervention. The Iraq intervention brought a million demonstrators into the streets of normally quiescent London, enflamed the suspicion and anger of hundreds of millions of Muslims, and toppled a European government. Intervention transformed the training, doctrine, and reputation of the wealthiest and most powerful military in the world. It took the United States, the United Nations, and the United Kingdom to a new pinnacle of international reputation and confidence and then heaved them into a humiliating mess.

Over the last two decades, intervention has been described, explained, and criticized by political philosophers, civil servants, human rights activists, journalists, development workers, film-makers, and ten thousand consultants. Parliamentarians from Edinburgh to Rio now refer confidently to the "Chapter VII resolutions," "no-fly zones," "the experience of the Kurds," and "the responsibility to protect." But the basic questions about intervention remain unresolved. People who cannot name four cities in Libya can deploy four arguments against or for an intervention there. These are the same arguments that crippled our response to Bosnia and Rwanda, emboldened us in Kosovo, and drew us deeper into the indignities of Iraq and Afghanistan. They were used in the 1960s for Vietnam, the 1920s for Mesopotamia, and the 1860s for Afghanistan. And they still provide little help in understanding those actions which we dub, so euphemistically, "intervention."

Intervention--from the Latin *intervenire*, means roughly "to come between." *Inter*/between does not reveal where you are, who or what is around or beside you, or the nature of your relationship with these people and things.[1] Often, the word has a neutral sense of just being somewhere (as in the word *interspersed*) or of bringing things closer together (as in *interweave* or *interconnect*). The other half of the word intervention—*venire*—doubles the ambiguity. It is not clear how you are coming: running, walking, or driving in a Humvee. But when *come* is attached to a preposition (such as *come between* or *come across* or *come by*), it often carries a sense of arriving accidentally.[2] And in its basic form *come here—come* implies welcome, an invitation from the person toward whom you are moving.

There are other words with which we could have defined our

advents and adventures in Kosovo and Iraq. We could have said we had simply *gone in*—using the Latin-derived word *invaded*. Or if we wanted to convey the sense of not simply being *in there* but *between*, we could have specified the action with the Latin words for *act between* or *go between*, *place between*, *throw between*, *speak between*, *break between*, or *strike between*: *interact*, *intercede*, *interpose*, *interject*, *interdict*, *interrupt*, *interfere*. But just as we don't call ourselves invaders, so too we don't call ourselves inter- ferers or interlopers.[3] Instead, we choose to cloak our action in a Latin word, which, even if translated, admits to nothing more than coming into a new relationship. It is silent on our right to be there, on whom we are meeting, on what exactly we are doing. But it implies that our movement may be gentle, driven by force of circumstance, and welcome.

But in truth, when we intervene we are there neither by invitation nor by accident. We are not passively present. We advance soldiers and we drop bombs and we fight to separate different parties. We have chosen to go in against the wishes of the sovereign government.[4] In short, we are not just interven- ers, not just "coming betweeners," we are also interlopers and interferers.

The two essays on intervention in this book emerge from a course and a study group that we each respectively led at the Harvard Kennedy School in 2010–11. But they are not academic essays on intervention—such as are written by lawyers, philoso- phers, human rights activists, and professors of international relations. We are not trying to debate the *jus ad bellum* and the *jus in bello* with the schoolmen, or challenge the think tanks with a statistical analysis of two hundred years of interventions and charts derived from the Tsarist Russian operations in Bul- garia in 1877 and the Americans in Haiti before the First World War; nor are we offering a legal interpretation of Chapter VII of the UN charter. We do not engage with the Marxists who criticize intervention as a form of economic colonialism and as a thin pretext for strategic bases, or the old conservatives who portray it as an illegal and dangerous challenge to the "Westphalian system." These are all important perspectives, but they are not the purpose of these essays.

Nor do these essays focus on the ethics of intervention. We both agree that there are certain occasions—such as genocide—that can justify an international intervention: that such horror can impose a form of duty on "the international community," and that state sovereignty need not confer total immunity. There may be countries that are too powerful to be tackled (China, for example), but this does not excuse non-intervention in East Timor. We agree with the philosopher Michael Walzer that there are occasions when the international community should remain for as little time as possible after an intervention, not to create a democratic, pluralist, liberal, or (even) capitalist government, simply a non-murderous government; but that in cases of mass extermination (such as in Cambodia), deep and enduring ethnic tension (such as in Rwanda), or total state failure, there is a case for the interveners not to leave too rapidly.[5] In other words, we accept the basic intuitions of many interveners around the world, and a worldview that seems to permit, for example, the intervention in Kosovo, even without the full legal sanction of the UN Security Council, and provides an account of our presence in East Timor and Cambodia. And we are comfortable with Bill Clinton's motto from 1995:

> We cannot stop all war for all time but we can stop some wars. We cannot save all women and all children but we can save many of them. We can't do everything but we must do what we can.[6]

Our aim is to understand, not as academics, but as participants in the interventions of the last twenty years, what makes
interventions work and fail.[7] In these essays we are not interested in whether we have an abstract moral right or even duty
to intervene, but whether and how to intervene in a particular
country at a particular time. This is a practical question which
rarely interests philosophers.[8] Perhaps they feel it is not their
subject. Perhaps it seems inconceivable that there is any war that
we couldn't win, provided we invested enough time and money.
Or perhaps—as the philosopher Bernard Williams suggested[9]—
there is something in the nature of ethics, its inheritance from
Kant, that makes it very difficult to incorporate practical ideas
of success, of context, and of luck into moral judgments.[10] Whatever the reason, the philosophers' arguments, about our moral
obligations and on our theoretical interests, have not prevented
our grand failures. The question of whether and how to intervene in Libya or Afghanistan is not fundamentally a question
of moral philosophy. It is not a question of what we ought to do
but what we can: of understanding the limits of Western institutions in the twenty-first century and of giving a credible account
of the specific context of a particular intervention. Hence, our
unapologetic focus on narrative—on the history of events, decisions, and individuals.

We have firm opinions on which interventions worked and
which didn't. Others will disagree. Some, for example, today
believe that Bosnia is teetering on the edge of collapse; others
argue that Kosovo was an illegal, reckless, and unnecessary
action. Some believe that the decision to invade Iraq will be
vindicated by history; others that it became a success with the
"surge" of 2006. Many believe that the problems in Afghanistan
were caused by "the light footprint" of 2001, that the deployment of more international troops was essential, that it may still

redeem the situation—and if it doesn't, it will be only because they came too late. We disagree with all these views. Both these essays assume that Bosnia and Kosovo were successes; that Iraq was from the very outset a humiliating mess; and that Afghanistan slowly became a failure. We do not have the space in these essays to argue against the contrary views.

Each of these essays is driven by the contrast between our particular experiences on the ground and the rhetoric of "the international community" (shorthand for the foreign institutions and individuals involved in an intervention, applied, often confusingly, to everything from the United Nations to non-governmental organizations and the U.S. military). Gerald began his career in Bulgaria in 1994, moved to Bosnia in 1996, and has continued to work in the region for the last fifteen years. The dominant international theory in Bosnia was that success had been due to a large foreign troop presence; that Bosnia was weakened by the international failure to confront war criminals and militias early and decisively; that it was endangered by elections held too early; that it was saved by charismatic foreign nation-builders with clear plans and almost limitless power; and that it is still dangerous. This theory had a decisive influence on the way the West has conducted interventions from Afghanistan to Iraq.

But Gerald's work in international organizations in Bosnia and Kosovo and his research as the director of an independent think tank (the European Stability Initiative, or ESI) convinced him that this theory of what did or did not work in Bosnia was misleading. ESI's detailed research revealed the surprising ignorance of the international institutions about the environment in which they operated, and highlighted the unintended consequences of their actions.[11] Some of his essays, such as one which argued that successive High Representatives in Bosnia had established a regime of enlightened despotism similar to that of utilitarian imperialists in nineteenth-century India—in Gerald's words "a European Raj"—created controversy.[12] His research ultimately convinced him that many of the lessons of Bosnia were almost exactly the reverse of those apparently "learned" by "the international community." The role of foreign troops in 1996 had been misunderstood—and what has often been perceived as their weakness, paid off. There were also positive effects of holding early elections. Delaying the confrontation with war criminals and allowing them to contest elections (while simultaneously strengthening the international war crimes tribunal) was surprisingly effective. The unlimited powers of international administrators soon created more problems than they solved. The most important institution in stabilizing the Balkans turned out to be one that was long considered one of the least impressive: the International Criminal Tribunal for the Former Yugoslavia (ICTY). And despite the pessimistic prophecies of some foreign analysts, Bosnia has been secure since 2000. Thus, Gerald concludes Bosnia was a success, but not for the reasons given by much of the international community.

Rory's first foreign posting, as a young British diplomat, was in Indonesia, and finished with the referendum for independence in East Timor in 1999. His second was in the Balkans, where he was convinced that the international community should have intervened earlier in Bosnia and that the Kosovo intervention had done some good. He still had a positive impression of intervention when he traveled through Afghanistan in 2002. But when he was posted to Iraq, his view changed. He arrived believing that the U.S.-led coalition could create a more stable, prosperous Iraq, but he soon realized that he was wrong: it should never have invaded. He returned to Kabul in 2005, convinced that the West should not send more troops to

Afghanistan, and found it very difficult to persuade anyone of this.

Rory has sought to describe how he and others were so wrong about Iraq, and why still others persisted in getting it so wrong in Afghanistan. Why had he—and others—been convinced that such interventions could work? Why did it take so long to acknowledge that they could not? Why did it take so long to withdraw? And what did this suggest about how we should do these things in the future?

Gerald's essay, therefore, is about a triumph misdescribed and misunderstood; Rory's is a story of failure, of a failure to acknowledge failure, and of the dangerous belief that failure is not an option. One essay explains how we got intervention right; the other, why we so often get intervention wrong. These different accounts reflect different temperaments, prose styles, backgrounds, education, and experiences. Rory warns against the almost irresistible—mesmerizing—pressures that lead to doomed and humiliating over-intervention; Gerald carefully records how international institutions misinterpreted an intervention which nevertheless worked.

Given these different perspectives, how could we teach together, still less write a book together? The answer is that these essays, which have their roots in our common experience of the Balkans and were developed through joint research at Harvard, ultimately reflect a single worldview. We both believe that it is possible to walk the tightrope between the horrors of over-intervention and nonintervention; that there is still a possibility of avoiding the horrors not only of Iraq but also of Rwanda; and that there is a way of approaching intervention that can be good for us and good for the country concerned.

THE DOMINANT POSITIONS FOR AND AGAINST INTERVENTION

Some people, of course, argue that one should never intervene. A few believe that states should be entirely free to do whatever they wish within their own borders. But more commonly the arguments against intervention are prudential. They are neatly listed by Professor Albert Hirschman as arguments from "jeopardy," "futility," and "perversity": an intervention will be dangerous (for the West or for the locals), or it will achieve nothing, or it will achieve exactly the reverse of what it intended (that is, create a more dangerous and unfriendly regime).[13] Such arguments can be bolstered by the language of medicine or commerce ("first do no harm," "it's none of our business," "we're broke"). Or even culture. Thus the Irish public intellectual Conor Cruise O'Brien said in 1992, "There are places where a lot of men prefer war, and the looting and raping and domineering that go with it, to any sort of peacetime occupation. One such place is Afghanistan. Another is Yugoslavia after the collapse."[14] These arguments ignore not only the strong moral and instrumental justifications for intervention but also the fact that intervention has in the past worked well: most notably (but not only, Gerald argues) in former Yugoslavia.

Our essays, therefore, are directed not against intervention, per se, but against two theories which seek to offer a universal formula for success in intervention. They are "the planning school" (epitomized by RAND Corporation's *Beginner's Guide to Nation-Building*), which prescribes a clear strategy, metrics, and structure, backed by overwhelming resources; and, second, "the liberal imperialist school" (epitomized by Paddy Ashdown, the High Representative in Bosnia), which emphasizes the importance of decisive, bold, and charismatic leadership. Each derives from and shares the language of business and military strategy. Each proposes a clear, confident, and unambiguous recipe for success in intervention.

Liberal imperialists in particular like to portray the country into which they intervene as terrifying and tragic: a rogue state, a failed state, a threat to its neighbors or a threat to our credibility. It is a place where "failure is not an option." They generally claim that the cause of this tragedy is "ungoverned space": ravaged by destructive indigenous forces (extremists, militias, corrupt governments) and shattered by predatory neighbors and international neglect. They assert that the end to this tragedy lies in "governance," "the rule of law," and the other elements of a state. And that there is a path to this end through a decisive and well-planned international intervention (with generous resources, a coherent strategy, coordination, staffing, communication, accountability, research, defined processes, and clear priorities).[15]

Both schools are deeply optimistic. But they are not optimistic about local capacity: the local population is often portrayed in a negative light—as criminals or victims. Instead, they are optimistic about "the international community" and its ability to measure, quantify, or define the problems; its ability to make informed plans, predictions, and decisions; and its power and capacity to implement successful programs. "The international community" is assumed to be highly likely to succeed, provided only that it has the right strategy, resources, and confidence. In the words of an eminent British general, intervention "is doable if we get the formula right and it is properly resourced."[16]

The credit for any success is, therefore, given to the heroic foreign intervener. Thus when in Iraq the deployment of more troops around Baghdad was followed by a decrease in violence, a strong causal connection was made. The drop in violence, according to the international community, was the result almost entirely of the foreign surge: not the internal features of the Iraqi government, Iraqi politics, or the region.

The international community is generally less willing to take responsibility for failure. Thus, in Afghanistan, when the deployment of more troops into Helmand Province in 2006 was followed by a spike in the number of insurgent attacks, no causal connection was made. The insurgency, according to the international community, had apparently not been caused by the foreign surge: instead it had been caused almost entirely by the corrupt Afghan government, fragmented Afghan politics, and provocation from the region, particularly Pakistan.

PRINCIPLED INCREMENTALISM / PASSIONATE MODERATION

Our two essays reject the models of heroic international planners and heroic international leaders on the grounds that they rest on a mistaken view of "the international community" and its interaction with local society. We argue that the foreigners who comprise "the international community" are usually much weaker than they imagine. They are inevitably isolated from local society, ignorant of local culture and context, and prey to misleading abstract theories. "The international community" often lacks legitimacy and local support because it is amorphous, unelected, and foreign (although the degree to which these institutions are perceived as foreign can depend on the context). Local political leaders are often far more competent and powerful than the foreigners think. Local institutions are far more resilient than the international theories (which treat post-conflict societies as blank slates) suggest. Local and regional factors tend to be far more important determinants of success than foreign analysts acknowledge. International attempts to impose foreign will through overwhelming force—or ever more absolute legal powers—tend to make the situation worse not better.

All interventions are intrinsically unpredictable, chaotic, and uncertain and will rapidly confound well-laid plans and careful predictions. The uncertainty in intervention is much more profound than the uncertainty in domestic policy (and the kinds of uncertainty which "business/management" models were designed to address). The Federal Reserve has difficulty predicting the consequences of a 0.5 percent rise in interest rates, even though thousands of civil servants have performed such relatively minor adjustments many times before, in a highly stable society and with the benefit of a century's worth of data. But an intervener has none of those benefits of stability, trained staff, or data, and the changes that they attempt to implement are far more profound. No one can predict what will happen in an intervention in which foreign armies topple a head of state, or turn society on its head.[17]

The international institutions that are part of the intervention are burdened and often crippled by the inherent problems of any bureaucratic institution in a foreign country.[18] At home, mechanisms exist to prevent civil servants from wasting public money and ignoring citizens. Politicians cut budgets and set up inspections and performance indicators; the media and civil society criticize; and the electorate can dismiss the government. Not so in an intervention, where the international community is often awash with money and lacks the time to develop a complex system of inspections or performance indicators, and where there is neither robust civil society nor media, nor fair elections to encourage accountability. International organizations whose legitimacy rests on their supposed superior knowledge of what is good for a society, and how to achieve it, also find it hard to admit to any mistakes.[19] In the twenty-first century, as Rory argues, these problems are exacerbated by the extreme isolation of international lives, their surreal optimism, and their abstract jargon.

As Gerald argues, the international policy-makers seem often unable to recognize or use the real strengths in local society and, therefore, are reluctant to delegate. They underestimate the intelligence and competence of local politicians and over-look their ability to compromise with their armed opponents. A sustained intervention, therefore, often prevents local leaders from taking responsibility; it does not put pressure on politi-cians to settle with their enemies, or broaden the kinds of deals they could offer. Instead, it sometimes strengthens the legiti-macy and popularity of insurgents.

Interventions are crippled by the political aims of the inter-vening governments, which change continually. In Iraq and Afghanistan, the goals lurched from toppling the old regime and leaving; to nation-building; to improving security through a surge; and then back to withdrawal. Sometimes all of these views exist simultaneously, as Richard Holbrooke, the U.S. diplomatist, later observed about Vietnam, the Balkans, and Afghanistan: "People sit in a room, they don't air their real dif-ferences, a false and sloppy consensus papers over those under-lying differences, and they go back to their offices and continue to work at cross-purposes, even actively undermining each other."[20] The problem is not that interveners adapt objectives in the light of changing conditions, which would be a good thing: they change their priorities independently of the local context.

International policy-makers have rarely articulated consistent views on how the security and interests of the West relate to the interests and rights of Iraqis, Yugoslavs, or Afghans (when they managed to do so in the Balkans after 1999, holding out a credible vision of a future integration of all Balkan states into the European Union, they dramatically increased their influence).[21] They lurch from a narrow to a broad definition of democracy, from an idea of democracy as elections to an idea of democracy as a liberal, stable, human rights–respecting, Western-friendly state. They then appear surprised that a simply elected government has none of the qualities of a "thick" established democracy. International policy-makers always have a muddled and half-understood picture of the country before intervention, perhaps an equally muddled and half-understood picture of their own society in the West, and some generally doubtful guesses about how to get from one to the other.

Finally, an intervention is not simply inherently unpredictable or chaotic—it includes dangers that would be unimaginable in a domestic context or in another sphere of life. Of these, the greatest is a widespread insurgency. In Kosovo, as in East Timor, Bosnia, and Sierra Leone, the local populations have mostly assumed that our failures were due to incompetence rather than malice. In Iraq, however, the population was not prepared to give us the benefit of the doubt. Many Iraqis assumed we had come to steal the oil, crush a potential rival, or stamp on Islam and Arabia. Twice in 2005, eighty to ninety percent of the voters in southern Iraq elected Islamist parties that had an anti-Western agenda, implemented conservative social codes, and kept armed militias. Most of the population disliked the U.S.-led coalition simply because it was the U.S.-led coalition. Neither development projects nor more flexible infantry tactics were going to turn that around.

All these factors contort and corrode the goals of the intervening powers. "The international community" ends by oscillating between exaggerated fears and an inflated sense of its own power, between paranoia and megalomania, reflecting in its lurches its half-conscious insecurity about its lack of power, knowledge, certainty, and legitimacy. Being unwilling to acknowledge the absurdity of heroic international plans and leadership, "the international community" perpetuates a misleading picture of the crisis, its causes, its solution, and the path to its solution.

Western politicians, diplomats, generals, and "policy-makers" traditionally describe the countries into which they intervene as the quintessence of terror and tragedy, a unique existential threat, or an inescapable obligation. This is true not simply of terrorism in Afghanistan or weapons of mass destruction in Iraq, but even of Balkan organized crime—which was presented as a vast global threat despite all evidence to the contrary. Such fears are almost always exaggerated: the country is only one obligation, and one interest among many, that must be balanced against other obligations and interests around the world. And neither Vietnam, nor Iraq, nor Afghanistan ever justified or required such an extravagant investment of money, lives, troops, and time. The causes of crisis are not, as the policy-makers assume, the result of universal structural flaws, blank "ungoverned" space, and helpless victims, but are instead specific to a particular place and time. Even the poorest, most fragile and traumatized nations—such as postwar Kosovo or even more dramatically Afghanistan—are densely patterned with functioning local forms of security, administration, and dispute resolution. These predated the crisis, continue to support communities, and will provide some of the solutions. Not all power-holders should be regarded by the international community as extremists or criminals, nor all citizens as helpless victims. Not every opposition to an international scheme is unforgivable

obstruction. And although there will be many long-term problems in a poor developing country at war—such as unemploy-
ment, poor education, or weak service delivery—these will not
be the prime cause of the conflict. The crisis will tend to be the
result of contingent short-term factors rather than the inevitable
doom or destiny of a particular culture or nation.

Finally—and this is the most difficult truth for the international
policy-makers to accept—intervention cannot always offer an end
to suffering. A modern intervener does not have the power, the
knowledge, or the legitimacy to "eliminate all the root causes
of conflict," let alone fundamentally reshape the structures and
cultural identity of a foreign land. Instead, intervention should
aim to provide protection and relief at a specific time and place.
And even such limited ambitions can often be defeated by a situation which is intrinsically unpredictable. No crisis is fixed or
permanent. But there are crises that "the international community" cannot address. Failure—however horrible—will always be
a possibility: an option.

Neither state-building, nor counterinsurgency, nor "inputs,"
nor leadership, nor any other formula, fixed theory, or doctrine
can therefore guarantee success. RAND's proposal that there
is a standard formula that can generate a fixed proportion of
troops, police, and money for a "hypothetical country with a
population of 5 million"[22] is absurd. The important questions
cannot be framed in hypotheses because they are "Which country exactly? And when? And why? And who?"

These essays recommend a theory of intervention, which
Gerald calls "principled incrementalism" and Rory, "passionate
moderation." Intervention in our view is not a scientific method
but a practical activity with a humanitarian purpose. Moral philosophy, theoretical models based on previous endeavors, and
heroic leadership are only small—perhaps the smallest—parts

of such an activity. The activity is inherently dangerous and uncertain. We believe success is dependent on the exact location and nature of the crisis and the capacity of the interveners (which is always limited) and the role of neighbors, the regional context, and local leadership (which is always more influential than is assumed).

Our experience suggests the following rules of thumb: that interveners must distinguish brutally between the factors they can control, the dangers they can avoid, and the dangers they can neither control nor avoid (whether permanent features of the place or specific to the crisis). An outsider can—indeed, should—provide generous resources, manpower, equipment, encouragement, and support. Courage, thought, and pre-planning are relevant. But they are not enough on their own. The best way of minimizing the danger of any intervention is to proceed carefully, to invest heavily in finding out about the specific context, particularly after the intervention, and to define concrete and not abstract goals. Power and authority must be given to local leadership through elections as soon as possible. Only local leaders have the necessary ingredient of knowing the situation well, over many years and in all kinds of conditions; only they can get around the dangers that cannot be avoided, and skillfully respond to them. Local leaders who are appointed by foreigners, rather than elected, will find it very hard to assume responsibility. The person intervening should not be so obsessive or neurotic about the activity as to ignore the signs that the intervention has become too dangerous, or the mission impossible, and that it is time to regroup, pause, or even withdraw.

Since intervention is a techne—to take a grand term from Aristotle—or, in more normal language, an art not a science, such advice will always seem underwhelming. Just as the military principle that "time spent in reconnaissance is seldom wasted" is seen by soldiers as an insight of great life-saving wisdom, but by a civilian as a glimpse of the blindingly obvious, so too advice on intervention. Few would have any theoretical disagreements with our recommendations. Even fewer would be surprised by them. The challenge is not to lay out the principles; it is to convey just how rarely they are implemented and why, how much damage has been done through ignoring them, and how difficult they are to uphold.

The difficulty is to show people how intervention—with its elaborate theory, intricate rituals, astonishing sacrifices and expenditure; its courage and grandeur and fantasy—can often resemble the religion of the Aztecs or the Soviet invasion of Afghanistan; to show how bad intervention can be: how far more absurd, rotten, counterproductive than any satirist could suggest or caricaturist portray. And that even when all the leaders have recognized that a policy is not working, how impossible it often seems for them to organize withdrawal.

An incremental approach may seem simply common sense. But overconfident policy-makers continue to be seduced repeatedly by the belief in the magic powers of planning, resources, and charismatic leadership. Intervention may be a necessary, indispensable ingredient of the international system. It is certainly capable, as in the Balkans, of doing good. And yet how easily it falls into excess. This is why the ultimate focus of these essays is on the particular context, temptations, predilections, and neuroses of twenty-first-century interveners. Rory's essay focuses exclusively on Afghanistan; Gerald's largely on Bosnia. But we hope they carry broader lessons because these essays aim to offer not an anthropology of the country into which the West is intervening, but an anthropology of the West—an anthropology of ourselves.

THE PLANE TO KABUL

Rory Stewart

TIME LINE

1839 First Anglo-Afghan War: Britain invades Afghanistan and installs Shah Shujah as king.

1841 British envoy Burnes is killed in Kabul, and his body is paraded through the streets.

1842 British retreat from Afghanistan: army of 16,000 is wiped out. British reinvade, burn Kabul bazaar, but then decide not to remain and instead depart, leaving their erstwhile opponent Dost Muhammed in place as ruler.

1857 Indian insurgency against British rule ("the mutiny") occurs. (John Lawrence is in Punjab.)

1867 Sir Henry Rawlinson and others press for Britain to reinvade Afghanistan. (Lawrence argues against and prevents the invasion.)

1878 Second Anglo-Afghan War: Britain invades.

1879 British envoy Cavagnari is killed in Kabul. Britain reinvades. One British force is destroyed in the Battle of Maiwand. General Roberts holds Kabul and relieves Kandahar, but then the British decide not to remain and instead depart, leaving their erstwhile opponent, Abdur Rahman Khan, in place as ruler.

1916 Britain invades Mesopotamia (Iraq).

1920 An uprising against the British occurs in Iraq. (Gertrude Bell is in Baghdad.)

1933 Zahir Shah becomes king, and Afghanistan remains a monarchy for the next four decades.

1973 Mohammed Daud (Zahir Shah's cousin) seizes power in a coup and declares a republic.

1978 April 28: General Daud is killed in a coup by the leftist People's Democratic Party. Nur Mohammed Taraki becomes president.

1979	September 14: Nur Mohammed Taraki is killed and replaced as president by Hafizullah Amin.
	December 27: Amin is killed by special forces from the Soviet Union.
1980	Soviet Occupation: Babrak Karmal becomes president. Various mujahideen groups fight Soviet forces; the United States, Pakistan, China, Iran, and Saudi Arabia supply money and arms.
1986	Babrak Karmal is replaced by Najibullah as head of the Soviet-backed regime.
1989	The last Soviet troops leave, leaving Najibullah in place as ruler.
1991	The Soviet Union stops aid to Najibullah.
1992	Najibullah is toppled. Civil war begins between mujahideen leaders.
1993	Rival mujahideen factions shell each other (including Hekmatyar) in Kabul.
1996	Taliban seize control of Kabul.
2001	Sir Michael Jay, head of the UK Foreign Office, revises management policies and removes foreign-language fluency and area expertise as criteria for promotion for diplomats.
	October: The United States and Britain launch air strikes against Afghanistan after Taliban refuse to hand over Osama bin Laden, after the September 11 attacks on America.
	November: Opposition forces seize Mazar-e Sharif, then Kabul.
	December 22: Hamid Karzai is sworn in as head of a thirty-member interim power-sharing government.
2002	General Karl Eikenberry is serving in Afghanistan. (Rory is walking across Afghanistan.)
	UN meeting in Kabul explores Afghan consensus to create a "centralized state based on democracy."
2003	U.S.-led coalition invades Iraq. (Rory serves as deputy governorate coordinator of two provinces in Marsh Arab region of Southern Iraq.)
	General Dan McNeill becomes ISAF commander in Afghanistan.

August: NATO takes control of security in Kabul, its first-ever operational commitment outside Europe.

2004　General David Barno succeeds McNeill as ISAF commander in Afghanistan.

April: Under guidance of Ashraf Ghani, seven hundred delegates from fifty-two countries meet in Berlin at a conference entitled "Sustaining Afghanistan's Future." Afghanistan secures $8.2 billion (£4.5 billion) in aid over three years.

August: American soldiers target militias, including "army" led by Ahmad Morghabi in Ghor Province.

2005　Eikenberry returns as ISAF commander.

September: First parliamentary and provincial elections are held after more than thirty years. (Rory returns to Kabul to set up NGO "Turquoise Mountain" and remains until 2008.)

2006　New ISAF commander General Sir David Richards increases troop levels to 18,500 soldiers from thirty-seven countries.

British government sends 3,000 troops into Helmand Province, Afghanistan, to supplement 200 U.S. troops.

Afghan National Development Strategy is created.

February: International donors meeting in London pledge more than $10 billion (£5.7 billion) in reconstruction aid over five years.

2007　United States doubles the number of its ground troops in Afghanistan.

2008　Afghan parliament implements Shia marriage law.

New ISAF commander General David McKiernan inherits a troubled war.

September: President George W. Bush sends an extra 4,500 U.S. troops to Afghanistan.

October: Germany extends Afghanistan mission to 2009 and boosts troop numbers in Afghanistan by 1,000, to 4,500.

Number of troops in Helmand reaches 9,000.

Total number of troops reaches 50,000.

2009   New ISAF commander General Stanley McChrystal replaces McKiernan.

February: Up to twenty NATO countries pledge to increase military and other commitments in Afghanistan after the United States announces a dispatch of 17,000 extra troops.

March: President Barack Obama unveils a new U.S. strategy for Afghanistan and Pakistan. An extra 4,000 U.S. personnel are deployed as "trainers."

September: Leaked report by the commander of U.S. forces, General Stanley McChrystal, demanding more troops.

October: Hamid Karzai is declared winner of the August presidential election, after second-placed opponent Abdullah Abdullah pulls out before the second round. Preliminary results had given Karzai 55 percent of the vote, but so many ballots are found to be fraudulent that a run-off was called.

December: President Obama decides to boost U.S. troop numbers in Afghanistan by 30,000, bringing the total number of U.S. troops to over 100,000 and total number of foreign troops in Afghanistan to almost 150,000.

2010   July: General David Petraeus replaces McChrystal as ISAF commander.

September: Parliamentary polls are marred by Taliban violence, widespread fraud, and a long delay in announcing the results.

November: Richard Holbrooke dies.

32,000 foreign troops stationed in Helmand are backed by 30,000 Afghans.

2011   May: Osama bin Laden is killed in Abbottabad, Pakistan.

It was April Fools' Day, 2011. The Afghan beside me on the plane was fifty-five, had a white beard and spikey black hair, and was wearing wool trousers and a V-necked jumper. He handed me a business card, having written on the back in English, "An Afghan Dilemma: Education, Gender and Globalisation in an Islamic Context: PhD dissertation." That was his book. But he didn't seem entirely pleased with it. "It is very long," he said. "Perhaps you won't have time to read it. Perhaps if you are having trouble sleeping."

He was one of only four Afghans on the plane to Kabul. The man in the shalwar kameez and jacket, with five stuffed plastic bags from Dubai duty-free, was an Afghan official. The man in a waistcoat looked like a businessman. And there was a younger Afghan wearing a black shirt and Gucci glasses who was carrying yesterday's *Frankfurter Allgemeine Zeitung*. Everyone else was a foreigner. There was a young Filipino woman with blonde highlights, ripped jeans, and a big gold necklace; an Iranian in a baggy suit and open-necked shirt, holding his cellphone away from his ear; and three African Americans in jeans, wearing desert combat boots and carrying Marine Corps camouflage packs. What did all the rest do?

Eight years ago, there would have been only a dozen foreigners on the plane, working for charities or the UN, and I would have known the majority of them. Now I could only guess. The sixty-year-old with a ponytail, paunch, collared shirt, and jacket seemed too relaxed for a businessman and too formal for an aid worker: he was probably a development consultant. The man asleep by the window had his International Security Assistance

Force badge strung from his neck in a clear-fronted wallet. The Indian with the highly polished shoes and the iPad, I stereotyped as working in finance—perhaps for the World Bank. The tall man who was smiling so much could only be a missionary: who but a Christian would bring a two-year-old blonde to Kabul? The men in cargo pants with crew cuts, untucked shirts, and massive upper bodies and tattoos on their bare forearms were bodyguards—or, if not, wanted to be.

But who were the hundred white men and women, aged between thirty and fifty-five, with sunglasses around their necks, sneakers on their feet, and small knapsacks—some listening to iPods, some asleep, others talking and sipping from cups with lids?

The Afghan next to me said, "I don't know either. I don't like to talk to foreigners on these flights anymore. I guess they're mostly working for companies." He shrugged, "Maybe they work for NGOs—but who knows anymore—what is an NGO and what is a company, given the salaries today?"

He had not been able to complete his degree in textile engineering before the Soviet invasion; he had fought in the jihad, gone into exile, studied abroad, and then returned to work with international aid agencies. The coalition-led invasion of 2001 seemed like the opportunity for which he had been waiting for over thirty years: the moment when all of his experience, his faith, and his learning could be put to the service of his country.

"We had a great chance in 2001—a great opportunity. We all wanted peace, even the Taliban had given up. So I thought hard about what Afghanistan needed and put it in a book. I considered writing in Dari: the language of our intellectuals," he said with a grin (he is not a native Dari speaker), "but a friend said, 'If you don't write in Pushtu who will?' So I wrote in Pushtu—it was a good book, though I say so myself—and I printed it privately for one thousand dollars. But no one would buy it. So I gave it away. And no one read it. Not even the man who told me to write it.

"I sent it to the Afghan cabinet. They were so busy working with the Americans and making money that they didn't have time. One mullah—who had been a Taliban minister—tried to read it, but he was offended because I had suggested that the Taliban attitudes to women were a reflection of their childhoods in single-sex boarding schools. I translated it into English for the foreigners who were interested in 'the context and application of educational theory.' But they didn't read it either."

It is difficult to convey his charm, the intonation and gestures with which he communicated his disappointment. He smiled a lot. He pinched my forearm for emphasis. He imitated voices and gestures: puffing himself up, dusting down his epaulets, and wagging his head when he was being Field Marshal Fahim, or putting on an oleaginously pious manner when being a former minister of education. Beneath the self-deprecation was a sense of his pride: as a Muslim, a Pushtun, an Afghan, an educated man with skill. But every anecdote emphasized his disappointment with the 2001 intervention in Afghanistan.

At first, I wondered whether he, like many analysts, thought the problem had been "the light footprint"—that the United States had been distracted by Iraq, that there had not been enough troops outside Kabul, that there had not been enough focus on "nation-building."[1] But he was not concerned about resources or formal strategy. The foreign presence was, he suggested, simply inherently corrupting—for the West and for Afghanistan—and his attempts to work with it had left him feeling powerless and humiliated. In fact, he suggested that the more that had been invested, the worse things had become.

"The U.S. ambassadors say, 'We will build this road; we will do that. You Afghans don't know anything—you are bearded and backward.' The Russians called us 'Black turbans.' And now the foreigners call us again"—he puts his hand on my forearm—"'Black turbans.' When I express traditional Afghan values, I am told, 'If you speak or write those things, they will not give you a single afghani—"yak rupee na bita." ' The foreigners thought they could spot anything eighty centimeters long from the air (although they couldn't find Osama bin Laden, who was 1.9 meters tall, if not longer). And they thought if there are any other problems: 'stupid Afghans—just give them money.' "

Many of his anecdotes concerned his encounters with the new Afghan ministers. One assured him that his book would bring God's blessings on him—but refused to read it. One accused him of being a religious fanatic. Each anecdote finished with him telling the minister he should be ashamed of himself. I was grateful I wasn't his minister. The doctor had different views from me about Islam, about women, about the West, and about Pakistan. And I thought he was wrong about most of those things. But he seemed a man of real wit, energy, and generosity. I thought that if an intervention loses a man like that, it is failing.

"My minister assumes he can please me by asking me to name my salary. In a poor country, where most Afghans are struggling to survive on two thousand afghanis [forty dollars] a month. As though I were a donkey for hire. People connected with the government can claim three hundred thousand dollars a year in housing allowance, and Afghan Americans can claim salaries of one thousand dollars a day, and never have to visit Afghanistan. And the corruption of the international community is worse than the corruption of the Afghans: 90 percent of the money goes back to the West and supports the people on this plane."

He reassured me that he was not Taliban, that he was highly educated, that he had worked for female education for thirty years, that he felt sorry for the president, and that he was not an ethnic bigot—and he insisted on each point, at least twice. It was clear that he was not just humiliated, he felt misunderstood. But his biggest concern was with what he called "buzzwords."

"I was at a conference four years ago in Sweden with the great foreign experts—famous men who care about Afghanistan—Ahmed Rashid, John Butt, Olivier Roy. But I said to them, 'You are listing all the problems in Afghanistan—and heaping up buzzwords like "tribalism" and "corruption." But actually these words have no connection to Afghan reality. You are trying to force Afghan reality into your theory—cutting the suit to fit the cloth." Perhaps because he had trained as a textile engineer, this analogy pleased him, so he extended it. "'You are forcing us to wear trousers that finish above the knee.'

"Recently I said to another foreigner, 'You insist that administrative reform is "comprehensible," "tailored to a local context," but even I—who has two masters and an international Ph.D.—don't understand four of the words in your opening pitch.' They replied, 'Don't worry, we will have them translated.' I replied there is no Afghan equivalent of these concepts. Even Ashraf Ghani—who is a famous international figure with a great academic pedigree who can say things like 'gender-sensitive . . . rule of law' in English—even he would not really know how to say them in his native language. This applies even to words you think are simple: like 'democracy' or 'market economy.' I promise you, no one in the Ministry of Finance, except perhaps for the minister, understands what a 'market economy' is.

"No one speaks about the reality of Afghanistan or its history. They act as though it was Pakistan not the Soviet Union who had invaded in the 1980s. They let India fool them. They forget how much Iran benefits from instability in Afghanistan—how Ayatollah Khomeini sounded just like Brzezinski when they were both inviting young Afghans to fight and go to Paradise." At this point another joke: "And paradise was good business—if one of us died, we could bring seventy others with us. During the communist period in Afghanistan we had holy words—such as proletariat—and no one could criticize them—even if they understood them. Today we have new holy words. Holy buzzwords.

"All of this," he concluded, "it is not just an Afghan phenomenon: it is a global phenomenon. I was in Sweden yesterday when they announced they were sending six planes to Libya—to bomb 'for humanitarian purposes'—what are they doing? They have no idea—we have become like children—a crowd of children is running and we join in and run along behind to see what we can see."

This short essay is in a sense only an appendix to my companion's remarks. Just as his own book is an appendix to his opening quote from the poet Rumi (who was born in what is now Afghanistan):

> *Oh how often have knowledge and keen wits and understandings*
> *Been as deadly as brigands or ghouls to the wayfarer*[2]

ISOLATION AND MODERN EXPERTISE

Each foreigner on the plane to Kabul would have his or her own experience of Afghanistan, and might well find it difficult to recognize mine. You could begin at dawn running in formation inside the perimeter of a military base; or pray in a secret church. You could eat your lunch at a chipped desk in an Afghan ministry office; or spend your afternoons gazing at a video-conference screen, linked to your country's capital; or your evenings, drinking Nescafé from a flimsy plastic cup around a Formica table with middle-aged South African consultants. You could sleep on a dark-wood bed, in a marble-floored room of the Serena Hotel, with a view of a mini-bar and wrapped French soap; or on a Chinese foam mattress on the floor of a Christian house in the 1970s suburb of Kartai-e-se; or in a tent with four other men on the military base at Kandahar; or in an eye hospital in the Pamir Mountains; or in a shipping container on the gravel flats near the Jalalabad Road.

But whatever the rhythm of your day, as a foreigner you were inevitably isolated from Afghan life: by your tour length, by security restrictions, by your career structures, by your education, and simply by being a foreigner. All this contributes to what, in Vietnam, former secretary of defense Robert McNamara dubbed "our profound ignorance of the history, culture, and politics of the people in the area, and the personalities and habits of their leaders."[3] And this was a central cause of the humiliating mess in Afghanistan.

Officials serving in the intervention in Afghanistan from 2001 to 2011—whether diplomats in an embassy, UN staff in a compound, or captains in a forward-operating base—were on very short tours. Even members of the U.S. military did not stay in Afghanistan for longer than fifteen months; the Italian military served four months; the British soldiers, six; and the British diplomats in Kabul were on a one-year term, extendable to two.[4] Such lack of continuity was difficult for political work because it stopped the development of trusting relationships with Afghan leaders, and for development work because it meant that any long-term project stretched impossibly far beyond any individual's tour.

Those civilians employed by Western governments were generally locked within guarded embassy compounds, which kept them brutally segregated from local life. In the 1960s, during the Vietnam War, Richard Holbrooke (then a young State Department officer) lived alone above a shop in the Mekong Delta.[5] But by 2000, the opportunities for experience and political understanding that such freedom of movement brought were no longer considered to outweigh the risks. Individual staff would have been willing to travel more (and often tried to do so behind the backs of their employers). But a new legal and insurance notion of "duty of care" imposed an overwhelming burden on ambassadors and managers to ensure their civilian staff took no personal risks.[6]

While soldiers went out on patrols, which often cost them their lives, civilian officials, therefore, spent most of their day in their embassies or in the air-conditioned and sandbagged shipping containers that served as offices and accommodations. Travel outside the walls of the British embassy, for senior staff, required booking a team of British bodyguards with two armored vehicles, twenty-four hours in advance. These teams frequently vetoed visits. One member of the U.S. embassy told me she had been in the country for two years without ever leaving the embassy property.

From 2008 to 2010 it was almost impossible to get security clearance for American, British, or Canadian civilians to even visit Murad Khane, a small historic neighborhood in the center of Kabul. This place had no record of attacks or violence and was a hundred yards from the door of the Finance Ministry and three hundred yards from the presidential palace. Even officials with the U.S. Agency for International Development (USAID), who had given ten million dollars to that part of the city, were not permitted to visit. When one senior visitor made it to the site, he was given twelve foreign bodyguards and fifty members of the Afghan police and security department as protection, and was allowed to remain exactly six minutes in the area before being "extracted." If they could not visit a safe neighborhood in central Kabul, it was out of the question for most foreign civilians to spend a night in a Pushtun village house.[7]

I experienced this directly when I returned to Kabul as a member of the British Parliamentary Foreign Affairs Committee. I was made to sit—in an armored vehicle—wearing a stiff eighteen-pound vest with giant Kevlar plates, crammed between two large British members of Parliament, each in their own body armor. I can still feel the pain under the left shoulder blade. We had all been lectured for two hours on what to do in the event of a mine exploding, a vehicle-borne improvised explosive device detonating, or the driver dying. We could not read the Farsi script, so even the billboards were incomprehensible. The British drivers navigated by grid coordinates and code names and therefore were unable to follow straightforward directions—understandable to any Afghan—such as "take the second left from Nader Pashtun before the Pul-e Khishti Mosque." I suspect the experience, for the visiting politicians, was too overwhelming for them to appreciate even the few details of Afghan life, which we could glimpse through the reinforced windscreen: the sugar-cane crusher on the trolley; the jeep with a militia commander and police lights; the miniature deer for sale on the road side; the Uzbek in a padded, floral, ankle-length coat; or the election poster of the Hazara MP.

And in the rare cases when diplomats were able to spend extended time with Afghans, they were often unable to speak to them. In nine years, I did not meet a senior foreign official in Afghanistan who spoke an Afghan language well. The British Foreign Office is an interesting example, if only because British diplomats once had a reputation for their linguistic and cultural expertise. Sir Michael Jay, the head of the UK Foreign Office in 2001, deliberately reduced the weight previously given to knowledge of languages and geographical areas (being an "Arabist" was once highly prestigious) in favor of administrative skills.[8] Linguistic or deep country knowledge became irrelevant for promotion. In 2010, one British diplomat, being interviewed for a post, was not allowed to even talk about the fact that he spoke the country's language and had already been posted in the country, for fear that it would prejudice the interview process against applicants who had not served there.

In 2009, according to the British Foreign Office's own assessment, the British required no Pashto speakers to work effectively in Afghanistan, even though it was the language of Helmand, where Britain was fighting.[9] The Foreign Office reckoned it required six "operational" Dari speakers, but only two of its diplomats in Kabul were proficient at this level. This was out of an embassy of more than three hundred staff, in a country where very few people spoke English.[10]

The workload of civilians did not leave them time to improve their scant knowledge of the country. Staff often worked fourteen-hour days at their desks, struggling to keep abreast of emails from their capitals, writing cables, and preparing press tours and official visits.[11] Development officials were absorbed in coordination meetings with "major donors," writing "strategic plans" and "feasibility studies," submitting reports, and ensuring the proper processing of "contracts, invoices and receipts."[12]

British civilians in Kabul were, therefore, well equipped for those processes of the international community connected with "management best practice" and "multilateral diplomacy,"

accounting, human resources, and "global" policy around climate change, trade, or heritage. But their knowledge about
Afghanistan itself—or indeed any other developing country—
was generally much more limited than that of a previous generation of foreign service officers.[13] And such problems were not
unique to the British foreign service.

Almost none of the modern employers in Afghanistan,
including the UN, sent their staff on extended Afghan language
courses.[14] In almost every organization, American or Swedish,
private or charitable, security advisers prevented staff from visiting remote areas and locked them at night in isolated guesthouses, under curfew. Few civilians were posted to remote field
offices and, when they were, found themselves often ignored
by the center. The leading international institutions in Kabul
employed far more short-term international consultants than
core staff. Managers—who were equally non-specialists—often
left the country long before their proposals could be tested, still
less fail. A culture of country experts had been replaced by a
culture of consultants.

Some foreigners in Afghanistan, such as NGO workers, journalists, and UN staff, were less restricted in their movements.
But they were as imprisoned by their education and twenty-first-
century worldview as they would have been by a bureaucratic
promotion structure or the razor wire on a compound wall. It
is easy—and would be unfair—to mock their attitudes and life-
styles. I was one of them. We sometimes went from listening to
French jazz by the swimming pool at L'Atmosphere to sitting
at the bar at Gandamack, festooned like a manor with muskets and hunting prints (though in this case the muskets were
Afghan jezails and the hunting prints were of Amir Habibul-
lah on his elephant). Some danced under spinning disco balls
and drank tequila in plastic cups at UN guesthouses while their

Afghan drivers waited outside in SUVs for the party to finish; others grew rocket in their Kabul gardens and imported charcuterie. All collected carpets.

Some of the young policy elite were paid well, but none, I think, were corrupt. They enjoyed having important jobs in a newsworthy country, but they were not simply narcissists: they were often dedicated to their idea of public service. They were generally cultivated, widely read, interesting, adventurous, kind to their Afghan staff, and loyal to their friends. Indeed, they were in some ways the cream of their culture: educated at Cambridge or Harvard, extroverted, successful in their fields.[15] They were employed in a wide range of institutions: research organizations, charities, private companies, and foreign or Afghan government departments, each with their own cultures and processes. They were mostly younger than thirty-five, but they were not from a single country: they were Finnish and French, East African, Canadian and Danish and more.[16] But they had a surprisingly uniform and narrow view of intervention and of countries like Afghanistan, which reflected the forms of education, experience, and values of the 1990s.

A friend of mine in Kabul—let us call him James—was in many ways typical. James had received his undergraduate degree in Britain and his graduate degree in the United States at an Ivy League school of government, taking classes in organizational theory, development economics, conflict negotiation, leadership, and human rights. At university, he had been exposed weekly to speeches by the most celebrated "international leaders." He worked very hard. He was highly optimistic about the possibility of reform. He had little time for people who emphasized uncertainty, ignorance, and contingency: he saw that as pessimism.

And the kinds of skills and knowledge he acquired appeared to relate to contemporary success, since on graduation he was offered a job as a management consultant with McKinsey. He eventually joined a multilateral institution, which sent him to Kabul, where he helped to write part of the development strategy. After two years, he left, and although he continued to visit occasionally as a consultant, his career shifted to Africa.

He was, of course, in many ways a great improvement on his colonial equivalent. He had no nineteenth-century prejudices about race or women or class. He would never have committed to paper the kind of insults (or indeed the kind of compliments) that Mountstuart Elphinstone showered when he wrote of the Afghans in 1805:

> Their vices are revenge, envy, avarice, rapacity and obstinacy; on the other hand they are fond of liberty, faithful to their friends, hospitable, brave, hardy, frugal, laborious and prudent.[17]

James was critical of injustice in traditional structures, and he tended to emphasize incidents of abuse, discrimination, and poverty. It was not clear how much he liked or admired or felt any kinship with Afghans.

He had little knowledge of Afghan archaeology, anthropology, geography, history, language, literature, or theology. He was not expected to know which ridge the commander Gulbuddin Hekmatyar used to shell Kabul in 1993, let alone that General Stewart took the same ridge in 1879. He was not expected to know how the commander of Kamenj was related to the commander of Barra Khana.[18] He may not have been aware why particular villages in Wardak Province had opened their arms to the Taliban. He did not know the Pashto poetry that celebrated the expulsion of foreign armies. He did not take an interest in the honor codes of gangsters in old Kabul, nor the exact content of the Sunni prejudices against the Ismailis. He

had no particular developed theories on how to work with traditional Afghan leaders. Again this was not his individual failing.
He could have learned all these things, but he was not given the
time to study them and he would not have been rewarded if he
had known them, promoted if he had been heavily influenced
by them, or listened to if he had written about them.

Instead, he, like most international civilians, was an expert
in fields that hardly existed as recently as the 1950s, and which
are hardly household names today: governance, gender, conflict
resolution, civil society, and public administration. They were
not experts in gender or governance in Afghanistan: they were
experts on gender and governance in the abstract. They had studied "lessons learned" by their colleagues in other countries and
were aware of international "best practice." Their focus was on
"cross-cutting themes"—issues that should be applied to all countries and integrated into any project—such as human rights, the
environment, and (to quote mission criteria for a Department for
International Development, or DFID, project in Iraq) "the political participation of the poor, the vulnerable and the marginalised,
particularly women."[19]

Curiously, although he was grandly optimistic about the
intervention as a whole, James could explain what was wrong
with every conceivable project within it. But his critique was
not related to the details of a particular place in Afghanistan
or derived from implementation of similar projects in the past.
Instead, it was a standard global catechism. He could undermine
almost any proposal by asking, "Is this project sustainable?" "Is
it replicable?" "What are your sources of funding?" "How does
it relate to the national strategy?" "What kind of community
consultation have you conducted?" "How have you sought to
involve the Afghan government in the project?" "What is the
role of women?" "What are your metrics?" "How transparent,

predictable, and accountable are your financial processes?" and so could ten thousand others like him.

Although our incomes were mostly derived from the programs or actions of NATO governments, we often seemed fiercely critical of the international intervention. When Ambassador Bill Wood considered eradicating poppy crops through aerial spraying, some called him "Chemical Bill." Others, equally unfairly, called General Dan McNeill "Bomber McNeill." Many despised the international security contractors, such as DynCorp, for the way they drove through the streets. We held forth on the iniquities of Afghan "warlords" and the Pakistani "ISI" (Inter-Services Intelligence). It was common to attack Afghan President Hamid Karzai, saying that he was corrupt, that he was weak, that his brother was a drug lord, or latterly, that he was mentally unstable. And we often criticized each other's programs as naive, extravagant, or unsustainable. Indeed, so aware were we of our disagreements that we were often unconscious of the uniformity of our views.

Almost all the foreign civilians, however, as late as 2005, seemed to share the same fundamental analysis of Afghanistan: that the solution to its problems lay in "governance" and "state-building"; that the intervention had been crippled by the lack of international effort ("the light footprint"); and that with a new strategy, new resources, and leadership, the international community could bring governance and "fix" the failed state in Afghanistan. These attitudes, career structures, and rituals, so common among policy-makers in Kabul, were also echoed by superiors in home capitals.

None of these views were permanent, inevitable, or fully rational: they were a particular phenomenon of the late twentieth century. Previous centuries had produced very different types of foreign policy-makers with different educations and career structures, which often made them much better informed about the history, language, culture, and politics of South Asia. Take the Viceroy John Lawrence, for example, who led only a slightly exaggerated version of the typical career of any British official working in India in the nineteenth century. It was not simply that he studied Indian languages and history at the East India College for two years, followed by further language training in Calcutta for a year, before his first posting in Delhi: it was that his first tour lasted sixteen years. He spent that posting taking measurements in agricultural fields and hearing domestic court cases in local languages. When Lawrence moved from rural Delhi to the Punjab for the next fourteen years, he was again absorbed in encouraging agricultural improvements, establishing a police force, laying roads and canals, mapping the province, forming courts, doing what would be called today "disarming, demobilising and reintegrating" former combatants,[20] negotiating deals with warlords, and patrolling the frontier with Afghanistan before being drawn into the Indian insurgency of 1857. He came from a system whose career structure repeatedly rewarded long experience in-country and promoted people who had served in remote posts and displayed detailed knowledge of specific cultures.

Compare Richard Holbrooke, who as presidential Special Representative for Afghanistan and Pakistan was perhaps the nearest twenty-first-century equivalent to Lawrence in terms of seniority and influence on Afghan policy. He began with an intimate knowledge of Vietnam, having learned to speak Vietnamese and then spending his first posting in the Lower Mekong Delta, supporting village projects, distributing food supplies, forming militias, and arguing with Vietnamese officials. But everything thereafter in his career detached him from the ground. Holbrooke spent less than sixteen months in that first posting, in which John Lawrence spent more than sixteen years. Within three years, Holbrooke was back in Washington, D.C. After an interlude at Princeton University and in the Peace Corps in Morocco, he returned to the States to edit *Foreign Policy* magazine and then work on Jimmy Carter's presidential campaign. Holbrooke became assistant secretary of state for East Asian and Pacific affairs at the age of thirty-six; Lawrence, at the corresponding time in his life, had just made his first move from Delhi to the neighboring district. By the time John Lawrence completed his tour as Viceroy, he had completed thirty-five years of service on the ground in India. Holbrooke was on a foreign posting for less than six years in his entire career: he spent three-fourths of his life in the States and more than twenty-four years of it on Wall Street.[21]

Holbrooke's focus was on Washington politics, and he felt he needed to be predominantly in Washington itself, to be absorbed in campaigns and in meetings with think tanks, journalists, and politicians. He served as a campaign adviser on foreign affairs for four presidential candidates, a role that extended to preparing them for television debates. *The New Yorker* observed in 1995 that he "shamelessly and effectively exploited the media, capitalizing on their natural attraction to indiscretion and swagger, in order to promote American policy aims and to intimidate those who stood in the way."[22]

So although each man worked hard, they directed their energies in very different ways and knew very different things. Lawrence's ideal (according to John Beames) was "a hard, active man in boots and breeches, who worked all day and nearly all night. . . . [T]he ideal Magistrate must show himself to all his people continually, must decide cases either sitting on horseback in the village gateway, or under a tree outside the village walls, write his decision on his knee, while munching a native chapatty or a fowl cooked in the hole in the ground; and then mount his horse and be off to repeat the process in the next village."[23]

The half of Holbrooke's working life that was spent in foreign service—as opposed to in journalism or finance—had a peculiar twenty-first-century rhythm and content. Despite the ease of modern transport—there are six civilian flights a day to Kabul from Dubai alone—he visited Afghanistan relatively rarely. He told *The New Yorker* that contact with the ground was so important that he aimed to visit the region at least every other month. When there, Holbrooke traveled by C-130 transport plane and Black Hawk helicopter (in a pink checked shirt, khakis, sunglasses, and a USAID baseball cap).[24] The hours he needed to work were legendary.[25] At dinner with Holbrooke, when he was Special Representative for Afghanistan and Pakistan, I noticed that when others were speaking, his hands were perpetually on his BlackBerry under the table sending what appeared to be hundreds of emails and texts every day—a necessity in the modern age if he were to remain ahead of the news and politics in Washington.

Holbrooke not only had to work very hard at cultivating members of Congress but also had to navigate his way through the labyrinthine strictures of budget and personnel management in a vast modern bureaucracy. Even with all of his determination and experience and the urgency of his role as Special Representative, it was eleven months before key members of his Afghan team were able to get the security clearance necessary to begin work. But none of this made him or his civilian staff in Kabul experts on the specifics of Afghanistan.

Such detachment from Afghan life extended even to those foreigners in Kabul who were most insistently adventurous: Louis who rode to Maimana, Eric who ski-toured on the Salang. Even the most determined foreigners had far less contact with the reality of daily life than the most junior policy-maker, working at home, on domestic affairs. Home civil servants have usually been born in the country and have spent their whole lives within its governmental and social institutions. They speak the language fluently (because it is their own), watch local television every night, travel on the buses, and inhabit the nuances of national manners and social expectations. In short, they have a kinship for the culture that surrounds them. And they are in it all the time: as a child or mother, as a voter, as a fisherman or clubber. We, by contrast, were so isolated from the reality of Afghan life, through tour length, security restrictions, linguistic and cultural barriers, and barriers of ideology, that we were hardly even conscious of the depth of our isolation.

SUCCESS

This isolation and ignorance proved to be a fundamental constraint on the intervention. But it did not make the intervention entirely useless. Some projects worked. The first two years after the intervention of 2001, for example, brought dramatic improvements in finance, health, public works, education, and telecommunications. These were things that either relied on technical expertise or could be done from offices in the capital. But because of their isolated lives, international policy-makers did much worse the closer they came to the real structures, and forms of resistance, in Afghan rural life. Thus, they did well at stabilizing the currency but very poorly at establishing honest local policemen; well at designing bridges, poorly at weaning farmers from opium poppy production.

The more narrow and technical the task, the better. The job of creating a central bank and stabilizing the currency, for example, was roughly the same all over the world and was not dependent on the exact social structure of an Afghan village. It could be done in an air-conditioned office in the capital. It was, therefore, ideally suited to the senior officials in the Ministry of Finance and their partners in the World Bank or Asian Development Bank. The new banking and currency structures were, therefore, established within months and have remained since. Not surprisingly, the international community also had rapid success in creating a central bank and a stable currency in Bosnia, Kosovo, and Iraq—and boasted accordingly. Such things were not "easy": they required considerable knowledge and skill. But they were things that foreign experts or Afghan experts in capitals were well qualified to do.

Similar factors accounted for the great improvement in high-level health care. Highly trained international physicians and modern medical equipment could—and did—rapidly transform survival rates in complex operations in Kabul hospitals. Seema, from my office, had to travel to Pakistan for a simple heart scan in 2006, but by 2008 she could receive all the treatment and monitoring she required in Kabul.

Highly trained foreign engineers and architects had a contribution to make in bridge design, generator construction, and even the restoration of historic monuments. When backed by enormous quantities of international money, they were able to erect a very large number of buildings and roads and through the construction industry contribute to double-figure GDP growth in the Afghan economy. (Costs rose accordingly—in 2002 the United States was paying one hundred thousand dollars to build a kilometer of road; by 2009 they were paying a million dollars for a kilometer of road.)[26]

In other cases, it was simply necessary to lift previous Taliban restrictions. Changing the Taliban law that prohibited female education brought one and a half million more children to school, almost overnight, well ahead of any real reforms in the curriculum, teacher training, or management in the Department of Education. And Afghan entrepreneurs responded quickly and confidently to the opportunities presented by a now-free media. Again, it was simply necessary to open the radio spectrum (albeit through a "responsible, centralized, and internationally supported" tender process) for there to be an explosion in mobile phone coverage. Under the Taliban there was essentially none. Immediately after the invasion the number of subscribers leapt to one million and then five million: different telecom companies competed to build masts across the country, pilot new forms of phone credit and applications, and encourage people onto the network.

Thus the international community was able to implement successful developmental, humanitarian, and commercial projects in Afghanistan. It did many of them within a few months of the intervention (though it still boasted of them years later). It even met its initial counter-terrorism goals, by driving Osama bin Laden and Al Qaeda out of Afghanistan and into Pakistan, in 2001; and then over the next nine years killing or capturing almost every senior member of the Al Qaeda leadership, including bin Laden himself.[27]

But the international community was not satisfied with development and counter-terrorism operations. They wanted "a sustainable solution." They felt that lack of international support and investment ("the light footprint") had left Afghanistan as "a failed state." They believed that if the state remained weak, or the Taliban reemerged, all the development would vanish, Al Qaeda would return and pose an "existential threat" to the United States and its allies. They, therefore, concluded that their only option was to fix the "root causes" of the conflict and the fundamental structures of the Afghan state. President Barack Obama was typical in conflating a number of different objectives in his Afghan strategy of 2009:

> The Afghan government is undermined by corruption and has difficulty delivering basic services to its people. The economy is undercut by a booming narcotics trade that encourages criminality and funds the insurgency. . . . For the Afghan people, a return to Taliban rule would condemn their country to brutal governance, international isolation, a paralyzed economy, and the denial of basic human rights to the Afghan people—especially women and girls. If the Afghan government falls to the Taliban—or allows al-Qaida to go unchallenged—that country will again be a base for terrorists who want to kill as many of our people as they possibly can.[28]

Obama's solution was to launch a counterinsurgency campaign, engage with Pakistan, and build an Afghan state. This latter mission, to "promote a more capable and accountable Afghan government . . . advance security, opportunity and justice . . . develop an economy,"[29] had been a priority for international policy-makers since at least 2004. And these goals, increasingly, dominated and distorted the intervention.

THE "TRAGEDY" OF AFGHANISTAN

President Obama and his predecessors were not, however, exaggerating the poverty, illegal activity, and lack of central control in Afghanistan. Leftist coups, Soviet intervention, and Islamist resistance, and the interference of superpowers and neighbors, had, since the 1970s, smashed Afghan government and society, killing millions and driving millions more into exile. When I walked through Afghanistan, shortly after the U.S.-led intervention, I barely recognized the economic and political structures of the country as structures at all.[30] The post-conflict society I knew best was Bosnia, but Bosnia was, of course, far more literate, and more developed. Countries such as Pakistan and Nepal, through which I had spent some of the previous eighteen months walking, were wealthier and much less isolated than Afghanistan.

If the ideal state of the international community included central control of finance and the military; and the development of legal livelihoods, infrastructure, state assets, and human rights: then central Afghanistan failed on every count. It appeared to be the quintessence of "ungoverned space," the antithesis of security, economic development, and good governance: the very failed state that was not just a danger to its citizens but also, through providing safe haven to Al Qaeda, "an existential threat" to the West.

On the first night of my walk, I was told that the fort at Sha'ede, where I planned to spend the night, was occupied by Al Qaeda terrorists. On the sixth day, I watched a dozen donkeys being loaded with opium poppy.[31] One of my hosts, Seyyed Umar, had worked with the Taliban; another, Commandant Bushire, looted antiquities. On the seventh day, Mullah Mustafa tried to shoot me. I didn't ask him on that occasion why. But when I returned eighteen months later, I was told that Nadir Shah, his cousin, had bet him that he couldn't hit me.

When I entered Hazarajat, it was threatened with famine, and food trucks were queuing on the snow-blocked passes, unable to bring relief. There was illegal quarrying of stone in Yakawlang District; Sar Jangal had not seen a civil servant for decades, and many of its villages had been fighting with their neighboring communities and could not visit their neighbors for fear of vendetta. Ismail Khan, the governor of Herat, kept the Herat customs revenue and dealt independently with the Iranian government. My lunch companion's father, Rais Salam Khan, cut off people's ears.

And international neglect seemed a clear factor in this failure. There had been little economic development since 1979. When I got sick in Sangizart, there were no clinics within a three days' walk. When the road was closed by snow, it was an eight-day walk to Bamiyan. And the international community had invested little in development—and often badly. Three separate international donors had spent money on wells and toilets in Kamenj, but all of them had been built in Haji Mohsin's private garden, on the other side of a fast-flowing river from their intended beneficiaries: the villagers of Kamenj. Médecins Sans Frontières (MSF) was running excellent clinics, but in 2002 it was not clear how they would relate to the priorities of the Ministry of Health, whether they did not potentially duplicate plans from other NGOs, or how sustainable such clinics would prove when MSF withdrew (which they did in 2003).

And "the light footprint"—or lack of international political, economic, and military focus on Afghanistan—was particularly evident after the intervention in 2001. Lakhdar Brahimi, the UN Special Representative for Afghanistan, prevented the establishment of serious UN field offices in provinces like Ghor. Some experienced staff looked in—I saw Michael Semple and Thomas Ruttig in the town of Chaghcharan—but they were very few, and they were forced to cover the whole country, so they came and went by plane in a single afternoon. There were no regular foreign troops in the province. Instead, there were four Special Forces soldiers on the airfield in Chaghcharan who had no mission related to population security or state-building, nor could have, being four of only eight foreign soldiers among a surrounding population of three million. They focused on the fight against Al Qaeda, and their presence aroused the suspicion of villagers. There were no regular Afghan soldiers or policemen in the province. All my hosts were armed and supported by armed militias. The new governor of Ghor, Ibrahim Malikzada, had no educated and trained civil servants in his administration and, it seemed, had fed a guest to his dogs.

The international community, therefore, was right to think Afghanistan was in trouble. If anything, it underestimated the enormity of the problems. As late as 2011, an American friend in Kabul—inspired by Egypt and Tunisia—spoke of a "Facebook revolution in Afghanistan." I had to remind him that there was hardly a village with electricity; that when the Helmand police trainers conducted an exam on their new entrants, 92 out of 100 men entering could not write their names or recognize numerals between 1 and 10 in their own language; and that you need electricity to be able to read and to use Facebook.

Nevertheless, the international community was confident that it understood the nature of Afghanistan's problems. And despite the depth and density of these problems, and despite its short tours, security restrictions, and lack of experience and knowledge, it was confident that it was in a position to transform the situation.

THE CIVILIAN VISION

The British ambassador to Kabul stated in 2011 that "almost by definition, good soldiers are irrepressibly enthusiastic, unquenchably optimistic."[32] But such optimism also characterized the civilian policy elite—both junior and senior. Perhaps the most articulate and influential civilian advocate of the policy consensus was the Afghan statesman Ashraf Ghani: one of the heroes of the international community, the architect of much of the international strategy, and a man whom Holbrooke saw as a potential Afghan president. I worked briefly for Ashraf in 2001, when he was a senior figure at the World Bank and was about to become Afghanistan's minister of finance. What the *New York Times* called his "academic's soft and careful manner" was allied with erudite epigrams, precise recall of financial statistics, organizational theory, and a focus on "strategy." His fierce commitment to the rebirth of his country, his highly philosophical monologues (which he interspersed with abstract questions), and his physique (he was a slight, bald man in his late fifties) made him appear almost like an Afghan Gandhi.

On Christmas Day, 2001, I joined Ashraf and a friend in the Pakistani hill resort of Murree at the great Cecil Hotel. The dining room was closed, so we sat in the garden on wicker furniture and ate chicken tandoori for our Christmas dinner. I don't remember the view, but I do remember the mesmerizing high-pitched voice in which he delivered his diagnosis. He described the war, first, as an economic catastrophe that had eliminated tens—even hundreds—of billions of dollars of value in Afghanistan. He described some of the leading commanders as "narco-mafia." He elaborated on how the burst of opium poppy cultivation turbocharged corruption. He explained how the programs of international charities and NGOs "undermined the accountability and credibility of the Afghan state."

But Ashraf had a new strategy and a new mission that could "fix the failed state" in Afghanistan.[33] This path to success required far more resources, channeled through the budget of the Afghan Ministry of Finance. At the table over the curry, he asked for support in presenting three choices to the international community in Afghanistan. The first was that (for three billion dollars) the international community could produce an impoverished wreck (I think he mentioned the Congo); the second was that (for a much larger sum) it could produce a peaceful middle-income country (he mentioned Costa Rica); and under the third (for many tens of billions) it could produce a Singapore. Each scenario and price tag needed to be summarized for international donors on a single piece of paper—as though we were seeking bids in a charity auction.

Every American and British general in Afghanistan over the next nine years believed there was a solution, and a path to that solution, or in the words of General Richards, "It is doable if we get the formula right and it is properly resourced."[34] But Ashraf did not speak like a general. His language and tone were saturated with management and international relations theory and enlivened with broad historical and comparative references. His analysis of successful state-building encompassed the tactics of a late-nineteenth-century Afghan king, property titles in Peru, crime policy in New York, new applications of fiber-optic technology, trade routes across Central Asia, and a cornucopia of statistics on Afghanistan's past, present, and future. His answers were frequently gnomic, and he liked to respond to a question with another question. Some of his references were too recondite and hypothetical to be challenged in conversation (he had calculated an exact figure for the economic benefit which would have accrued to Afghanistan over sixty years if there had been no partition between Pakistan and India). But his proposals could also be tough, challenging, and concrete. And, sometimes—particularly in his program of trusting villagers to choose their own development programs (the National Solidarity Program)—he was genuinely inspired and highly constructive.

There was no doubting his faith: that if allowed to implement his new strategy with the right resources, he could deliver a decisive success. He drew comparisons with the speed of development in Dubai and Singapore, reminded me that Korea had been poorer than Afghanistan in 1950, and observed in passing that Afghanistan could be turned into the insurance capital of Central Asia in seven years.

Ashraf's views were not those of an eccentric academic: he was perhaps the most influential Afghan voice of the time, and as the minister of finance he shaped the new international theory, through a dozen daily meetings, through strategic plans, with academic papers and consultancy reports, in op-eds and international seminars, with charm, mystification, hard statistics, and blazing arguments. And the international community made a start at putting some of his ideas into practice. In April 2004, largely under the guidance of Ashraf Ghani, seven hundred delegates from fifty-two countries, including the whole of the European Union, the G8, and NATO, met in Berlin to sign on to a strategy largely of his devising.[35]

ABSTRACTION: DEFINING THE GOAL

But what exactly was the end goal in Afghanistan? There were a hundred. In 2002, at a UN meeting in Kabul, I was told that the goal emerged from an Afghan consensus to create a "gender-sensitive, multi-ethnic centralized state, based on democracy, human rights and the rule of law."[36] Five years later, when my friend Minna was given the astonishing title of "Secretary of the Joint Coordination Monitoring Board of the Interim Afghan National Development Strategy," the central headings of the strategy appeared as follows: "5.2 Security; 5.3

Governance, Rule of Law, and Human Rights; 5.4 Economic and Social Development; 5.5 Achieving Our Vision Through a 'Social Compact'; 5.6 Linking Strategy to Sectors; 6.1 Crosscutting Themes; 6.2 Gender Equity . . ."

This specialized language—what my Afghan friend called "buzzwords"—drawn from development theory and overlaid with management consultancy, before being inserted into the multilateral policy-drafting process, was bewildering. But the three most popular definitions of the "goal" seemed to revolve around the words *government, state,* and *governance.* In a speech in 2009, Obama defined his goals as "a more capable and accountable Afghan government." The U.S. White Paper talked of "effective local governance." NATO agreed unanimously at the sixtieth anniversary summit in April to create "a stronger democratic state."[37] The new UK strategy for Afghanistan in 2009 wanted all three simultaneously, calling within thirty-two pages for a "legitimate, accountable state," a "legitimate and accountable government," an "effective and accountable state," and "effective and accountable governance."[38]

What exactly did this mean?[39] Ashraf Ghani attempted to clarify by listing "ten functions of the state." These were "the legitimate monopoly on the means of violence; administrative control; management of public finances; investment in human capital; delineation of citizenship rights and duties; provision of infrastructure services; formation of the market; management of the state's assets (including the environment, natural resources, and cultural assets); management of international relations (including entering into international contracts and public borrowing); and maintenance of the rule of law."[40] But how clear or helpful were these definitions? Or Ashraf's suggestion that it was to be achieved through:

(1) the alignment of the internal and external stakeholders (2) to the goal of a functioning sovereign state that creates internal and external legitimacy (3) through the formulation and calibration of rules of the game (4) mobilization of sufficient resources (5) establishment of processes and organizations (6) designation of critical tasks, by (7) credible leadership and management, (8) measured through iterative monitoring.[41]

Even its greatest advocates must have sensed that this was hardly everyday language, and it was certainly not a program that any Western politician would have ever attempted to present or sell to an electorate. Nevertheless, this was the theory that was largely enshrined in the first comprehensive formal statement of the Afghan government, presented in Berlin in 2004. This document, entitled "Securing Afghanistan's Future," reflected the work of "over a hundred international experts" nearly three years after the invasion. This document became the foundation of the Afghan National Development Strategy of 2006. It was formally endorsed and supported by all of the major multilateral institutions, including the Asian Development Bank, the International Monetary Fund, the United Nations Development Programme, the United Nations Assistance Mission in Afghanistan, and the World Bank. It was then approved by more than forty nations and became the fundamental rationale and channel for billions of dollars of international aid. But the goal remained, for me at least, an enigma couched in an abstraction.

Among the sixty-nine separate tables and charts in this 137-page plan, including ones on "predicted teledensity" and "status and accomplishment, national police and law enforcement," the following words did not appear: *Pushtun, Hazara, Tajik, Islam, Sharia, jihad, communism, Northern Alliance, warlord, democracy, equality, insurgency, resistance,* and *consent.*[42] Were you to delete the word *Afghanistan* from the document, and replace it with the word *Botswana,* it would be very difficult to know of which country you were speaking.

Ashraf, who was himself acutely aware of many of these problems, cannot be held responsible for their surreal flourishing. He resigned as minister of finance and produced aggressive critiques of the international system. But the juggernaut of international abstraction rolled on regardless. Vagueness and imprecise phrases were heaped in countless combinations in "strategic plans" and "mission statements" to justify hundreds of billions of dollars of expenditure. The new UK strategy for Afghanistan in 2009, five years after Ashraf's resignation, proclaimed itself as

> international . . . regional . . . joint civilian-military . . . coordinated . . . long-term . . . focused on developing capacity . . . an approach that combines respect for sovereignty and local values with respect for international standards of democracy, legitimate and accountable government, and human rights; a hard-headed approach: setting clear and realistic objectives with clear metrics of success.[43]

Such language was no longer just an abstraction. It had become a negation. It was not a plan: it was a description of what we had not got. It revealed an approach that was short term, one that had struggled to develop Afghan capacity, to resolve regional issues, and to overcome civilian-military divisions; that had struggled to respect Afghan sovereignty or local values; that had failed to implement international standards of democracy, government, and human rights; and that had failed to set clear and realistic objectives with clear metrics of success.

The United Kingdom apparently believed that describing what it did not have constituted a plan on how to get it.

Nevertheless, such language, although a largely futile proposal for Afghanistan, had many other benefits for its users. Because it did not directly address the question of how much our institutions actually knew, could afford, or knew how to do, and because it included few uncomfortable realities from Afghanistan itself, it suggested possibilities. It allowed policy-makers to sketch indistinct utopias of "state-building" and "counterinsurgency," and promise voters a final dream of "legitimate, accountable governance." The language was so unexceptional and morally appealing that it proved as captivating for Norwegian aid agencies as for Delta Force, and the new U.S. Army and Marine Corps counterinsurgency doctrine began to read like a World Bank policy document, replete with commitments to the rule of law, economic development, governance, state-building, and human rights.[44]

And since there was no real definition—still less concrete agreement on the definition—of an Afghan state, the Taliban, terrorism, development, security, or governance, all these phrases and categories could be arranged in every conceivable sequence and relationship to justify whatever they were claiming to do at the time. You needed to defeat the Taliban to "build a state" and you needed to "build a state" to defeat the Taliban. There could not be "security" without development, or development without "security." If you had the Taliban, you had terrorists; if you didn't have "development," you had terrorists; and as President Obama informed *The New Yorker*, "If you have ungoverned spaces, they become havens for terrorists."[45]

These connections then spread around the world, linking American or European voters to villages in Afghanistan. Gordon Brown asserted that they were locked to each other by a "chain of terror."[46] In Obama's words, "Our security and prosperity depend on the security and prosperity of others."[47] Or as a British foreign minister rephrased it, "Our security depends on their development."[48] Indeed, at times it seems that all of these activities—building a state, defeating the Taliban, defeating Al Qaeda, and eliminating poverty—were in fact the same activity. In Obama's words, "Security and humanitarian concerns are all part of one project."[49]

These euphemisms and evasions, this web of tautologies and negations, gradually coalesced into the worldview formalized in Obama's speech of 2009. For Obama, the defeat of Al Qaeda required the defeat of the Taliban, which in turn required him to "promote a more capable and accountable Afghan government . . . advance security, opportunity and justice . . . develop an economy." In other words, state-building and its related concepts—governance, the rule of law, and "the legitimate monopoly of the use of violence"—had become the essential core of the intervention. But what did any of this jargon have to do with Afghan reality?

Which existing state did the spinners of such phrases have in mind as a model for Afghanistan? With a great deal of investment and luck, and many years of effort, they might have hoped to turn Afghanistan into a poorer version of its neighbors.[50] (Afghanistan was at least twenty years behind even Pakistan in the development of its military, its private sector, its civil service, and its media.) And which neighbor would that be? Pakistan, Iran, Turkmenistan, Uzbekistan, and Tajikistan presented a bewildering variety of states: a military dictatorship cum democracy, an Islamist theocracy, a surreal mock-tribal autocracy, a repressive secular dictatorship, and a country trembling on the edge of civil war.[51]

And what was to be the role of the security forces, for example, in this new dispensation? By 2010, the U.S. government was spending fourteen billion dollars a year, just on training the Afghan National Army and Police. The entire annual fiscal revenue of the Afghan government at that period was a billion dollars, so more was being spent each month on training the army and the police than the Afghan government raised in a year. Some policy-makers pointed out that this cost was unsustainable and would leave Afghanistan dependent forever on the largesse of the international community.[52] But curiously few asked how this powerful military complex was supposed to relate to the other international objectives such as state formation, development, counter-terrorism, and a "free society." When British Prime Minister Gordon Brown predicted in a speech in 2009 that "there can be only one winner: democracy and a strong Afghan state,"[53] did he believe it? Or did the international community perhaps assume, without ever confessing (like many members of the Afghan cabinet), that an authoritarian military state was a necessary phase in state-formation, or a precondition for rapid economic development, or a lesser evil in the fight against modern terrorism?

And what in the end did all this talk of state-building, or of any of these goals, buzzwords, or calculations mean to Haji Mohsin, sitting with other elderly bearded men, who were mostly his cousins, on a mud floor, leading his community? How exactly did "ungoverned space" or "the rule of law" or "the legitimate monopoly on the use of violence" apply to the province of Ghor? What exactly was the international community intending to change in Haji Mohsin's life and his village? Did it have a clear answer to that question? Did it have the skill and knowledge to succeed? Would Haji Mohsin let the international community do what it wanted?

UNGOVERNED SPACE

My own experience on the walk in 2002 was that Afghanistan was far from being "ungoverned space," still less a white spot on the map. It was true that there were no police or civil servants in the villages of central Afghanistan, and there had not been for over twenty-five years. Yet I walked entirely safely alone and unarmed for three hundred miles through them without being robbed or murdered, because the area was generally densely controlled, in a way that had little resemblance to the descriptions or prescriptions of the international community.

On the one hand, there were the international slogans of "governance" and "chains of accountability linking the citizen to the state."[54] On the other hand, there was the role of the fifty men in whose houses I ate or slept during my walk, well-known men whose reputations spread for fifty miles on either side: Shia and Sunni, from the Hazara, Aimaq, Pushtun, and Tajik minorities, young and old, literate and illiterate.

My hosts had fought and collaborated with and resisted the Russians, Taliban, and Karzai and had been financed by many different groups, sometimes simultaneously. Almost all had trekked into Iran or Pakistan at some time, to take refuge or gather supplies or ammunition. Almost all had lost close relatives during the jihad. All were backed by armed followers, many of whom were their relatives. They all prayed five times a day and engaged me in earnest conversations about Islam. They all expressed their resistance to foreign occupation. Some had hosted Al Qaeda.

Almost all of them provided justice and security to their communities. I watched them preside at meetings, impose punishment on villagers, respond to threats from neighboring communities, organize groups to gather grain, and distribute money. They exercised something close to the power of life and death over their villages. They generously put me up in their houses and fed me, night after night, and they almost never requested anything from me—or from the development community.[55]

The name of one host, Commandant Moalem Haji Mohsin Khan Kamenji (whom I mentioned earlier), sounded like a lot of names, but instead contained a lot of titles: commander of the militia, school teacher, pilgrim to Mecca, hereditary chief of the Taimani Aimaq, and landlord of Kamenj. His own career illustrated the real effect of constitutional and governance changes over thirty years. Mohsin had been an official under the king's cousin, Daud Khan. When Daud was assassinated in 1978, Mohsin became an official under the pro-Soviet leftist government of Nur Muhammad Taraki; when Taraki was assassinated in 1979, Mohsin became an official under the mildly anti-Soviet government of Hafizullah Amin. When Amin was assassinated by Spetsnatz (Soviet Special Forces) storm troopers, at the end of 1979, Mohsin became an official under the new Soviet occupation. In 1986, Mohsin became a commander of the CIA-backed resistance to the Soviets. In 1996 Mohsin was a Taliban commander.

When I stayed with Mohsin, he was in hiding, having recently tried to assassinate Ismail Khan, the governor of Herat; but within months, Mohsin was back in power again under Karzai as the education director of his local district of Shahrak. There had been many regimes in the last thirty years, backed by Americans, Soviets, Saudis, Pakistanis, and now the UN mandate: royalist, nationalist, Marxist, Soviet, theocratic, and pro-Western, with many constitutions. But there always seems to be one power in Kamenj. Mohsin's was not the state that the international community or indeed many

Afghans wanted—it was conservative and patriarchal. But did the international community understand it, or have the formula to transform it?

THE RULE OF LAW

"The rule of law" was one of the most popular goals of the international community in Afghanistan. In 2007, the Italian government held a conference on "stato di diritto" in Afghanistan, and German Chancellor Angela Merkel of Germany gave a speech, emphasizing "Rechtsstaatlichkeit." In 2009, French President Nicolas Sarkozy wrote to Karzai praising him for his progress toward "l'etat de droit," and UK Prime Minister Gordon Brown emphasized "the rule of law" in Parliament. Obama highlighted it again in a speech in Kabul in 2010.[56] Indeed, I am not aware of a head of government or a general in NATO who did not apply the phrase to Afghanistan at that period. It was so ubiquitous that it hardly ever seemed to demand definition.[57] The World Development Indicators (sponsored by the World Bank), however, defined "the rule of law" as "the quality of contract enforcement, the police and the courts, as well as the likelihood of crime or violence."[58] Characteristically, the international community considered that in this respect—as in so many other respects—Haji Mohsin's province of Ghor and Afghanistan in general were a disaster. Equally characteristically, every year, the international community had a new strategy to transform it.

Eighty-five percent of Afghans and almost 100 percent of people in Ghor operated through traditional structures, without police, courts, or prisons. Such things existed in the cities—along with a detailed corpus of civil and criminal law, a clear constitutional delineation of citizens' rights and responsibilities—but most villagers encountered none of these things. Village detection of crime (in the absence of police) was largely based on the assumption that many people in the village "knew what was going on," and, of course, in most villages there were no formal procedures for serving a warrant, charging, or arresting. The "cases" were "heard" (of course, all these words are highly misleading) on a village floor by elders or mullahs. The informal "jury" consisted of the people who were generally related to both victim and culprit.

The "judges" were often illiterate, and even if they could read, they had rarely mastered a detailed corpus of legislation. The laws they implemented were a distinctive blend of Sharia Islamic law and Afghan tribal custom. These could differ dramatically between communities. Shia family law, for example, when codified for the Afghan parliament, required a wife to have sex with her husband, except under certain specified medical conditions. The Taliban banned televisions and hung them from trees. Different sectarian groups and different mullahs within a single group could disagree on crime and punishment. There were some judicial mutilations and executions, but generally communities preferred to award fines, even for criminal offenses, and people were rarely incarcerated, in part because there were no prisons.

For most of the foreign consultants—and, indeed, most of the formally educated Afghan judges and lawyers—this existing system, insofar as they were aware of it, seemed to have little to do with what they meant by the rule of law. Indeed, the definition of *the rule of law* by the great legal philosopher Joseph Raz seemed almost a direct attack on the practice in Afghan villages: "There should be clear rules and procedures for making laws; the independence of the judiciary has to be guaranteed; the principles of natural justice should be observed, particularly those concerning the right to a fair hearing; the courts should have the power of judicial review over the way in which the other principles are implemented; the courts should be accessible."[59]

The international community spent hundreds of millions attempting to create "the rule of law" in Afghanistan. The World Justice Project, created by New York law firms, and propagated through seminars in Vienna, wanted to ensure that in Afghanistan "access to justice is provided by competent, independent, and ethical adjudicators, attorneys or representatives and judicial officers who are of sufficient number, have adequate resources, and reflect the makeup of the communities they serve."[60] As with many programs, one of the most sophisticated aspects of their program was its feasibility study, which boasted that it had "developed a robust and cost-effective methodology to measure more than 100 variables."[61]

The USAID programs on the rule of law were more costly. A friend of mine who was employed as a rule-of-law consultant in one of them calculated that the total cost of himself, his single colleague, their accommodation, their support, and their security team was one and a half million dollars a year. The hundreds of millions of dollars spent over a decade allowed the international community, among other things, to train lawyers and judges; to take Afghan judges to meet state judges in the Midwest; to hold seminars; to republish Afghan laws; to introduce new codes and administrative regulations; and to build prisons and train policemen.

At the end of the period, the justice delivered by young Taliban commanders under trees was consistently rated as fairer and more efficient than that of the infrastructure of the state to which the international community had devoted so much time and money. The Afghan judiciary was astonishingly corrupt. A

senior Afghan judge conceded in 2009 that the only reason anyone came to his court in Helmand was to get a passport application form. And more and more Afghans said, "At least there was
security and justice under the Taliban." Across the country, 85
percent of Afghans continued to focus on informal systems.[62]

Many in the international community came to recognize their
failure, and after 2008 more energy was invested in understanding "traditional and transitional justice." But they were never
able to determine what role foreigners could usefully play at a
village level, given the isolation and limits of the foreigners and
the huge variety and family-specific nature of those processes.
The Afghan formal judiciary in the cities continued to be hostile to "backward" methods. An Afghan supreme court justice
told me in 2010 that this was not "justice at all." So, although
the international community belatedly acknowledged the problem (even U.S. Secretary of Defense Robert Gates talked about
"minimal methods of dispute resolution"), it was far from clear
that it had a "solution"—or whether its new interest in informal
structures was really going to help its stated objective of "fixing
the failed state" in Afghanistan.

DISARMAMENT, DEMOBILIZATION, AND REINTEGRATION

"The rule of law" was the last of the ten functions of the state
that underpinned the 2004 strategy on Afghanistan. The first
was "the legitimate monopoly on the use of violence." This
was a phrase used by the early-twentieth-century sociologist
Max Weber to explain the importance of centralized armies to
nation-states in Western Europe in the seventeenth century. But
Weber was now firmly in Afghanistan. A report commissioned

by the UK government cited him in 2003.[63] Fareed Zakaria wrote in the *Washington Post*, "Max Weber once defined a state as that entity that has a monopoly of the legitimate use of force in the country. In Afghanistan, the state has no such monopoly. Winding down militias is the only path to that goal."[64]

But the programs that attempted to realize Weber's description were often not simply surreal but reprehensible. I remember, for example, in August 2004, watching some American soldiers leading a column of the Afghan army into Ghor, in the central highlands. Their aim was "DDR," to "disarm, demobilize, and reintegrate" the militia of Ahmad Morghabi, a key commander in the province. Ahmad had been armed by the United States, Saudi Arabia, and Pakistan to fight the Soviets in the 1980s. In 2001, he had again become an ally of the international community in the fight against the Taliban, and his militia group had been given a formal role as "the 41st Division" of the Afghan army. Now the international community was planning to disarm him.

He had not been selected at random: he had been selected by ministers in Kabul because he was an ally of their former friend and now enemy, Ismail Khan, the governor of Herat. The militia, who would be promoted in Ahmad's place, included that of Haji Mohsin's brother-in-law, Rais Salam Khan (who cut off ears), whose major income came from control of the central opium routes, and Governor Ibrahim Malikzada (the man who apparently fed his guest to his dogs). Human Rights Watch meanwhile had just mistakenly described Rais Salam Khan as an ally of Ismail Khan (he was a sworn enemy), and the UN had just been convinced into releasing him from jail.

I saw the U.S. soldiers resting by a landslide in the road and particularly noticed a blond man taking photographs of a beautiful young girl who was scouring cooking pots, near a round yurt. Later that afternoon the column was ambushed, two U.S.

soldiers were wounded, and an A-10 "Warthog" tank-buster air-craft covered the retreat (with a thirty-millimeter cannon that can fire 3,900 depleted uranium rounds in one minute). The villagers estimated that at least twenty Afghans were killed. This chaos was tidied up in a speech by the UN spokesman into a mission "to discuss various issues, including potential disarmament plans, with a faction that had originally been part of the 41st Division."[65] Major Jon Siepmann, the U.S. military spokesman in Kabul, added that the bloody retreat conveyed "an important message that DDR here in Afghanistan is more than just talk."[66]

The next month, inspired in part by this action by the international community, Rais Salam Khan the ear-cutter was confident enough to attack Ismail Khan, Ahmad's ally, in Herat and take over from Ahmad as commander of Chaghcharan. Ismail Khan retreated to Kabul, and his supporters took to the streets and set fire to UN offices. Seven people were killed in the rioting. A senior official in the Afghan government told me this was all "a virtuous circle, away from illegitimate fiefdoms towards a legitimate central authority and a secure, stable, free, prosperous and democratic Afghanistan."

In truth, the DDR mission against Ahmad was not just a surreal abstraction: it was a policy of imperial divide and rule, which was as foolish as it was morally disturbing. It was directed against a group previously armed and supported by the international community. It was interfering violently with a fragile microsystem of vendettas in a distant province, and destabilizing the region around Herat, which was at the time the best-administered, most stable, and most prosperous province in the country. In the name of disassociating itself from warlords, the international community was in fact forging public alliances with even more unpopular and cruel men at a great cost to its own legitimacy—and ultimately (since many of these men had been Taliban commanders) to its security.

Within a few years the international community was rearming militias such as Ahmad's again. This was because it had lost confidence in the ability of the Afghan security forces to protect villages. The rearmed groups were called "local defence forces." And the international community wanted to disarm them again a year later.

As for human rights, it is worth noting that the commander Gul Agha Sherzai, whose notorious child abuse in 1995 had been one of the major reasons for the Taliban's early popularity, was well established by 2009 as governor of Jalalabad, where he became the toast of the international community. Mullah Mustafa, who shot at me in 2002, continued to terrorize people on the main highway, effectively closing it to all international NGOs. (A predator drone tried to kill him in 2008 but missed and killed twenty others.) Rais Salam Khan, the ear-cutter whom the international community had brought back to power, was finally killed in Barra Khana not by the international community but by a rival, in December 2009. His brother-in-law Haji Mohsin remained the sole power in Kamenj. In 2002, when I walked safely alone as a foreigner from Herat to Chaghcharan, there was no Taliban threat in the area. By 2011, after hundreds of billion of dollars had been spent on security and state-building, the Taliban operated freely around Herat and it would have been almost suicidal to walk the route again.

But the same abstraction that doomed the international community's projects to failure also prevented it from recognizing its failure. Lofty abstractions such as "ungoverned space," "the rule of law," and "the legitimate monopoly on the use of violence" are so difficult to apply to an Afghan village that it was almost impossible to know when they were failing. And since it had perhaps not yet succeeded (what after all would success look like?), the international community sent in more money and more troops and more plans.

MILITARY OPTIMISM

Nowhere was this tendency clearer than with the military. Each new general in Afghanistan from 2002 to 2011 suggested that the situation he had inherited was dismal; implied that this was because his predecessor had had the wrong resources or strategy; and asserted that he now had the resources, strategy, and leadership to deliver a decisive year.[67]

General Karl Eikenberry, whom Richard Holbrooke supported to be the new ambassador in Afghanistan, had served there before. In 2002, as a general in Afghanistan, he said he had inherited a position in which "the mandate was clear and it was a central task, but it is also fair to say that up until that time there had been few resources committed."[68] In 2003, the new commander, General Dan McNeill, like almost all his successors, said he had inherited no strategy: "We had nothing in any book."[69] McNeill, however, had a new strategy,[70] and he predicted that "most parts of the country will soon begin to realize some reasonable degree of security and stability." The year 2004 might be a turning point during which the United States could reduce troop numbers.[71] His successor agreed: "Without question," 2004 would be "a decisive year."[72]

In 2004, the new ISAF commander, General David Barno, said he had inherited a situation in which "there was no major planning initiated to create long-term political, social and economic stability in Afghanistan."[73] But he had a new strategy: "What we're doing is moving to a more classic counterinsurgency strategy here in Afghanistan. That's a fairly significant change in terms of our tactical approach out there on the ground."[74] General John Abizaid, his commander, thought 2005 would be a "decisive year."[75]

In 2005, the new commander, General Eikenberry (returning), said he inherited a situation in which "the institutions of the Afghan state remain relatively weak." But he had a new strategy: "Our longer-term goal of strengthening good governance, the rule of law, reconstruction and humanitarian assistance, and economic development."[76] He was confident that 2006 would be a turning point.[77]

In 2006, the new ISAF commander, General Sir David Richards, said he had inherited a position that was "close to anarchy."[78] But he had a "new strategy": "establishing bases rather than chasing militants."[79] ISAF doubled its presence in Afghanistan to 18,500 soldiers from thirty-seven countries,[80] and the troops under his command increased from 9,000 to more than 33,000. General Richards predicted that for the Taliban 2006 would be the "crunch year."[81]

In 2007, the new ISAF commander, General McNeill (again), had inherited a position[82] defined by "shadows cast by former power brokers or warlords . . . lack of effective governance . . . a lack of unified effort amongst the international community and lack of effective police." As for counter-narcotics, "We're not trained, we're not equipped, we don't have the requisite number of helicopters, and we're not manned to do it."[83] He was much more cautious about giving press interviews than his predecessor, so it is WikiLeaks that confirmed his private views in a confidential U.S. telegram:

> [McNeill] was particularly dismayed by the British effort. They had made a mess of things in Helmand, their tactics were wrong,

and the deal that London cut on Musa Qala had failed. That agreement opened the door to narco-traffickers in that area, and now it was impossible to tell the difference between the traffickers and the insurgents. The British could do a lot more, he said, and should, because they have the biggest stake.[84]

But the general had a new strategy, which included, it seemed, a shift to a more "kinetic strategy" including aerial bombardment.[85] The United States doubled the number of its ground troops in Afghanistan.[86] Norwegian Foreign Minister Espen Barth Eide predicted that 2007 would be "a decisive year."[87]

In 2008, the new ISAF commander, General David McKiernan, said he had inherited a position in which "we are seeing an increase in violence . . . there are unacceptable levels of corruption," and the Afghan government "is ineffective in many areas of Afghanistan."[88] But he had a new strategy. In his Joint Campaign Plan of 2008, he introduced more counterinsurgency terminology (as opposed to the previous "stability" strategy).[89] "The fact is that we are at war in Afghanistan. It's not peacekeeping. It's not stability operations. It's not humanitarian assistance. It's war."[90] Defense Secretary Robert Gates approved the deployment of a further 3,200 marines to southern Afghanistan,[91] bringing the total number of troops during 2008 to 50,000. Canadian Major General Bernard S. Champoux predicted 2008 would "be a decisive year."[92]

Richard Holbrooke was not impressed in 2009 by the strategy or the resources that had preceded his arrival. Shortly after Holbrooke took office as the presidential Special Representative for Afghanistan and Pakistan, General McKiernan was fired. "From a military perspective, we can and must do better," Defense Secretary Gates said.[93] And Holbrooke's new team brought "a new strategy, a new mission and a new ambassador."[94] President Obama had already approved the deployment of a further 17,000 troops to Afghanistan. In 2009, the new ISAF commander, General Stanley McChrystal, talked about the situation he had inherited in terms of "resilient and growing insurgency . . . weakness of Afghan government institutions."[95] He unveiled his comprehensive assessment, stating, "The new strategy will improve effectiveness through better application of existing assets, but it also requires additional resources." The Canadian ambassador, Ron Hoffman, predicted that 2009 would be "a decisive year."[96]

General David Petraeus, then commander of U.S. Central Command, confirmed, "For the first time we will then have the tools and what's required in place to carry out the kind of campaign that [is] necessary here with our Afghan partners."[97] In the last interview before he too, like his predecessor, was fired, General McChrystal stated, "The Taliban . . . no longer has the initiative. . . . We are knee-deep in the decisive year."[98]

In 2010, the new ISAF commander, General Petraeus, inherited a position characterized by insurgent attacks on coalition forces spiking to record levels, violence metastasizing to previously stable areas, and the country's president undercutting anti-corruption units backed by Washington.[99] But Petraeus had a new strategy, which involved moving back to a more kinetic approach (combined with counterinsurgency).[100] President Obama had already agreed to send 30,000 additional troops, and troop levels reached almost 150,000. Both the NATO secretary-general and the UK foreign secretary, David Miliband, predicted that 2010 would be "a decisive year."[101]

Reading all of the interviews, testimonies, strategies, and reports of the ISAF commanding generals from 2002 through 2010 is to stray into the congregation for an astonishing chanted liturgy. Year after year, those leading the ceremony condemned the demons of narcotics and corrupt government and reaffirmed the goals of state-building and counterinsurgency. Different commanders heralded new approaches in their ceaseless struggle to empower district or central officials, build up local defense forces, improve the police, and win the confidence of the population. Every year from 2005, more and more money was spent, more and more troops were deployed. Each year was to prove decisive. None was. How could this have been possible? Why was no one ever exposed? Why did neither colleagues nor bosses nor the public ever challenge such sublime "cautious optimism"? How could it have been allowed to continue?

These attitudes were not confined to the center: they echoed down the hierarchy in every province. In Helmand Province every departing commander celebrated his unit's achievements. Every new commander believed he had inherited a situation characterized by corruption, insecurity, tribal tensions, lack of local support, poor Afghan government, and lack of development. Every commander wondered if his predecessor had not worked, perhaps unknowingly, with the wrong power-holders—the wrong subdistrict officials, the wrong policemen, the wrong tribes—and launched "unsustainable" development projects. To each commander, the problem was clearly that the previous strategy had been wrong. So each introduced a new strategy.

When the predecessor emphasized central government, the successor emphasized decentralization. Predecessors and successors oscillated between emphasis on local militias and emphasis on the national army; action on counter-narcotics and inaction on the same; spread-out isolated positions to concentrated bases; keeping distance from the population to being among them. The commanders went from "ink spots" and "Afghan Development Zones" (a concentrated approach) to remote, thinly spread forward operating bases. Musa Qala is taken and lost and taken again (so is Panjwai); troops clear, hold, leave, clear, hold, and leave again. Governor Sher Muhammad Akhunzadeh is replaced by Governor Daud, and Governor Daud by Governor Mangal, and then there is pressure to reappoint Sher Muhammad Akhunzadeh. The people are disarmed, and then rearmed as local defense forces, or as arbakai, or as local police. We go from training the Afghan forces, to mentoring them, to partnering with them.

All of which heralds a decisive year. And during this time, great progress is announced: previously unsafe areas are cleared, "the bazaars are opening again," the soldiers are building strong relations with the Afghans, our "knowledge of tribal structures" is improving, we are more "coordinated," smarter with our deployment of money, more aware that there is "no purely military solution," "more realistic" about our expectations.[102] Meanwhile, the commander presses relentlessly for more resources, and more resources are granted. In Helmand in 2005, there were 200 American soldiers. By 2010, there were over 32,000 foreign troops in the province of Helmand alone, backed by more than 30,000 Afghans. The province accounts for only 1 percent of the landmass and 3 percent of the population of Afghanistan. Each time a commander hands over control of an area in a ceremony, he is praised by his successor for the transformation. And then almost immediately we hear the new commander privately confess that he has inherited a dismal situation but has a new strategy, requiring new resources, which will usher in a decisive year.

Britain is just one of forty-nine coalition partners and provides about 8 percent of the foreign soldiers in the country. Up and down the country, from the Spanish in Maimana to the Germans in Kunduz, from the Dutch in Uruzgan to the Lithuanians in Ghor, month by month came ripples and eddies of improvisation, hope, and despair as each separately inherited a bad situation, developed a new strategy and mission, and increased the resources.

This manic-depressive lurch meant that generals were often the very best critics of the policy that they championed, and frequently explained why they couldn't succeed. In the words of General McChrystal in his assessment of 2009,

> Many indicators suggest the overall situation is deteriorating. We face not only a resilient and growing insurgency. There is a crisis of confidence among Afghans . . . that undermines our credibility and emboldens the insurgents. [Problems include] weakness of Afghan government institutions, the unpunished abuse of power by corrupt officials and power-brokers, a widespread sense of political disenfranchisement and a long-standing lack of economic opportunity.[103]

Yet, he insisted that with more troops, all this could still be transformed. And eighteen months later, President Obama still reassured the American people:

> We are making considerable gains toward our military objectives. . . . [M]ore Afghans are reclaiming their communities. Targets for the growth of Afghan security forces are being met. . . . [W]e've dramatically increased our civilian presence, with more diplomats and development experts working alongside our troops. . . . We're going to have to continue to stand up. . . . And we will continue to do everything in our power to ensure the security and the safety of the American people. . . . [T]hanks to the extraordinary service of our troops and civilians on the ground, we are on track to achieve our goals.[104]

Richard Holbrooke died in November 2010. Three weeks after his death, the U.S. administration paid tribute to his service and then reinforced this optimistic doctrine. After all of the strategic reviews, and all of the effort and expenditure over the previous nine years, Secretary of State Hillary Clinton said, in 2010, that they had still "inherited an extraordinarily difficult situation. There was *no coherent strategy* to unify America's efforts in the region. There was *no clearly defined mission*. And our people, both our military and our civilian forces, *lacked the resources* they needed to get any progress . . . we had to *adopt a new strategy*, we had to *resource it more*."[105] President Obama had a new strategy that "defined a clear *mission* and committed the *resources* needed." The president concluded that "for the first time in years, we've put in place the *strategy* and the *resources*," and "we'll continue to give our brave troops and civilians the *strategy and resources* they need to succeed."[106] German Foreign Minister Guido Westerwelle predicted that 2011 would be an "entscheidendes," or a "decisive," year.[107]

More than forty years earlier, in a secret report dated 1966, Richard Holbrooke, a young State Department officer at the time (long before he was to play such a dominating role in the Balkans or Afghanistan), described his view of the situation at the other end of Asia: "Sitting in on the mission and hearing the same tired old arguments, visiting the Delta and listening to the same recital of difficulties and shortcomings, getting the constant refrain from each part of the Vietnam mosaic produced as if by rote . . ."

Holbrooke's secret report shows that he cannot escape chanting some of the litany himself. The U.S. administration had inherited a dismal situation: "There is no real government in Vietnam in the sense of a functioning administrative and political structure which can get the job done. . . . I have never seen the Americans in such disarray. This is the result of a rapid build-up, great pressure from higher headquarters, rapid personnel turnover. . . . [W]e are going to need a cadre of superior officers who are willing and interested to serve extended tours out there." He celebrates a new strategy: "I think the reorganization plans look good. They will put every American civilian in the provinces into a single operational line of command, reporting directly to the Deputy-Ambassador. . . . In each Region/Corps . . . a Senior Civilian Representative . . . will command all US civilian operations in the area. And it is a decisive moment. . . . [W]ithin ninety days we will be able to see whether or not this new organization holds promise of more effective management of the US mission. I believe it does." [108]

ELEVEN LESSONS

In 1995 former U.S. secretary of defense Robert McNamara recorded "eleven lessons" from the Vietnam War. Leaders in Afghanistan today tend to blame the problems, which they inherited: corruption, poor governance, and the absence of the rule of law.[109] Such problems were as present in Vietnam as in Afghanistan, but McNamara does not list them. In Iraq, commentators have tended to blame the tactical errors of the United States in 2003: disbanding the Iraqi army, de-Ba'athifying, and allowing looting. There were similar tactical errors in Vietnam, but McNamara does not emphasize them. Nor does he propose that there was a solution such as "engagement with neighbors" or "a political settlement with the insurgents." Nor recommend a new strategy of "state-building" or "counterinsurgency." Nor ask for more resources.

Instead he emphasizes that the problems in Vietnam were much more structural. They stemmed from the intrinsic limitations of the foreign administration: its absence of political decorum, solid research, independent civil servants, and "first-class" policy analysis. He insists that more deep country and language expertise was required.[110] He argues that the political leadership struggled to cope with explaining uncertainty and complexity:[111] "We did not explain fully what was happening and why we were doing what we did. We had not prepared the public to understand the complex events we faced and how to react constructively to the need for changes in course as the nation confronted uncharted seas and an alien environment."[112]

McNamara's deeper analysis, however, raises points that are still unwelcome and unsettling today. Fundamentally for McNamara, the real problem of the intervention did not lie simply in poor preparation, planning, decisions, resource deployment, or even the absence of a specialized cadre of interveners. The failure was predetermined by modern Western culture—by attitudes and worldviews of which the policy elite would have been hardly conscious. These included a materialist worldview whose gods were technology and progress, which denied the reality of cultural difference and which was driven by a bizarre optimism:

> We failed to recognize that in international affairs, as in other aspects of life, there may be problems for which there are no immediate solutions. We failed to recognize the limitations of modern, high-technology military equipment, forces, and doctrine in confronting unconventional, highly motivated people's movements.[113]

The most profound part of Robert McNamara's analysis of Vietnam reaches far beyond a conventional policy book and provides explanations for the West's behavior that are psychiatric or even spiritual. He points to our sins in the language of the confession:

> We viewed the people and leaders of South Vietnam in terms of our own experience. We do not have the God-given right to shape every nation in our own image or as we choose. We did not recognize that neither our people nor our leaders are omniscient. We exaggerated the dangers to the United States.[114]

FEAR

It is McNamara's last observation on the "exaggerated . . . dangers to the United States" that explains in part why interventions from Vietnam to Afghanistan have persisted far beyond the moment at which it should have been obvious that they had failed.[115] Afghanistan, Vietnam, and indeed Iraq were each presented as a unique threat to global security: a nation that could endanger the very survival of the United States and the global order, not simply one troubling country among many. In the words of Ronald Reagan in 1964, "We are at war [in Vietnam] with the most dangerous enemy that has ever faced mankind in his long climb from the swamp to the stars."[116] Or in Donald Rumsfeld's phrase, "No terrorist state poses a greater or more immediate threat to the security of our people and the stability of the world than the regime of Saddam Hussein in Iraq."[117] In Obama's words, the Afghan border region was "the most dangerous place in the world."[118] In every case, therefore, failure seemed "not an option."

The exact object of our fear changes over time; the structure of that fear does not. During the Cold War we were afraid of communism.[119] There was a brief moment when, as an eighteen-year-old British infantry officer with a short-service limited commission, at the end of the Cold War, I felt we were struggling to find our new demon. My regiment, apart from tours in Northern Ireland, had not seen action since the Korean War. Senior officers had served full careers without ever going into battle. I felt we were rehearsing for a play that would never be performed.

But when, twelve years after my first rainy Remembrance Sunday parade in England, I next laid a wreath on Remembrance Sunday, it was in the cemetery in Al Amarah, in Iraq. The security establishment had found its new threats and deployed accordingly. Genocide, organized crime, weapons of mass destruction, terrorism, and failed states had now replaced communism as our target. The Black Watch adjutant who attended that parade in 1991 was about to command the battalion in Fallujah and then a brigade in Helmand. The European diplomat Robert Cooper now fluently analyzed Afghanistan in the light of "non-state actors, notably drug, crime, or terrorist syndicates . . . using premodern bases for attacks on the more orderly parts of the world."[120]

Once a country has been named as an existential threat, the fear could be extended in four well-established directions. The first category of fear was of the country itself: the fear of the rogue state, which was often perceived as posing a direct threat to the homeland. Iraq, according to Tony Blair, had weapons of mass destruction that could be "launched within 45 minutes" against targets in Europe.[121] Vietnam, Lyndon Johnson said, was behind an invasion, whose purpose was "to conquer the south, to defeat American power and to extend the Asiatic domination of Communism."[122] And in the words of British Prime

Minister Gordon Brown, "There is a chain of terror that comes from the Pakistani and Afghan mountains, right across Europe, and can end up very easily on the streets of Britain."[123]

Second, there is the fear of what is not in the country—the vacuum into which outsiders or rogue elements can flow. This is the fear of the failed state. For Lyndon Johnson the communist international movement had infiltrated Vietnam and was using it as a base.[124] For Paddy Ashdown, the High Representative in Bosnia, it was "crime and corruption," which "follow swiftly . . . like a dark shadow. They seep into the space that wars leave almost as the last firing stops."[125] The major threat in Iraq, after the invasion, was often defined as coming from foreign fighters such as Abu Musab al-Zarqawi (a Jordanian). Afghanistan mattered because foreigners like the Saudi Osama bin Laden had once based themselves there.[126]

Third, there was the fear of the effect on the neighbors. Bush's ambassador to the UN, John Bolton, *Time* magazine's Joe Klein, and the *Economist* magazine each argued that if Afghanistan fell to the Taliban, nuclear Pakistan could fall to extremists too.[127] U.S. Deputy Secretary of Defense Paul Wolfowitz insisted that the political system in Iraq had a catalytic effect on the neighboring countries, such as Iran and Saudi Arabia (and if it became a democracy, so should its neighbors).[128] And there was no more important rationale in Vietnam than the effect on neighboring Southeast Asia, for as Eisenhower claimed, "You have a row of dominoes set up: you knock over the first one, and what will happen to the last one is the certainty that it will go over very quickly."[129]

Finally, there was the fear for our own credibility and that of our coalition partners. As the deputy head of the UN in Kabul insisted, "We have our credibility on the line not just as individual nations but as a community of nations."[130] Sherard

Cowper-Coles, the British ambassador to Afghanistan, asked, "How would you explain [troop reductions] to our NATO partners? We would do severe, perhaps fatal, damage to the international alliance. No responsible British prime minister could support such a policy."[131] Richard Nixon explained, "What concerns me more than anything else [in Vietnam] is what happens to the U.S. If a great power fails to meet its aims, it ceases to be a great power. When a great power looks inward, when it fails to live up to its commitment, then the greatness fades away."[132]

President George W. Bush's concept of the "war on terror" often led him to speak about Iraq in a way that combined many such different fears: "The terrorists regard Iraq as the central front in their war against humanity, and we must recognize Iraq as the central front in our war on terror." He added in the same speech that we should not dismiss militants who "believe that controlling one country will rally the Muslim masses, enabling them to overthrow all moderate governments in the region, and establish a radical Islamic empire that spans from Spain to Indonesia."[133]

The Pakistani scholar Ahmed Rashid could also portray Afghanistan as almost the sum of all our fears:

[Withdrawal of troops] would be an abandonment of the Afghans. It would be an abandonment of the region. I think NATO would start unravelling. Helmand would immediately fall into the hands of the Taliban and they would get their hands on the biggest asset for extremism—drugs and money. If this kind of money was really made available to Al Qaeda and the extremist Taliban, I think it would have a devastating effect not only in Afghanistan but across the region.[134]

Such worst-case scenarios were generally not presented as one possibility among many—but as the inevitable and inescapable result of any block on troop increases (still less proposed reductions). The verb was always *would* or *will*, not *might*. In the more restrained rhetoric of President Obama in 2009,

> For the Afghan people, a return to Taliban rule *would* condemn their country to brutal governance, international isolation, a paralyzed economy, and the denial of basic human rights to the Afghan people—especially women and girls. The return in force of al-Qaida terrorists who *would* accompany the core Taliban leadership *would* cast Afghanistan under the shadow of perpetual violence. . . . If the Afghan government falls to the Taliban—or allows al-Qaida to go unchallenged—that country *will* again be a base for terrorists who want to kill as many of our people as they possibly can.[135]

Two years earlier, Ambassador Cowper-Coles—one of the most enlightened and critical analysts of the intervention—predicted the consequences of reducing troop numbers in language redolent of the apocalypse, or the closing battles of *The Lord of the Rings*:

> The people—especially the women—of the Pashtun belt *would* be plunged back into a new dark age. The warlords *would* regroup, and come down from the north. A new and even bloodier civil war *would* erupt. . . . War, and probably famine, *would* stalk the land again.[136]

Holbrooke understood how exaggerated and imprisoning our fears had been in Vietnam, saying, "The mission itself was based on a profound misreading, by five presidents and their advisors, of the strategic importance of Vietnam to the U.S."[137]

But he believed that the paranoia which had been irrational in Vietnam was now entirely rational in Afghanistan:

> The President put the stress on Al Qaeda because that's the reason we're there, and that's the core difference between Iraq and Vietnam, on the one hand, and Afghanistan, on the other. Americans cannot think of a situation where, in the face of attacks by Al Qaeda, they would give up, they would say, "The hell with it, we have to leave." It's just not an acceptable course of action.[138]

In Afghanistan—as in so many previous interventions—because of our fears "failure was not an option."

LAWRENCE AND HOLBROOKE

None of this was entirely new. Many nineteenth-century public figures saw Afghanistan as a fundamental threat. There were fears of Afghan rulers raiding or attacking their neighbors. Then there was the fear of the "failed state" or vacuum. In the words of Prince Gorchakov, the Russian foreign minister on Afghanistan in 1864,

> The position of Russia in Central Asia is that of all civilized states brought into contact with half-savage nomad populations possessing no fixed social organization. In such cases it always happens that the more civilized state is forced, in the interest of the security of its frontiers and its commercial relations, to exercise a certain ascendancy over those whose turbulent and unsettled character makes them undesirable neighbours.[139]

For the British Empire, the main fear was of foreigners exploiting Afghan soil (at this time, not, of course, Saudi terrorists, but the Russians). But neither the Russians nor the British ever felt that "failure was not an option." Despite their colonialist agenda, each ultimately resisted the temptation of persisting in a full occupation of Afghanistan or trying to press on with a program of state-building in the face of widespread insurgency. Thus, John Lawrence, the British Viceroy of India, said in response to demands to occupy Afghanistan in 1867,

> I am firmly of opinion that our proper course is not to advance our troops beyond our present border, not to send English officers into the different states of Central Asia; but to put our own house in order, by giving the people . . . the best government in our power, by conciliating, as far as practicable, all classes, and by consolidating our resources.[140]

This belief that Afghanistan did not pose an existential threat, and that intervention might be unwise reflected, in part, the structures within which Lawrence and his colleagues operated. His employers in British India, on whose border Afghanistan lay, were often racist, harsh, destructive, and justifiably despised, but they were deeply immersed in local reality. British India was not a rapidly improvised ad hoc collection of internationals, with extravagant budgets, limitless power, and very short-term postings. It favored staff with long experience who served in remote posts, spoke languages well, and reflected on local culture. This was inculcated in every cadet, factored into every promotion and medal. And experience also characterized the institutions at home. More than sixty members of Parliament in 1805 had served in India, and by law the majority of the Council of India, which controlled Indian affairs in London, had to have served more than ten years on the ground in India. (By contrast, in late 2010, not a single staff member of the Foreign Office team responsible for Afghanistan in London had served on a posting there.)[141] This institutional culture and this cadre of specialists in Parliament, the military, and the media provided a well-informed challenge to exaggerated ambitions or fears about Afghanistan.

Victorian journalists like Archibald Forbes, or administrator-politicians like John Lawrence, or generals like Frederick Roberts were more critical of intervention than their equivalents are today. Forbes, for example, who was in some ways a loyal establishment journalist, wrote in 1890 about the murder of the defenseless, civilian British envoys whose corpses were paraded through the streets of Kabul: "Burnes and Macnaghten had met their fate because they had gone to Kabul the supporters of a detested intruder and the unwelcome representatives of a hated power."[142] In the 1920s, Gertrude Bell, serving as the senior political officer in the British occupation of Iraq, wrote a series of semi-private letters to government ministers and journalists that were never muffled in platitudes:

> . . . There's no getting out of the conclusion that we have made an immense failure here.
>
> No one knows exactly what they do want, least of all themselves, except that they don't want us.
>
> [In talking to an Arab nationalist leader] I said complete independence was what we ultimately wished to give. "My lady" he answered—we were speaking Arabic—"complete independence is never given; it is always taken."[143]

None of this wisdom saved them from failure. Some British officials remained keen on intervention and the British stumbled into a humiliating mess in Afghanistan in 1842 and 1879. But they were much quicker than their modern equivalents to acknowledge their failure and withdraw. This was not because of a lack of public pressure to remain. Many Victorians insisted that the Afghans wanted them to remain; that if the British left, it would become a failed state, exploited by Russia and endangering the whole region; and that if the British were seen to be driven out by the Afghans, the credibility of the British Empire would be destroyed around the world. In short, all of the fears for British national security, Britain's relationship with the Afghans, and British pride required Britain to remain.[144] But General Roberts, the hero of the Second Anglo-Afghan War, was able to summarily reject these views, in a way that Holbrooke could not. Despite all the fears and the guilt, and the losses and expense that Britain had incurred in its campaign in Afghanistan, he argued,

> We have nothing to fear from Afghanistan, and the best thing to do is to leave it as much as possible to itself. It may not be very flattering to our amour propre, but I feel sure I am right when I say that the less the Afghans see of us the less they will dislike us.[145]

CHANGING POLICY

I returned to Afghanistan (after spending a short time at Harvard) in 2005. And when I heard that the British government was about to send three thousand soldiers into Helmand, I was confident that there would soon be a widespread insurgency. I also predicted that the military would demand more troops, and would get dragged ever deeper. It wasn't that I had any particular skill in predicting the future. I failed to predict that Egypt's President Hosni Mubarak would fall. I was wrong about Iraq. And my prediction for Helmand wasn't based on any knowledge of Helmand. It was simply that I recognized the mindset and the actions of the NATO governments from Iraq. And I wasn't alone in warning against the deployment. Many others predicted the same thing in Helmand. A military friend of mine had returned from a recce saying, "There isn't an insurgency, but you can have one if you want one." The Helmand surge continued regardless. The British government seemed to have a momentum, quite distinct from any individual politician or policy-maker. Troops were increased from two hundred U.S. Special Forces in 2005 to three thousand British soldiers in 2006.

At the time, senior officials reassured me that they understood the danger of being dragged in too deep. Two offered to sign a document saying that if the three thousand troops didn't "establish governance, economic development, and security" within six months, they would admit the policy was a mistake, rather than claim that the problem had simply been *strategy* and *resources*. But I did not force them to sign. And when six months passed and the situation had worsened, the same officials supported the call to increase the number of troops to five thousand, and a few months later to seven thousand. I began writing and speaking publicly against the policy. I argued that what was needed was not a surge but a reduction to a light long-term footprint.

This put me in a difficult position because the policy-makers were my friends and I lived in Kabul, where I had just started an NGO, restoring part of the historic city and establishing an institute for traditional crafts. My personal life and work indebted me to many of the people whose policies and governments I was criticizing. I found myself writing op-eds against generals who had been my hosts; giving academic lectures mocking the books and theories written by friends; and publicly debating an ambassador whom I admired. I was calling on the governments that were giving money to my NGO to send less money to Afghanistan. I was arguing against fighting the Taliban while many of the philanthropists who supported my work did so out of hatred of the Taliban. Many of my upper-class Afghan friends who had returned from the West to Kabul and were relying on the international community to build a state were particularly confused and hurt by my arguments. In retrospect and in the circumstances, I am astonished how forgiving they all were. Only one ambassador gently asked whether I could stop criticizing his country, in return for the millions his nation's taxpayers were giving to our NGO. But when I wouldn't make the commitment, the money still came.

Most of the internationals I knew in Kabul disagreed with me strongly. They said that I didn't know what I was talking about. And in many ways they were right. I was certainly not an expert on Afghanistan. Academics such as Tom Barfield and Barnett Rubin are truly scholars of Afghanistan. Afghan statesman such as Ashraf Ghani and the Afghan-American Zalmay Khalilzad have a much more detailed sense and understanding of Afghan history and politics. Journalists such as Ahmed Rashid have a much better sense of the language, the recent past, and the regional context. People who have run projects on the ground, from Andrew Wilder and Antony Fitzherbert to Michael Semple and Martine van Biljert, have a much more detailed sense of the reality of international assistance in Afghanistan. Generals and ambassadors and development directors know far more about military tactics, practical diplomacy, and development theory. There are, most importantly, thirty million Afghans who intuitively understand far more about Afghanistan than any foreigner. And, as the British pointed out gleefully, I had traveled only in the north and center of Afghanistan—I had been to Helmand only once.

Nevertheless, I was confident that I was right. I tried to explain that this was not based on any special insights about Afghanistan, but instead on a sense of ourselves: the international community. I felt I had learned in the Balkans and particularly in Iraq that we—the foreign government organizations and their partners—know much less and can do much less than we pretend. I knew the international community underestimated the reality of Afghan rural life: they did not grasp just how poor, fragile, and traumatized Afghanistan was; just how conservative and resistant to foreigners, villages could be. Our institutions were too inherently optimistic, too ad hoc, too isolated from the concerns and realities of Afghan life, too caught up in metaphysical abstractions of "governance" and "the rule of law" ever to succeed—or to notice that we were not succeeding. But I don't think I ever convinced a single international in Kabul that "counterinsurgency" or "state-building" was doomed to failure.

I began, from my base in Kabul, to travel to the bewildering international policy conferences to try to make the same arguments, but I had no more success. In 2007, for example, I spoke in Tartu, Estonia, at a government conference on Afghanistan. There were German generals, Italian diplomats, and representatives from European think tanks. The three Afghans present were almost the only native English speakers in the room, having been brought up in California and Virginia. The participants were reminded that there was "no military solution"; lectured on the need for a "comprehensive approach," including economic development and good government; and taught the intricacies of Pashtun tribal structures. I argued for my belief that there should not be troop increases but a "light long-term footprint." The conference concluded that more resources and a new strategy were needed.

Not only did I have no impact, but I also ceased to understand why such conferences were held in the first place. The Estonians did not, it seemed, see Afghanistan as vital to their future. They were there primarily to deepen their relationship with NATO and particularly the United States. So why were the Estonians or I or any of the representatives of America's allies, such as Germany, France, and Italy, producing PowerPoint presentations on Helmand government structures, papers on police training, and principles for tackling Pakistan? If we drew different conclusions from the United States, would we really be willing to present them, or able to implement them? The European Afghan debate seemed almost a ceremonial activity preserved to divert the public and to please visiting Americans—preserved for the same reasons that the Horse Guards still salute with their swords outside Buckingham Palace.

In 2008, I stopped working for the NGO and began to spend more time outside Europe trying to argue against troop increases. This gave me a glimpse of the frenetic activity and movement that comprised the natural living environment of people like Richard Holbrooke. I just found, doing my tax return, that I took a flight every two days, moving between Afghanistan, Europe, and the States, and participated in 104 separate meetings, lectures, and interviews[146] on Afghanistan in a single month. I got jet lag and I got nowhere. By 2008, the number of troops in Helmand had risen in three years from two hundred to three thousand to nine thousand.

At the end of 2008, I moved back to the United States to teach and to run a center at the Harvard Kennedy School. This was, I felt, the best chance I would ever get of convincing the international community to stop increasing the number of troops and adopt a "plan B." I expected the debate to be more open in the United States because America carried so much more of the responsibility and costs of the operation. It certainly seemed more alive. The new administration was conducting a "fundamental review" of the Afghan strategy. Very senior figures were beginning to express doubts about the troop increases. Even the most committed U.S. general told me that creating an effective, popular Afghan government alternative to the Taliban was "challenging." Holbrooke assured me that he had learned in Vietnam about generals who always assume that they need only to have more troops, new tactics, and more time. President Obama was acutely aware of the parallels between his position in Afghanistan and that of Bush in Iraq.

And my real advantage was that I was not alone. The center I was in at Harvard included six fellows who between them had spent over a century in the region, and who were, therefore, unlike me, real experts on Afghanistan. They covered every subject, from agriculture to tribes and counterinsurgency; they spoke Afghan languages fluently and were continually deep in the field. They were now also arguing, with their own hectic travel schedules, and through every conceivable channel and medium, against the current strategy of further troop increases, and in favor of a lighter, more moderate approach. Between us we briefed almost all of the major international policy-makers, diplomats, generals, and foreign ministers. But in March 2009, seventeen thousand more troops were sent. We redoubled our efforts to ensure that those were the last, and that the administration would now adopt a different strategy. Then, in October 2009—four years after I had begun a path where I did almost nothing other than argue against troop increases—Obama sent another thirty-four thousand troops.

Our failure with the administration was echoed by my failure in the classroom. Sixty students had signed up for a class on intervention, and in addition to the policy-makers who came to speak (we had George W. Bush's deputy national security adviser, Meghan O'Sullivan, and his deputy secretary of defense, Paul Wolfowitz), we allowed each of the six specialists to deliver detailed arguments based on their decades of experience of working in Afghanistan, talking about exactly what was not working with the elections, or rural development, or narcotics. And my friend Gerald Knaus led a whole section on the Balkans. I hoped to illustrate the lack of knowledge, power, and legitimacy in the engagements in the Balkans, Afghanistan, and Iraq. I wanted to show how policy was distorted by surreal, misleading, and fraudulent assumptions about counterinsurgency and state-building.[147]

The students were experienced and open-minded. And their attitudes were representative of the most ambitious policy professionals of the time, many of whom went to such institutions. (In 2009, the Harvard Kennedy School had more than twenty students or fellows who had recently served in Afghanistan and many more who were on their way there.) The military officers who had served in Afghanistan were among my best students. Erik, who had lost three men under his command in Waigal, was self-aware, critical, and focused. He wrote, "I am indescribably proud of my service, but can never feel good about it. I did the best I could with an impossible situation, but left behind what has become one of the most violent and unstable valleys in Afghanistan." He was not shy about offering criticism of the commanding general: McChrystal's "strategy is directly at odds with the goals. . . . Its presence stunts the growth of the Afghan state, institutions, and civil society. It enables the Karzai government's corruption, laziness and ineffectiveness."

He was far from alone in mounting powerful, cogent arguments that were very aware of the broader political process. Jake, for example, wrote imaginatively about the narrative of the war, the importance of accepting failure and the introductions of false crises. He explored the paradoxes of "localization" ("gaining the initiative makes strategic consolidation more difficult"). He discussed the need for different time lines for different audiences.

One student who went on to work for USAID wrote in a more abstract tone than the soldiers, with more organizational theory and language ("Since the inputs between Afghanistan and Iran are not analogous, the same outcomes should not be expected of the former as was seen in the latter"). She was sometimes tempted to assume that something like good governance in Afghanistan was achievable with time, rather than contemplating the practical obstacles that would probably prevent the United States from achieving it. But again, she made excellent, original, and convincing observations on the growth rate in Afghan army recruitment and on the tensions between short- and long-term goals.

But almost none of these experienced, able students agreed with me that the mission to defeat the Taliban or to build an Afghan state was not simply difficult but impossible. I failed even to convince them that because of the dramatic differences between Iraq and Afghanistan, "the surge of Iraq" would not work in Afghanistan. My attempt to argue that the international community necessarily lacked the knowledge, the power, and the legitimacy to engage with politics at a local provincial level, was mocked.

One student assured me that contrary to my claim that it was impossible for anyone to understand the complexity of Iraqi politics, "the key issues at the time had all been covered, in the

Washington Post, The New Yorker, and other mainstream media."
When I tried to suggest how much had been left out by even the
best journalistic descriptions of Iraq (the question, for example,
of why the Badr brigades were strong in Samawah and the Sad-
rists much stronger in Amarah), the same student accused me of
"moving the goal posts" and speculated, "I suspect one reason
why you oppose interventions is because you were never present to see them stop massacres of civilians, as in Kosovo, and
only came along some years after the fact of interventions to see
Clowns without Borders, U.N. offices, etc., move in."

The majority of students did not enjoy the detail about the
specifics of Afghanistan from the six fellows who had spent years
on the ground there. They preferred hearing from the public figures who had served in Washington. The articulacy, focus, and
clear itemized strategies of these senior officials impressed the
students, who were apparently not troubled by the officials' lack
of experience on the ground. Friends and colleagues of mine
who were interested in Afghanistan also spent surprisingly little
time with the fellows in the center. One distinguished former
State Department officer and professor who took the lead on
South Asia seemed to find my and the fellows' views unhelp-
fully nihilistic. Our arguments, therefore, had little impact on
the policy debate on Afghanistan, in Washington or at Harvard.
By the time I left Harvard to stand to be a member of the British
Parliament in 2010, the number of foreign troops in Helmand
had increased from their initial level of two hundred in 2005 to
thirty-two thousand. And my two teaching assistants, who had
loyally assisted my attempt to explain the futility of the surge in
Afghanistan, moved to guarded compounds in Afghanistan to
run governance programs for USAID.

MOUNTAIN RESCUE

Can we develop a new approach to intervention, one that could avoid the horror of Iraq or the absurdity of the Afghan surge? There can never be (*pace* the RAND Corporation) a universal formula for intervention, specifying the exact quantity of resources required for each hypothetical country. There is no use in relying, like the Organisation for Economic Cooperation and Development (OECD), on global indexes, which count and rank the governance indicators of Chad against those of Afghanistan. The answer is not more quantification, more data, or the search for more universal, replicable, and predictable models.

The knowledge required for intervention is not theoretical knowledge—it is a form of practical wisdom: an activity in which there is no substitute for experience. The ideal instructors are those who have spent a long time getting to know a particular place and have seen it at very different times and under different conditions. The ideal education is through an ever more detailed study of the history, the geography, and the anthropology of a particular place, on the one hand, and of the limitations and manias of the West, on the other.

You should not, therefore, teach intervention in the way that you teach natural science, but in the way that you teach mountain rescue. Although there is a humanitarian purpose—to save life—the central question is not "What ought you to do?" but "Where are you and who are you?" If you were advising an attempt at a high-altitude mountain rescue, you would say that mountains are intrinsically risky and dangerous: they can defeat and kill even the best. Therefore, if you can avoid climbing, do. A well-informed guide could present alternatives. Instead of remaining obstinately focused on one grand rescue climb, the guide could use flares, lay out caches and tents, and summon teams from other directions. Part of the decision-making process is to consider whether you can actually do any good: if the climber has been stuck at twenty-three thousand feet for twenty-four hours, the chances are that there is nothing you can do for him or her. If you decide you must go, then you minimize the risks through preparation and planning; carry suitable equipment; learn the environment; are honest about your capabilities; and trust an experienced and thoughtful guide.

The most important assessments and reassessments are made after you have launched the attempt. You have to remain alert for any dangers in the environment, some of which—like frost on a steep grass slope—may not have been present a day earlier. You need to go a very long way to avoid them. And you need to recognize that there are problems—such as bad weather, exhaustion, and hypothermia—that you may not be able to predict or control or avoid, but only monitor. And finally you need to understand the powerful forces of guilt, fear, and overconfidence, which will tempt you to ignore and reinforce a dangerous and futile attempt—or worse, to believe that there is no alternative, and that, whatever the cost, "failure is not an option." A good guide, someone with practical knowledge, who is not too isolated from the ground is able to spot more quickly the signs of danger and failure; can be more confident in changing course; and may not be too intimidated by the prospect. In the straightforward words of the English Mountain Rescue, "Be prepared to turn back if conditions turn against you."[148]

Such an analogy should not be used to stop all interventions any more than it is intended to stop mountain rescue. The standard of preparation, knowledge, and caution required should not be so impossibly high that you never act. Not all action is futile. But your moral obligation is both practical and limited. It is easy to think that we cannot intervene in Bosnia unless we also intervene in Burma; or that we cannot withdraw from Afghanistan—however futile and costly and destructive our presence might be—because we "have a moral obligation to the Afghan people." But in intervention, as in a mountain rescue, the moral right and duty to protect lives does not require futile or destructive adventures.

Modern heroes—whether policemen, firemen, or mountain rescuers—are expected to be brave, selfless, but intelligent risk-takers: they are not supposed to rush into a situation without protection and backup, or charge into a falling building, or leap blindly over a cliff. "Ought implies can"—you don't have a moral obligation to do what you cannot do. And the most useful thing we can do in the long term is to build a corps of more experienced guides for foreign policy: people who are absorbed in the political reality of a particular country.

Of course, better-informed staff do not guarantee success. Consider Gertrude Bell, Gerard Leachman, and Bertram Thomas, in the British occupation of Iraq in 1920. The resources at their disposal would have been, as Gerald points out in his essay, praised as exemplary by the RAND Corporation. And they had many of the qualities admired by "liberal imperialists." All three were fluent and highly experienced Arabists, all three won medals from the Royal Geographical Society for their Arabian journeys, and all three were greatly admired for their political work. They had an imperial confidence. They were not unduly constrained by the press or by their own bureaucracies. They were dealing with a simpler Iraq and a smaller, more rural population, at a time when Arab nationalism and political Islam had not yet developed their modern strength and appeal.

But they failed. Thomas was driven from his office in Shatra by a tribal mob. Colonel Leachman, who was famed for being able to kill a tribesman dead in his own tent without a hand lifted against him, was shot in the back in Fallujah. Iraqis refused to permit foreign political officers to play at founding their new nation. Bell's defeat was slower but more comprehensive. Of the kingdom she created, with its Sunni monarch and Shia, Sunni, and Kurdish subjects, there is today no king and no Sunni government, and there are tensions that hover on the edge of civil war. Perhaps one day there will be no country. Even highly intelligent, articulate, courageous, talented, creative, well-informed, and determined figures can fail. The task is chaotic and unpredictable, and there is an intrinsic absurdity and horror in building nations for peoples with other loyalties, models, and priorities.

If, however, you have to intervene—and there will be many situations where you believe that your moral duty is overwhelming and many cases where you have much stronger ethical grounds than the dubious British mandate in Iraq—then there are steps you can take to reduce the chances of failure. The most important remains to find, listen to, and trust the right people. Of course, the people who know the country best are its nationals: and as Gerald argues (and as I witnessed in Iraq), the sooner responsibility and broad scope are given to the locals, the better. But since there will always be a role for foreigners in international intervention—sometimes because domestic taxpayers demand it, sometimes because they have skills or resources that locals lack—we need to find, listen to, and trust the right foreigners.

CONVERSATION WITH HOLBROOKE

At the beginning of 2009, I gathered some such people to meet Richard Holbrooke in the Tabard Inn in Washington, D.C. They were the Harvard fellows and they included Andrew, who had been born in Pakistan and spent most of his working life there and in Afghanistan; Paul, who had begun working in Afghanistan in 1978; Michael, who had been in Afghanistan since there late 1980s; Nigel, who was born in Iran and grew up in Pakistan; and David, who had been working on counter-narcotic policy during the Taliban period. Holbrooke arrived with General Petraeus.

David was asked about counter-narcotics. I expected the kinds of comments generally made by development workers ("You need to develop alternative livelihoods") or by ambassadors ("Counter-narcotics cannot work without the rule of law") or by journalists ("It's all about Karzai's brother and the drug trade").[149]

Holbrooke began, "Surely you agree that it is ridiculous to attempt to eradicate poppies." I and others around the table nodded our heads. Of course, we muttered, it would be counterproductive and dangerous.

But David replied, "Well it depends where you are doing it. Eradication has had some success as part of a broader strategy in the eastern province of Nangrahar but it probably would work much less well in Helmand (in the south)."

Holbrooke seemed surprised. But he didn't pursue the point. Instead he said, "Surely you agree that it is ridiculous that Afghanistan is importing 70 percent of its wheat when it used to be a net–wheat exporter. Surely we should be subsidizing wheat?"

"Well," replied David, "I would suggest that it's better to subsidize inputs such as fertilizers because wheat subsidies would be stolen by village chiefs."

Again Holbrooke paused in thought. "In which case," said Holbrooke, "which alternative crop should we be planting? Pomegranate?"

"Well in provinces like Ghor," continued David, "it makes sense to plant a mixture of onion, potato, apricots, and wheat, rather than poppy. Such a mixed legal crop has a longer growing season, is less labor-intensive, and allows a couple of family members to get a job in the city, so overall the family income would be higher than planting poppy. But then the poppy is short-stemmed in Ghor."

Although Holbrooke's questions were insistently abrupt and binary, David's responses suggested a much more complicated, more promising world: in which there was a different answer in each province, in which instead of looking at a final crop, we should be looking at fertilizer, or at labor and income, instead of seed.

David's work on farming had not left him cynical and impotent. His message was one of possibility and small practical success. But his knowledge was not limited to particular villages. David could also discuss the latest global commodity prices, or the situation in Colombia, and he could show photographs he had taken of crops in the same field in central Afghanistan every year for a decade.

There were few foreigners who knew as much as David. There were even fewer foreigners—no more than fifty out of ten thousand—who had spent years living in Afghanistan; who spoke Afghan languages fluently; who had seen it pass through the Soviet period, the civil war, and the Taliban; who had tried to implement projects year after year in rural areas; who knew the main political players, men like Michael, Andrew, Paul, and Nigel, or people not at the table such as Tomas, Martine, or Jolyon.[150]

Their judgments were not infallible, but they were consistently more reliable than those of someone such as myself who had arrived in the country in 2001. It was not simply that these people had seen similar projects before, so that when someone proposed a self-composting toilet, they could show them the abandoned wrecks of self-composting toilets in the suburb of Khair-Khane. Or that they knew the minister of defense from when he was shelling Kabul in 1994, and when he was stealing the land in Shirpur in 2002. Or that they knew that the new police chief in Helmand was from the Popalzai tribe and that this would cause problems with the Barakzai community. Or that they could sit in their offices and talk fluently to people from Bamiyan whom they had known for fifteen years. Paul, Andrew, Jolyon, and Michael had met hundreds of rural leaders in almost every province of Afghanistan. They had not just sat with them in a short, structured interview, with an agenda and an interpreter. They had spent long hours sitting on the floor in their houses, listening to their conversations with other Afghans in Dari or Pashto. They had slept in their houses and absorbed the rhythm of their days. They had bumped along with them in old Russian jeeps and ridden on horses alongside them. They had done this week after week over twenty or thirty years. They could sense when an international project would fail. They understood the rural reality that faced the promise of salvation through international state-building.

Andrew would have been able to provide ideas—as detailed and compelling as David's—on the relationship between security and development programs; Paul, on health clinics; Michael, on tribal structures; Nigel, on project management in Helmand.

And you could hear equal wisdom from hundreds of people not around the table at the Tabard Inn that night in 2009: about the Afghan parliament, immunization programs, education,[151] the relative peace in one part of Kunar compared to the violence in the Korangal Valley, the implications of the electoral system, attitudes toward women, civilian casualties from aerial bombardment, the role of the Pakistani Inter-Services Intelligence agency in the insurgency, or the performance of the minister of electricity. In almost every case, experience brought prudence, meaning that although these people never supported abandoning Afghanistan—they loved it—they were generally strongly opposed to surges and over-intervention. They believed less is often more.

Such people are not avatars of "heaven-born" colonial officers. The international community should not be looking to recruit people with a Victorian background. It should not be trying to replicate a nineteenth-century ethos; nor its academic qualities, forms of seniority, medals and promotions; nor Edwardian security restrictions, policy priorities, and rhythms of daily work. Even if it could replicate the types of a previous generation, Western governments would not support them, nor would Western or Afghan society. Nor should they: colonial officers could be racist, harsh, and unpleasant.

But there are already twenty-first-century people like Paul, Michael, Jolyon, and Andrew who could provide advice on intervention: people much more focused on the history and culture of Afghanistan, more attentive to the realities of rural life. The massive influx of international money and staff has made this group of specialists a tiny minority. They are drowned by vast, rapidly expanding organizations with eye-watering budgets. This was the phenomenon Holbrooke noticed in Vietnam when he wrote, "I have never seen the Americans in such disarray. This is the result of a rapid build-up, great pressure from higher headquarters, rapid personnel turnover."[152] And yet this was exactly the situation Holbrooke replicated in Afghanistan by forcing through a civilian surge.

The international community must learn to bring such outsiders, who have worked for years in the field, back into the policy center. We need to reform "the corporate culture" of international bureaucracies to allow the recruitment, retention, and promotion of what Holbrooke called in Vietnam "a cadre of superior officers who are willing and interested to serve extended tours out there."[153] We should ensure that the emphasis in promotion is less on how well candidates get on with their own staff or superiors, and more on how well they get on with "foreigners."

Such people can minimize the abstraction and isolation of our policy elites. They know what the relationship is between the grand objective of "state-building" and the reality on the ground. They alone can ask the right detailed questions: What is the purpose of this state? What exactly does it look like? Where has this been done before? Why do you think we can succeed? What is the opposition? And how much are you prepared to spend in money and in blood? They alone understand what the relationship is between concepts such as "accountability" and "the rule of law" and the actual daily life of Haji Mohsin and the villagers of Kamenj and can, therefore, ask what exact part of Haji Mohsin's environment the international community proposes to change and how.[154]

They should not tempt us to intervene more, still less entice us with a promise of "better occupations."[155] Frequently the role will be to make the detailed, country-specific arguments on why we cannot intervene in a particular place, or why we should not intervene too deeply (as we did in Afghanistan after 2005).

Their role would include limiting our initial interventions, reassessing them, spotting the dangers, acknowledging the failures, and having the confidence, if necessary, to pull back. But in cases such as Bosnia, where intervention was the right policy, giving us the confidence to continue, to innovate and exploit fresh, unpredictable political opportunities.

In early 2011, the international community often seemed to believe it could avoid putting "boots on the ground" in Libya simply because of the language of the UN resolution authorizing force to protect civilians. But it had almost no idea of what it should do if Gaddafi were still in place in three months' time, or if a humanitarian catastrophe were to occur despite the no-fly zone, or if there was a civil war in which both sides killed civilians, or if former regime elements in a post-Gaddafi state mounted an insurgency. These scenarios were best imagined and understood by people who knew the Italian colonial history, who were informed about the last ten years in Benghazi and the sorts of networks Gaddafi still possessed. They could judge whether the power of tribal groups was fading and how much emphasis to put on Islamist parties and how much to trust them. And do this in situations of stress and chaotic unpredictability. But such people were in short supply.[156]

Our international institutions, which have for so long lectured developing countries on "governance" and "civil service reform," need to heal themselves. And they may have to turn away from their obsessions with contemporary "management best practice" and the abstract theories of governance, development, and state-building and look at more "traditional" types of knowledge. In the nineteenth century, European governments introduced reforms to overcome the problems of eighteenth-century policymakers: problems of amateurism, nepotism, and corruption. They did so through new entrance examinations; professional schools; legal requirements that the majority of those controlling policy in the capital had served a posting in the country for which they were responsible; and by ensuring that the most senior posts in a country went to people with long experience on the ground.[157] Our reforms should be as ambitious and targeted at the problems of the twenty-first century: problems of deep isolation, optimism, and abstraction. These reforms must happen not just in the United States, but also in the United Kingdom and throughout the United Nations. If we reform our institutions to achieve these things, we can responsibly exercise noble options like humanitarian intervention. But if not, these adventures will only become more ill-informed and more dangerous. Failure will become increasingly inevitable, invisible, and inconceivable. And we will discredit the interventions and, ultimately, ourselves.

HOLBROOKE

Richard Holbrooke called me in January 2009. It was after midnight—although we were both in Washington, D.C. He had been Special Representative for Afghanistan and Pakistan for a week, and he wanted to quiz me on Afghanistan.

After each reply, Holbrooke paused and then—just as I suspected he was texting someone else—growled, "Okay, so what do we do?" "How can you prove that?" "What do we do about Pakistan? Iran? Russia? Karzai?" We spoke for an hour. Then he said, "You've lost your argument against the seventeen-thousand-troop increase. But Petraeus is asking for another forty thousand in September, and if you think that's wrong, you should say so." He encouraged me to model myself on a general who had spoken against Vietnam. He concluded, "I am sitting you next to

Secretary Clinton at dinner. Say exactly what you think. If you don't, I never, ever want to hear you criticize the policy again." And then he hung up, I guessed, to call someone else.

I was left standing half to attention in my boxer shorts at the end of the bed, unsure about what had just happened. The energy of this man, thirty years older than I am, shook me. But it was not his alertness, or the charm of his sustained attention, or his flattering comparisons that captivated me. Nor was it even his revelations (I had thought that a decision on seventeen thousand troops was a month away and had no idea a further forty thousand was remotely likely.) I was suspicious of his encouragement. But I was conquered by his contradictions. He was listening intently to someone with whom he disagreed and giving a platform to someone who argued against his own position. He wanted to transform the approach of the Pakistan, Afghan, and U.S. governments, while I argued that this could not be done. He felt Afghanistan was vitally important and that we had a moral obligation to continue; I, that we had no moral obligation to do what we could not do. But he poured his energy into me and gave me, I felt, a charter to fight against his Afghan policy.

Many political leaders had been hesitant to invest as much, emotionally or intellectually, as the bewildering intervention in Afghanistan demanded (although they were always happy to invest more money and troops). Perhaps because they felt stuck with it, they had little desire to examine its foundations. They preferred writing objectives to rubbing their faces in the intractable stuff of Afghanistan. Europeans and Afghans implied it was the Americans' responsibility. American politicians deferred to military advice; generals blamed politics.

But Holbrooke was different. He seemed to want both to expose the truth and to take full responsibility for the policy.

He wasn't interested in tinsel triumphs. He had a real historical imagination, displayed in his surprisingly modest and scrupulous account of his role in the Balkans. I had heard him assess the weaknesses of early-twentieth-century Arabists with the insight, fondness, and sparks of envy that one might apply to a childhood friend. And he was aware of history's questions, the kind of questions he posed of Vietnam: How important was it really? Did it make sense? Could it be done? And believing in Afghanistan that it did and could, he nevertheless wanted to give space to those who did not agree. In saying to a young foreigner, with whom he disagreed, "Say exactly what you think. If you don't, I never, ever want to hear you criticize the policy again," he seemed to be, in an unusual fashion, taking responsibility for both a position and the truth of that position.

If anyone, therefore, had the self-confidence, the stubbornness, the experience, and the intelligence to resist the Afghan surge, it was Holbrooke. But he did not. He did not acknowledge failure, and he did not resist the surge. Instead, he felt his only option, eight years in, was to support the decision to send more soldiers and more money. Under his leadership the operation grew to nearly 150,000 troops and $130 billion of annual expenditure: an operation that was still fighting the old demons of "rogue state" and "failed state," still protecting "dominoes" and "Western credibility," and pursuing the goals of "governance," "the rule of law," and a "legitimate, accountable state."

You, whose business is with intervention,

You who turn the wheel and look to windward
Consider Phlebas who was once handsome and tall as you.

THE RISE AND FALL OF
LIBERAL IMPERIALISM

Gerald Knaus

TIME LINE

1992   April: War starts in Bosnia—Sarajevo siege begins.

May: Omarska prison camp is opened by Bosnian Serbs near Prijedor for Bosniak and Croat prisoners.

August: Human Rights Watch publishes report on war crimes in Bosnia and Herzegovina, and calls for an international criminal tribunal.

September–October: Colin Powell, chairman of U.S. Joint Chiefs of Staff, comes out against any military intervention. So does UK Foreign Minister Douglas Hurd.

December: The term *ethnic cleansing* is introduced in a UN General Assembly resolution on Bosnia-Herzegovina (Resolution 47/121). By the end of the year Bosnian Serbs control more than two-thirds of Bosnia's territory and there are hundreds of thousands of displaced persons.

December: The United States sends 37,000 troops to Somalia as part of UN-mandated Operation Restore Hope.

1993   April: U.S. President Clinton rules out deploying U.S. ground troops in Bosnia. A U.S. proposal to arm Bosnian government troops and to carry out air strikes against Bosnian Serbs ("lift and strike") is rejected by European allies.

April: Bosnian Croat forces launch a war within a war against Bosniak (Muslim) civilians with the backing of Croatia. A massacre in the Central Bosnian village Ahmići on April 16 leaves 115 Bosniak civilians dead.

May: The International Criminal Tribunal for the Former Yugoslavia (ICTY) is created by the UN Security Council; it will remain without a prosecutor for the next fourteen months.

October: Eighteen U.S. Army Rangers are killed following an attempt to arrest a Somali warlord in Mogadishu. The United States decides to pull its troops out of Somalia.

1994   April: Rwanda genocide begins. Eight hundred thousand people are killed between April and July. The genocide only ends when Paul Kagame's Rwandese Patriotic Front rebels defeat the Hutu-extremist regime in July.

July 31: UN Security Council resolution authorizes the use of force to restore the elected president in Haiti. The U.S.-led intervention gets underway in September.

1995   Bosnian Serb army still controls 70 percent of Bosnian territory.

July 12: Srebrenica genocide begins, as Bosnian Serb forces under General Ratko Mladić kill 8,000 Bosniak men in what had been a designated UN safe haven.

July 17: U.S. National Security Adviser Anthony Lake reveals American "endgame strategy," a variation on the previously proposed policy of "lift and strike."

August: Croatian government forces launch Operation Storm (*Oluja* in Croatian) and retake territory occupied by Croatian Serb troops for almost three years. More than 200,000 Croatian Serbs are expelled from Croatia. NATO Operation Deliberate Force begins on August 30, with three weeks of air strikes against Bosnian Serbs.

October: Bosnian Croat and Bosnian government forces continue their offensive and retake 20 percent of Bosnian territory from Bosnian Serb army.

November: U.S.-led peace talks begin at an American air force base in Dayton, Ohio, moderated by the U.S. lead negotiator Richard Holbrooke. Three delegations are led by Croatian President Franjo Tudjman, Serbian President Slobodan Milošević, and Bosnian President Alija Izetbegović. The Dayton talks end with an agreement on November 21.

The war in Bosnia leaves almost 100,000 people dead; an estimated 1 million people are displaced within the country; 1.3 million refugees are abroad.

November: President Clinton explains the deployment of 20,000 U.S. troops as part of an international peacekeeping force.

December: An international Implementation Force (IFOR) of 60,000 is deployed to Bosnia to aid peacekeeping efforts. It has a mandate for one year. An Office of the High Representative (OHR) is established in Sarajevo without formal powers. Carl Bildt becomes the first High Representative.

1996   March: National Security Adviser Anthony Lake argues in a presentation that "it is dangerous hubris to believe that we can build other nations. But where our own interests are engaged we can help nations build themselves."

June: Radovan Karadžić, indicted for war crimes, is reelected leader of the SDS (Serb Democratic Party). Diplomatic pressure then leads him to give way to his former hard-line deputy Biljana Plavšić to succeed him as president of the Bosnian Serb entity.

IFOR resists efforts to organize assessment visits for displaced persons to visit their former homes in Bosnia.

September: The first postwar national elections are held in Bosnia. They are won by the three dominant national parties.

November: The UN reports that two hundred Bosniak houses have been blown up in the Bosnian Serb entity.

December: IFOR is replaced by the smaller Stabilization Force (SFOR), with some 40,000 soldiers.

1997   March: An international supervisor is appointed to govern Brčko, a town disputed between Bosnian Serb and Federation entities.

July: Operation Tango in Prijedor leads to the first arrests of Bosnian Serbs by SFOR troops on the basis of "sealed" (secret) indictments.

August: SFOR troops prevent a coup against Bosnian Serb President Biljana Plavšić after she breaks with Radovan Karadžić. SFOR gradually asserts control over special police forces in the Bosnian Serb entity.

September: Displaced person Aziz Ibraković is elected deputy to the Doboj municipal assembly in the Bosnian Serb entity in the first Bosnian local elections.

November: Elections in the Bosnian Serb entity lead to the loss of power of Radovan Karadžić's SDS. A politician with no roots in wartime politics, Milorad Dodik, is elected prime minister of the Bosnian Serb entity.

December 9–10: An international conference in Bonn, Germany, grants "Bonn powers" to the OHR, to impose legislation and replace elected and appointed officials obstructing peace.

1998   May: Aziz Ibraković returns to his village in Doboj after six years in displacement. First returns to Prijedor and to other locations in the Bosnian Serb entity begin.

September 12–13: Second Bosnian national elections are held.

1999   March: NATO air strikes begin in Kosovo. Following the war the United Nations Interim Administration Mission in Kosovo (UNMIK) is created on June 10 to govern Kosovo (UN Resolution 1244).

March: A special Brčko District is set up in northern Bosnia with unlimited powers for the American supervisor.

March: OHR dismisses elected Bosnian Serb president Nikola Poplašen to help Milorad Dodik remain in power.

May: Slobodan Milošević is indicted by ICTY.

Summer: David Rieff publishes an article titled "A New Age of Liberal Imperialism."

September: An international peacekeeping force for East Timor (INTERFET) is deployed. In October the United Nations Transitional Administration in East Timor becomes the interim administration until May 2002, when East Timor becomes independent.

November: The UN secretary-general issues a report about the UN's failures in Srebrenica. This is followed in December by another report on the UN and the genocide in Rwanda.

December: Croatian President Franjo Tudjman dies in Zagreb. This leads to profound changes in Croatian policy toward Bosnia.

December: The European Union Helsinki summit promises "big bang" Eastern enlargement and offers a concrete EU integration perspective to South East European nations. Bulgaria and Romania begin accession talks; Turkey becomes an official candidate for accession.

2000   October: Slobodan Milošević is overthrown in Belgrade following protests by his own compatriots.

November 11: The third postwar national elections are held in Bosnia. Displaced persons begin to return across Bosnia.

2001   March: Former Serbian president Slobodan Milošević is arrested by Serbian police and handed over to ICTY.

2002   April: Senior British diplomat Robert Cooper writes about "postmodern imperialism" in the *Observer*.

May: Paddy Ashdown arrives as the fourth High Representative. He tells the Bosnian parliament that the choices facing the elected deputies were not "whether to reform. But how fast, how soon and, above all, who will drive the process of reform—you or me?"

December: The UN Police monitoring mission leaves Bosnia after seven years. The number of SFOR troops is down to 12,000.

Samantha Power's *"A Problem from Hell": America and the Age of Genocide* is published.

2003   March: Iraq invasion begins.

May: Paul Bremer arrives in Baghdad as head of the Coalition Provisional Authority.

2004   March: Violent two-day riots break out in Kosovo. The international community begins to accelerate steps toward Kosovo independence.

June–July: Paddy Ashdown dismisses sixty Bosnian Serb officials.

October: Local elections are held. In Doboj a mayor representing the SDS wins with support from Bosniak returnee voters.

December: SFOR and U.S. troops leave Bosnia, to be succeeded by a small EU-led peacekeeping force of 7,000.

2005   October: Croatia begins European Union accession talks.

2006   January: Military conscription is abolished in Bosnia.

June: Paddy Ashdown tells the British House of Lords that Bosnia is "a remarkable success story."

December: New U.S. Army/Marine Corps *Counterinsurgency Field Manual* is published.

2007   May: Paddy Ashdown's book *Swords and Ploughshares* comes out.

2008   February: Kosovo declares independence, which is recognized by the United States and most but not all European nations.

May: Serbian national elections produce a pro-Western government. Former Bosnian Serb leader Radovan Karadžić is arrested in Belgrade in July and handed over to the ICTY.

April: Richard Holbrooke writes about Bosnia as a success story in the *Washington Post*.

October: Richard Holbrooke and Paddy Ashdown describe Bosnia as on the brink of disaster in the *Guardian*.

2009   April: Croatia joins NATO as a full member.

December: Serbia submits its application to become an EU member.

2011   April: Ante Gotovina, former Croatian chief of General Staff, is sentenced by ICTY to twenty-four years for war crimes related to the 1995 Operation Storm. In total the ICTY has indicted 161 people.

May: The number of EU peacekeepers in Bosnia is below 2,000. There is still an international supervisor in Brčko and an Office of the High Representative with "Bonn powers" in Sarajevo.

May: Ratko Mladić, the former Bosnian Serb military leader indicted by the International Criminal Tribunal for the former Yugoslavia (ICTY) in 1995 for genocide and crimes against humanity, is extradited by the Serbian government to The Hague to stand trial. This leaves only one indictee still on the run.

THE AGE OF INTERVENTION

The last two decades have been an age of intervention. Hope for a new era of international peace following the collapse of communism in 1989 was shattered by the outbreak of the Balkan wars. A period of impotence and despair in the face of large-scale ethnic cleansing and genocide was followed by the astonishingly successful military interventions in Bosnia and Herzegovina (here referred to as Bosnia) in 1995 and Kosovo four years later. Among advocates of intervention, the Al Qaeda attack on the World Trade Center in 2001 dramatically increased the sense of urgency. As the United States and its allies invaded Afghanistan and Iraq, lessons supposedly learned in the Balkans were transposed onto a new playing field.

At the beginning of the new millennium, it seemed that the United States and its allies had both the right and the capacity to intervene anywhere. The key lesson of the Balkans in the 1990s—that it was within the power of the international community to "end mass atrocity crimes once and for all," as Gareth Evans, the former Australian foreign minister, put it—seemed at once intellectually gratifying and emotionally appealing.[1] The hope was that international organizations, arriving fast on the heels of military intervention, could tackle the longer-term root causes of violence and instability and build effective, accountable, and democratic states. Regime change in Afghanistan and Iraq not only was achievable but also could lead to a democratic domino effect in the Middle East, passing through Iran to Syria, Saudi Arabia, and Egypt.

A series of publications by practitioner-scholars set out to distill lessons on using external power to reshape post-conflict societies. American political scientist Francis Fukuyama wrote about nation-building in *Nation Building 101*.[2] Robert Cooper, a British author and an adviser to former prime minister Tony Blair, published an article calling for a postmodern imperialism.[3] RAND Corporation, the United States' biggest think tank, published a wide range of case studies to outline a formula for success in future interventions, summed up in its own *Beginner's Guide to Nation-Building*. This includes rules of thumb to estimate the resource requirements for both heavy peace enforcement missions and light peacekeeping. Articles celebrated the dawn of a new era of benevolent U.S. imperialism.[4] While only a few went so far as to claim that intervention and post-conflict state-building were easy, by 2003, the year the United States invaded Iraq, a growing chorus suggested that it was feasible—anywhere. As the RAND *Beginner's Guide* put it, "The more sweeping a [nation-building] mission's objectives, the more resistance it is likely to inspire. Resistance can be overcome, but only through a well-considered application of personnel and money over extended periods of time."[5] If the United States and its allies only wanted it badly enough, they could end atrocities, overthrow hostile regimes, rebuild states, introduce democracy, and impose the rule of law. Thus was born the liberal imperialist vision of the early twenty-first century.

Two factors above all else explained the hold this vision was to have over Western policy-makers. One was the experience in the Balkans. A disaster zone whose future once seemed to belong to warlords and ultra-nationalists saw war criminals arrested and hundreds of thousands of men under arms demobilize. The second was the state of heightened anxiety over failed states, non-state actors, and hostile regimes following the 9/11 attacks. The first experience supplied policy-makers with the confidence that interventions could work; the second motivated them to assume greater risks and costs than ever before.

The red thread that runs through these recent policy debates on intervention is the reassuring notion that all fundamental problems have solutions. It is the belief that lessons learned in one place can be transferred to any other, and that what works in one intervention is likely to work elsewhere. It is the conviction that in the end everything depends mainly on good management, resources (troops, money), and political will, and that the key to success lies with the intervener: with the nature of the domestic political debate in the West and with the wisdom of military and civilian leadership.

"Can intervention work?" remains today a question at the very center of global politics. To answer it, let us return to the Balkans, the crucible for the emergence of twenty-first-century doctrines of humanitarian intervention, for the modern principle of "the responsibility to protect," and for liberal imperialism. Let us go back to the killing fields of Bosnia in the 1990s and to the ultimately successful international campaign to bring mass atrocities in the Balkans to an end. Let us revisit the successes and failures of what were then the most ambitious post-conflict missions ever undertaken—and examine the difficult question of whether lessons learned in one place and context can be applied in another. Policy-makers and analysts are not condemned to stumble on in darkness, overly cautious at one time and overly confident at another, relying on luck to make up for the incapacity to control events and on ideology for the inability to understand them. A critical look at the Balkans and at the actual impact of one of the most ambitious international protectorates established in the past half century will help us understand when and under what conditions interventions can work.

THE UNNECESSARY DEFEAT

> Let me recall, in conclusion, that in French law there is a crime called "failure to assist a person in danger" (*non-assistance à personne en danger*).
>
> UN SECRETARY-GENERAL KOFI ANNAN,
> "INTERVENTION," 1999[6]

Today's international debate on intervention is shaped by powerful experiences that haunt and guide individuals and nations. Some policy-makers are haunted by the trauma of *failed interventions*. The iconic one is Vietnam, America's biggest post–Second World War nation-building experience, which ended in failure amid some sixty thousand killed U.S. soldiers. Another is Somalia, where eighteen American soldiers died—trapped in a Mogadishu slum—trying to capture a hostile warlord in 1993. Confronted with television images of a mob dragging a dead U.S. soldier's body through the streets, U.S. policy-makers swore never again to attempt a military mission in which U.S. national interests were not clearly at stake.[7]

Throughout the late 1990s, by contrast, ever more individuals were haunted *by the failure to intervene* in time. Roméo Dallaire, a Canadian major general, headed a small UN peacekeeping force in Rwanda in early 1994. Disaster struck the Central African nation only a few months after the shock of Mogadishu. This time around, the West responded by withdrawing embassy staff and peacekeepers. Looking back at a frenzy of killing that left eight hundred thousand people dead within a few months, Dallaire relived the moment when the world decided to ignore Rwanda:

> Could we have prevented the resumption of the civil war and the genocide? The short answer is yes. If UNAMIR [the UN peacekeepers already on the ground in Rwanda at the time of the genocide] had received the modest increase in troops and capabilities we requested in the first week, could we have stopped the killings? Yes, absolutely. Would we have risked more UN casualties? Yes, but surely soldiers and peacekeeping nations should be prepared to pay the price of safeguarding human life and human rights.[8]

In December 1999 the UN secretariat in New York issued an agonizing report looking back at its failure in Rwanda five years earlier. It warned that "acknowledgement of responsibility must also be accompanied by a will for change: a commitment to ensure that catastrophes such as the genocide in Rwanda never occur anywhere in the future."[9]

A generation of politicians has also been haunted by memories of Bosnia: by images of Bosnian Serb concentration camps in the summer of 1992; by the shelling of Sarajevo civilians during a siege that lasted more than three years; by the expulsion of hundreds of thousands of people and the destruction of their homes and heritage by Bosnian Serb and Bosnian Croat troops; and finally, by the image of Dutch UN peacekeepers in Srebrenica, a UN safe haven, standing by as Bosnian Serb General Ratko Mladić sent some eight thousand Bosniak (Bosnian Muslim) men and boys to their deaths in the summer of 1995. A report on Srebrenica commissioned by the UN secretary-general and published in November 1999 was also unflinchingly critical. It concluded that

> the cardinal [lesson] of Srebrenica is that a deliberate and systematic attempt to terrorize, expel or murder an entire people must be met decisively with all necessary means, and with the political will to carry the policy through to its logical conclusion. . . . Srebrenica crystallized a truth understood only too late by the United Nations and the world at large: that Bosnia was as much a moral cause as a military conflict.[10]

Like the Rwanda report, it is the imperative that is striking: future mass atrocities "must be met . . . with all necessary means."

This new tone reflected the way in which the debate over intervention in the Balkans had evolved. Its first phase consisted of years of agonizing soul searching as to whether there was anything outsiders could have done to stop the bloodshed in this small part of Europe. David Rieff, a young reporter in the Balkans in the 1990s, argued that what made Bosnia a moral disaster was the fact that this tragedy could so easily have been prevented: "the unnecessary defeat, the defeat that could have been averted, the genocide that need not have taken place, or, once it had begun, could have been cut short, are things to which it is obscene to be reconciled."[11]

However, most military experts and politicians cautioned otherwise. Nothing short of a full-scale invasion with hundreds of thousands of ground troops would make a difference in a place like Bosnia, they argued. In the summer of 1992, Colin

Powell, chairman of the U.S. Joint Chiefs of Staff, came out strongly against any military intervention. He also argued against limited air strikes against Bosnian Serb forces, which some had proposed: "You bet I get nervous when so-called experts suggest that all we need is a little surgical bombing or a limited attack. When the desired result isn't obtained, a new set of experts then comes forward with talk of a little escalation."[12] Many experts backed him up. In February 1993, Colonel Michael Dewar, deputy director of the prestigious International Institute for Strategic Studies in London, published a two-page article with the title "Intervention in Bosnia— The Case Against."[13] Underlining that difficult decisions ought to be made on the basis of "coldly calculated criteria," Dewar explained that if a large enough force was raised, the ethnic cleansing in Bosnia could *theoretically* be brought to an end. He then proceeded to demolish the idea, pricing intervention out of the market. Dewar noted that separating the combatants would be an immensely complex undertaking since "these communities are seemingly no longer able to co-exist." The force required for this would have been huge:

> The defeat of the Serbian militias in Bosnia and the subsequent military occupation of Bosnia and Herzegovina would require something in the order of 500,000 men. . . . [I]t is not so much the defeat of all opposition that would be the most manpower-consuming; rather the subsequent peace-enforcement exercise throughout the whole of Bosnia in every city, town and village. And that is assuming Serbia remains neutral.[14]

Britain could not have provided more than a few thousand soldiers. The French might have been able to raise an additional ten to fifteen thousand troops. Due to constitutional limitations at the time, Germany would have been unable to provide any. Without the United States, Dewar noted, "one way or another it might be possible to raise 20,000–30,000 troops." There was then no political will in Washington for a full-scale military intervention involving U.S. ground forces, although for the United States "it would be theoretically possible to raise 200,000 men." Since even this would have fallen far short of the necessary half a million troops, all that could really be done was to hope to broker a peace agreement. "There are only two answers: full-scale military intervention, which is most unlikely and, in any event, could also be counter-productive, or a continuation of current peripheral action. The latter is the lesser of two evils." Thus, Dewar concluded, "it would be wise to ease the passage of history, not try to reverse it."[15]

The real debate from 1992 to 1995 over intervention was not over a massive invasion by ground forces led by the United States, however. It was whether evidence of mass slaughter should have brought the United States and its allies to support the victims of genocide through arming the Sarajevo government and weakening the Bosnian Serb army through air strikes. As Bosnia's Muslim president Alija Izetbegović told U.S. President George H. W. Bush in August 1992, "I completely agree with Mr. Bush's statement that American boys should not die for Bosnia. We have hundreds and thousands of able and willing men ready to fight, but unfortunately they have the disadvantage of being unarmed. We need weapons."[16] Colin Powell's main objection to a policy that President Clinton was to call "lift and strike" (lift the weapons embargo against the Bosnian government, limited air strikes) was, in the end, less military than political: the reasoning was that even trying to stop Serb forces in this manner would create expectations and pressures that would then make it impossible for (U.S. or UK) leaders to resist further escalation if—as seemed certain to these experts—air strikes alone would be insufficient. The lesson from Vietnam haunting Powell and others was that once bombing starts, and the credibility of a big power is at stake, nothing could stop a further slide into total war and costly occupation. Skeptics focused on the complexities of what was happening in Bosnia and the difficulty for outsiders even to understand the conflict. They emphasized the irrationality of the peoples of the Balkans. As British military expert John Keegan put it, "The war is understood by no one . . . in so far as it can be given a name, it is a primitive tribal conflict, of a sort known only to a handful of anthropologists." Reports from Bosnia, he noted, "might be taken from a field report on the Yanomamo, one of the [most] primitive and savage tribes known."[17] Such critics discounted claims that the atrocities that occurred in Bosnia were far from irrational, but followed a clear and openly stated logic familiar from modern European history: a history in which ethnic cleansing, as it came to be called, had long been an instrument in the service of the policy of creating ethnically homogeneous nation-states with enlarged borders. The human rights group Human Rights Watch had provided detailed material to indicate the extent of systematic slaughter already in the summer of 1992, meticulously documenting ethnic cleansing and citing by name ten responsible Serb and Bosnian Serb military officials and political leaders, at the time to no avail.[18] In December 1992, then U.S. Secretary of State Lawrence Eagleburger had publicly called for charges against Serbian leader Slobodan Milošević and the Bosnian Serb leaders Radovan Karadžić and Ratko Mladić for "crimes against humanity."[19]

The experience of late 1995—the Srebrenica massacre of eight thousand Bosniak civilians followed by a successful military intervention that brought to an end three years of war—in the end proved wrong all those who had argued that there was no halfway house between a full-scale invasion and watching the atrocities from the sidelines. In doing so, it gave birth to a new phase in the debate on intervention. One of the seminal texts to emerge from this period, capturing both the despair and the hope of the time, is Samantha Power's *"A Problem from Hell": America and the Age of Genocide.* Power had covered the war in Bosnia as a young journalist. As she told an audience at a university commencement address in May 2006, "I consider myself a member of the Bosnia generation. Out of college, at the ripe old age of twenty-two, I trekked to the Balkans."[20] Shocked by the West's seeming indifference, she also set out to study previous international reactions to the genocides carried out in the twentieth century. There had been a persistent failure of U.S. policy in the face of genocides. "America's non-response to the Turkish horrors," Power wrote, referring to the Armenian genocide in 1915, "established patterns that would be repeated. Time and again the US government would be reluctant to cast aside its neutrality and formally denounce a fellow state for its atrocities."[21] In such a situation, "the sharpest challenge to the world of bystanders is posed by those who have refused to remain silent in the age of genocide." Speaking out was central to tackling the fundamental problem: the lack of political will.[22]

Power noted that in the face of any mass atrocity there was a "continuum of intervention" that policy-makers could employ, ranging from clearly condemning the act, to naming those responsible, imposing sanctions, establishing tribunals, imposing no-fly zones, and finally, intervening militarily.[23] It was only in Bosnia and later Kosovo, however, unlike previously in Rwanda, Cambodia, and northern Iraq, that the United States actually proceeded to the final stage. The killing of some eight thousand civilians following the fall of the UN safe haven of

Srebrenica in early July 1995 finally created sufficient public pressure. The U.S. press corps became merciless. There was a sense of U.S. humiliation and shame, and for the first time there appeared to be a real domestic political price to pay for the failure to intervene. By the summer of 1995 the future of Bosnia and the credibility of American foreign policy were inextricably linked. Under those conditions—on July 17—U.S. National Security Adviser Anthony Lake unveiled an "endgame strategy": to back muscular U.S. diplomacy by threatening to bomb the Bosnian Serbs and to arm the forces of the Bosnian government through covert arms shipments by third parties.[24]

When a shell landed in a crowded Sarajevo market at the end of August 1995, killing thirty-eight people and wounding many others, weeks of NATO bombings followed. Soon Bosniak and Croat forces managed to take back some 20 percent of Bosnia. Within another few weeks, the international community successfully pressured representatives from all parties to come together in November at a U.S. Air Force base in Dayton, Ohio, to negotiate a peace agreement. After such an agreement was signed by all parties, a sixty-thousand-strong peacekeeping force was deployed to Bosnia by the end of 1995. A three-year long war had come to an end.

So why was U.S. diplomacy in 1995 successful? After all, one thing that had not changed was a commitment by U.S. policymakers that there would be no deployment if there was no peace to keep. This reflected a long-standing U.S. policy and conformed with public expectations. Already in April 1993, President Clinton had noted that "at this point I would not rule out any option except the option that I never ruled in, which was the question of American ground troops."[25] In 1994, Holbrooke, a senior diplomat at the time, had observed that "using American ground troops to fight the war was . . . out of the question."[26] In 1995, U.S. public opinion remained heavily opposed to military deployments. Seventy percent of Americans did not want troops in Bosnia under any circumstances.[27] Richard Holbrooke, in 1995 the chief U.S. negotiator at the Dayton talks, noted that "in any case, we would not deploy American or other NATO troops absent ironclad guarantees from all three parties concerning their safety, access and authority."[28] During the Dayton talks, the Republican leadership of both the Senate and the House of Representatives sent a letter to President Clinton underlining that support in Congress for sending U.S. troops to Bosnia, even in support of a signed peace agreement, was "virtually zero."[29] As a result, walking away in the absence of a peace agreement signed by all sides remained a real option, as far as the United States was concerned. At one tense moment during the Dayton negotiations—when it looked as if there would be no agreement—George Stephanopoulos, the White House spokesperson, summed up the administration's conflicted attitude, telling Holbrooke, "Our polls show the public overwhelmingly opposed to sending American troops to Bosnia. . . . [I]f Dayton failed, there would be a combination of relief and disappointment. If you succeeded, there would be a combination of pride and apprehension."[30]

What changed the situation on the ground and the dynamic in Bosnia following the Srebrenica massacre was a successful attack by the army of the Republic of Croatia in August 1995, followed by a sustained ground offensive by Croatian and Bosnian government forces in Bosnia. In 1994 Croatia had turned to a U.S. military consulting firm, Military Professional Resources Incorporated (MPRI), based in Virginia, in which former U.S. generals held key positions. MPRI's instruction coincided with a major boost in the potency of the Croatian armed forces, demonstrated in August 1995 when Croat forces launched Operation Storm, a turning point in the war. In a lightning offensive, Croatia's U.S.-trained troops managed to retake most of the territory of Croatia that had been under the control of a Croatian Serb rebel state for three years. While liberating their territory Croatian troops also expelled more than 200,000 Serbs, who had lived in this region for centuries. It was the largest single act of ethnic cleansing of the war.[31] Croatian President Franjo Tudjman himself triumphantly raised the Croatian flag in the former Croatian Serb mountain capital of Knin.

In early 1995 the Bosnian Serb army had controlled 70 percent of Bosnia's territory, but already then its lines of defense were stretched thin. During the summer, its army lost large swaths of territory. The Bosnian Serb leaders had before their eyes the dramatic fate of the Krajina Serb statelet within Croatia, which collapsed in August 1995 after only a few days of fighting. The myth of Serb military invincibility had collapsed. Feeling the pressure, Bosnian Serb wartime leaders—all of whom were later indicted for war crimes—began to fall out with one another. During October 1995, NATO bombed Bosnian Serb positions. At one moment it looked as if even Banja Luka, the largest city held by the Bosnian Serbs, might fall. It was clearly time to sue for peace. As Mark Danner put it, Slobodan Milošević came to Dayton in November because

> the tide had turned against his Bosnian Serb protégés; because Franjo Tudjman's American-supported Croatian army had driven the Serbs out of Krajina, which they had occupied during the war's first days; because under the umbrella of their new NATO air force the Croats and Bosnians had fought and begun to win on the ground.[32]

British historian Brendan Simms later argued that the U.S. air strikes would very likely have worked at an earlier stage in the war with similar effect. He also noted that "it seems unlikely that the Croats would have been able to defeat the Krajina Serbs and the Bosnian Serb army in north-west Bosnia without US training . . . the military success of *Operation Storm* and *Deliberate Force* in August-September 1995 suggests that 'lift and strike' should have been tried earlier."[33]

This final phase of the war had many consequences for the talks about peace. Croatia's success on the battlefield led David Owen, former co-chair of the conference for the former Yugoslavia, to comment in 1995 that "the victors in the Yugoslav wars of 1991–1995 have been the Croats and President Tudjman."[34] Croatia's president was the strong man in Dayton and arrived in the United States in a state of nationalist euphoria. Tudjman was convinced that history was dominated by the clash of civilizations, a belief that had gained plenty of international notoriety when Harvard political scientist Samuel Huntington published an essay on the subject in 1993.[35] This view led Tudjman to conclude that cultural and ethnic separation was the only way toward stability in a region in which three different "civilizations"—Western Christianity, Islam, and Eastern Christianity—allegedly clashed. Tudjman told his Western interlocutors that he was seriously concerned about a "Muslim peril" to Europe. On the eve of the Dayton talks, he delivered long lectures to U.S. negotiators on the "futility of any thoughts of Bosnia as an independent, unified state."[36] In late 1995 Croatia's strategy inside Bosnia remained unashamedly to maintain the structures of a Bosnian Croat para-state controlled by Bosnian Croat hard-liners, who for all practical purposes treated their territory as a part of Greater Croatia. This para-state was directly funded, supported, and controlled by the Croatian Ministry of Defense. It maintained separate armed forces (the Bosnian Croat army, called HVO). It had its own separate governing bodies and resisted any attempt to create functioning multiethnic institutions or to allow the return of displaced persons of other ethnic groups (either Bosniaks or Serbs) to its territory.

The second basic reality about making peace in 1995 concerned the role of Slobodan Milošević. The Serbian president's crucial role in Dayton stemmed from the fact that he offered a way out of an acute dilemma. U.S. negotiators insisted on getting guarantees from the Bosnian Serbs not to attack their peacekeepers in case they would be deployed. They also refused to talk directly to Bosnian Serb leader Radovan Karadžić and General Ratko Mladić, who had already been indicted for war crimes. Milošević could speak on their behalf. He was able to coerce them to accept the deals he was negotiating. Richard Holbrooke referred to the relationship between U.S. negotiators and the Serbian president as "bonding with the godfather." When asked, at Milošević's request, to sit down with the Bosnian Serb leaders responsible for horrible atrocities, he reminded himself about Wallenberg sitting down with Eichmann during the Holocaust to save Hungarian Jews.[37]

What made a peace agreement possible in 1995 was the fact that the United States had some leverage over all three parties.[38] The Croats had achieved their territorial objectives with tacit American support. The Bosnian Serbs had reason to fear defeat and could be motivated by a promise that a peace deal would help them retain the territory they had conquered during the war. This explains why much of the drama in Dayton lay in persuading the Bosniak leadership of the Republic of Bosnia and Herzegovina, President Alija Izetbegović and Prime Minister Haris Silajdžić, to accept the provisions of the peace agreement. They were compelled to come to a deal with Milošević

They were forced to accept the continued existence of a Bosnian Serb entity within the future state. They also had to accept a priori the idea that this Bosnian Serb entity would control some 49 percent of Bosnia's territory. In late 1995, following three years of horrendous violence, the Srebrenica massacre, and the shelling of civilians in cities such as Sarajevo and Tuzla, Bosniak leaders had little reason to reconcile with Bosnian Serbs. As their troops advanced for the first time since the beginning of the war, regaining control of cities, they were tempted to hold out for a longer war. At the same time they were extremely vulnerable to threats that had been there from the very beginning of the conflict: a possible accommodation between Croatia and Serbia, and Bosnian Croat and Bosnian Serb hard-liners, at their expense, and the loss of international support. So after hesitations, Bosnia's President Alija Izetbegović set out to wrestle three vital commitments from international mediators: there would be no partition of the country; those who had lost their homes would enjoy the right of return; and the United States promised a training program for the Bosnian armed forces similar to the one that had dramatically strengthened the Croatian army by 1995.

All of this also had profound consequences for the kind of state that would emerge from Dayton. The Dayton Peace Agreement foresaw the creation of a very limited central state with a collective presidency consisting of one Bosniak, one Bosnian Serb, and one Bosnian Croat. Central institutions had very few responsibilities.[39] The state consisted of two entities, a Bosnian Serb entity ("Republika Srpska") and a (largely) Bosniak-Croat entity referred to as "the Federation." The Dayton constitution even allowed the three wartime armies to remain in place. The concept of a state whose stability was supposedly guaranteed by an internal balance of military power was unprecedented. Richard Holbrooke admitted at the time that "in an ideal world, the several armies of Bosnia-Herzegovina should have been sharply reduced in size and merged into a single force controlled by the central government."[40] But in 1995 that was not an option: "Sadly we would have to allow each entity within a single country to maintain its own military force—a fundamental flaw in our postwar structure, but nonetheless inevitable, given the self-imposed constraints on what the outside powers were willing to do."[41]

Once all of the parties had signed on to the Dayton Peace Agreement, President Clinton made his plea to the U.S. public in November 1995 to support the deployment of twenty thousand U.S. troops—an essential part of the agreement. In affirming a bounded commitment by the United States, this speech spelled out the doctrine of limited humanitarian intervention. Clinton started from the premise of limited American power. He reminded his audience that "implementing the agreement in Bosnia can end the terrible suffering of the people, the warfare, the mass executions, the ethnic cleansing, the campaigns of rape and terror." He noted that the United States "must help the nations of Europe to end their worst nightmare since World War II now." He stressed that this was within the gift of the United States in this particular situation: "There are times and places where our leadership can mean the difference between peace and war and where we can defend our fundamental values as a people and serve our most basic strategic interests."[42] Clinton added that there were limits to what the United States was willing to do in Bosnia: "Let me say at the outset America's role will not be about fighting a war. It will be about helping the people of Bosnia to secure their own peace agreement. Our mission will be limited, focused, and under the command of an American general. . . . Our troops will make sure that each side withdraws its forces behind the front lines and keeps them there. They will maintain the cease-fire to prevent the war from accidentally starting again." U.S. troops would use their weapons only under very narrow circumstances: "to respond with overwhelming force to any threat to their own safety or any violation of the *military* provisions of the peace agreement." One goal of this mission, Clinton said, summing up his strategy, was to buy time to change the balance of forces on the ground in Bosnia. The United States, Clinton explained, would now provide "breathing room, space for the Federation forces to rearm."[43] The U.S. exit strategy was to arm one side to allow it to better defend itself after the international troops leave, within the foreseeable future. In the meantime, U.S. troops would monitor a narrow "zone of separation" between the entities.[44] The mission objectives were concrete: to remove weapons, to separate armed forces, to hold elections within the space of one year, and to avoid U.S. casualties. This met the requirement to deploy U.S. forces only for "clearly defined political and military objectives" and with a clear exit strategy.

In hindsight it is striking what was not mentioned in Clinton's speech. Clinton did not refer to the ideologies that led to and fueled this war (the dreams of Greater Serbia or Greater Croatia). The U.S. intervention in Bosnia was not a nation-building effort, as the chairman of the Joint Chiefs of Staff, General John Shalikashvili, explained to Congress: "IFOR [the international Implementation Force] will not be responsible for the conduct of humanitarian operations. It will not be a police force. It will not conduct nation-building. It will not move refugees."[45] This was a limited intervention that expressed the foreign policy vision presented by National Security Adviser Anthony Lake in a speech in March 1996: "It is a dangerous hubris to believe we can build other nations. But where our own interests are engaged *we can help nations build themselves*—and give them time to make a start at it."[46]

So what was the real lesson from the Balkans for future humanitarian interventions? U.S. policy in 1995 was characterized by forceful diplomacy taking place within clear (domestic) constraints. Later accounts of U.S. peacemakers as bulldozers, prepared to knock regional leaders' heads together, while U.S. planes bombed recalcitrant Bosnian Serbs into accepting a peace deal, are misleading. Making peace in Bosnia in 1995 required that U.S. diplomats deal directly with the men most responsible for mass atrocities, even if they did not allow those already indicted by the International Criminal Tribunal for the Former Yugoslavia (ICTY) to participate in the Dayton peace talks. Ending the genocidal campaign by Bosnian Serb forces in 1995 also *did* involve (Croatian and Bosnian government) ground troops putting military pressure on their opponents. This was, in the end, not so different from previous interventions to stop mass atrocities, which Samantha Power describes in her book. After Pakistani troops killed between one and two million Bengalis in the spring of 1971, she writes, "only the Indian army's invasion, combined with Bengali resistance, halted Pakistan's genocide."[47] In Cambodia it was a Vietnamese invasion that in January 1979 finally dislodged the regime of Pol Pot.[48] In Rwanda it was Tutsi (Rwandese Patriotic Front) rebels under the command of Paul Kagame who eventually brought the genocide committed by Hutu extremists to a halt. "In so doing they sent Hutu perpetrators, among them an estimated 1.7 million Hutu refugees, fleeing into neighboring Zaire and Tanzania."[49] The use of ground forces was a necessary ingredient in all of these interventions to eventually stop genocidal regimes and bring mass atrocities to an end.

Humanitarian interventions are, by their very nature, matters of limited commitment for outsiders, involving limited interests and objectives to be pursued at limited risk. As Mark Danner wrote, Clinton in 1995, "in one of the more eloquent speeches of his presidency, had explained to Americans why they must send their sons or daughters to Bosnia. Still, approval ratings stayed low; his audience remained concerned about the risks. Given such inescapable realities, American officials sadly concluded, as they had in Haiti the year before, that the loss of even one soldier might threaten the mission."[50] The United States did not seek regime changes in Belgrade or Zagreb, or even in Pale (the wartime capital of the Bosnian Serbs outside Sarajevo) and West Mostar (the center of radical Bosnian Croat separatists). Many critics of Dayton have rightly highlighted these trade-offs; some have suggested that they went too far, creating a Potemkin state with no chance of survival once international troops were withdrawn. This simply reflected the fact that Bosnia remained for U.S. leaders a matter of important but not vital interest, which justified a limited and not open-ended commitment.

However, the fundamental fact about 1995 is that U.S. leaders, under pressure from public opinion and following an effective campaign by civil society, put their minds to it and managed to bring a terrible war to an end. There was no new Srebrenica. After one hundred thousand deaths in Bosnia and Herzegovina, the killing stopped. As a result the experience of late 1995 was a turning point in the international debate over humanitarian intervention. In the end, Samantha Power noted that for all of the dithering that preceded it for more than three years, the intervention in Bosnia was the most robust U.S. response to mass atrocities in a century. Once the United States *did* intervene in the summer of 1995, the argument that the worst could have been averted through more timely action seemed even more obvious. As Samantha Power put it:

> The best testament to what the United States might have achieved is what the United States did achieve. For all the talk of the likely futility of US involvement, in the rare instances that the United States did act, it made a difference. . . . NATO bombing in Bosnia, when it finally came, rapidly brought that three-and-a-half-year war to a close.[51]

The war came to an end as a result of an effort that mixed military force and diplomacy. It was a military intervention without any U.S. casualties. Bosnia held out the vision of a "good intervention," the use of military power in defense of the defenseless, and the use of bombs to stop evil and genocide.

A REMARKABLE OCCUPATION

Amir Abdur Rahman, who ruled Afghanistan from 1880 to 1901, was, according to former World Bank anthropologist Ashraf Ghani, one of the most successful state-builders of the late nineteenth century. In an essay published in 1978, Ghani described the secret of the Amir's long rule: "During the twenty-one years of his reign, he was to be constantly engaged in large and small-scale wars, carrying the power of the State to the remotest corners of the country. At his death, he passed on to his heir a State that had never been so centralized." The Amir challenged the autonomy of tribal aristocracies. He imposed taxes on everyone who had previously been exempted. He propagated a form of Islam that justified centralization. He also imposed a unitary form of religious worship on his subjects, and pushed those who resisted into exile. For Ghani, who has made a name for himself in recent years as an international expert on state-building, the Amir's experience showed one way—this was how one could go about forging a modern bureaucratic state in Afghanistan.[52]

The challenge of building a functioning state in postwar Bosnia in 1995 was very different. At the very outset there were no functioning and legitimate central state institutions. At the same time, there was neither a charismatic state-builder, nor a common external enemy, nor a unifying national vision. There was certainly no appetite for another twenty-one years of small-scale wars. The task facing the international community in Bosnia was to help build the institutions of a highly decentralized state as foreseen in the peace agreement reached in Dayton and to do so without coercion, while helping to rebuild the country's infrastructure and address the concerns of a huge number of displaced persons.

In terms of either refugee return or the extent of the state-building challenge, there were precious few precedents for what was being attempted in Bosnia after 1995. The UN had previously been successful in easing the transition to independence and democracy in Namibia between 1989 and 1990. In 1992, it had set up a Transitional Authority in Cambodia (UNTAC), where it also assumed nominal responsibility for governing. Yet these missions were limited. There were never more than two hundred UN civil administrators on the ground as part of UNTAC, and the whole operation ended in 1993. Parallel to the international mission in Bosnia, the UN also took over—for a limited period of two years—the transitional administration of Eastern Slavonia in Croatia.[53] All of these missions lasted for short periods of time. They involved neither U.S. leadership nor anything close to the resources and international ambitions in Bosnia. Initially, the assumption was that the mission in Bosnia would be similar. It would focus on specific concrete goals (withdrawing weapons, holding elections, and beginning the rebuilding of destroyed infrastructure); it would have a clear time horizon for international peacekeepers of one year. There was a civilian mission whose task it was to facilitate the efforts of local institutions, and about two thousand UN police observers without any executive powers. As the first High Representative of the international community in Sarajevo, Carl Bildt, put it, Bosnia was not going to be a protectorate. Or so it seemed in 1996, before Bosnia turned into one of the most ambitious state-building missions ever undertaken.

When the RAND Corporation published a series of eight case studies in *America's Role in Nation-Building—From Germany to Iraq* in 2003, the only two recent precedents examined were far from encouraging: Somalia (1993), which ended in retreat and withdrawal, and Haiti (1994), where the United States managed to restore a democratically elected leader, ousted by a coup, in an operation that "left little residue in the way of transformation." To find models of nation-building success, the RAND analysts had to go back to the U.S. occupations of Germany and Japan after World War II. These, they argued, had set "a standard for post-conflict nation building that has not since been matched." Both demonstrated "that democracy was transferable; that societies could, under certain circumstances, be encouraged to transform themselves; and that major transformations could endure."[54]

Yet there is good reason to think that both Germany and Japan were irrelevant as models for the Balkans. U.S. troops had entered these countries after they had been defeated. Germany was to experience a "stern all-powerful military administration of a conquered country, based on its unconditional surrender,"[55] not a peacekeeping operation to implement a peace agreement accepted by all parties. In Germany the military occupation authority appointed all officials, while the leading civilian authority in postwar Bosnia, the Office of the High Representative (OHR), initially had no executive powers. Both Germany and Japan were vital to U.S. national security interests in ways no Balkan country was half a century later. Finally, for all of its other successes, the U.S. occupation of Germany did not focus on the return of millions of refugees to their former homes (in fact, the policy decided by the victorious allies had favored the expulsion and resettlement of millions of Germans from Eastern Europe to Germany). In the end, the occupation authorities in Germany also did not prevent the country's partition into two states.[56]

All occupations require military interventions, but not all military interventions lead to occupation—with good reason, writes David Edelstein in another recent study, since "military occupation is among the most difficult tasks of statecraft."[57] A successful occupation is one where an occupying power can withdraw after a certain period without concern for the security of its interests. However, Edelstein underlines, "most military occupations have ambitious goals that take a long time and substantial resources to be accomplished." What makes this even more difficult, he writes, is that "both occupied populations and occupying powers grow weary of extended occupations, undermining their success."[58] As a result, there have been only a few successes. Edelstein counts twenty-six completed military occupations in the world since 1815. On his count, only seven succeeded.[59] The United States was involved in five of these:

Germany and Japan, but also Austria, Italy, and the Japanese Ryukyu Islands (Okinawa), all of which took place after World War II. Edelstein sees a clear pattern to the rare cases of successful occupations:

> When an occupied population perceives that another country poses a threat to its future security, it will welcome an occupying power that is both willing and able to protect it from that threat . . . allowing the occupier time to rebuild political and economic institutions.[60]

In the case of all U.S. Cold War occupations, the threat was posed by the Soviet Union. One example where the occupied population did not perceive a common threat and the United States remained doubtful about the commitment it was prepared to make was postwar South Korea—and here, even at a time of its greatest successes in occupation in Western Europe and Japan, America did not succeed in reaching its objectives.[61]

This did not bode well for Bosnia, where the main threats right after the war, as perceived by each side, came from other ethnic groups. From the outset, the most important challenge to implementing the relatively narrow provisions of the Dayton Peace Agreement was the undiminished strength of ultra-nationalist (Bosnian Croat and Bosnian Serb) power structures, which could count on significant material and political support from neighboring countries. Putting Serbia's Slobodan Milošević, and Croatia's Franjo Tudjman partly in charge of building a functioning Bosnian state and reversing ethnic cleansing was like putting the foxes in charge of the chicken coop. As a result of the Bosnian war and the way it ended, local warlords and their political masters remained firmly in control throughout much of the country in 1996. Local politicians, police chiefs, and party leaders who owed their wealth and influence to the legacy of ethnic cleansing remained unchallenged. As their hold on power endured, so did their ideas and political programs—a nationalist ethic of sacrifice and murder in the name of ethnically pure nation-states. Those who had ripped apart the pluralist fabric of Bosnian society in the name of ethnic purity—and had often profited from it—did not see any reason in 1996 not to defend what had been gained.

And so in the period following the war, as the large group of foreign journalists in Sarajevo who had covered Bosnia thinned out, it appeared as if nothing much was happening. At the end of 1996, following Clinton's reelection, IFOR, the initial Implementation Force, was replaced by SFOR, the Stabilization Force, which was given a two-year mandate that would be extended repeatedly thereafter. One reason for this had been the absence of any American casualties. Seemingly endless rounds of elections, national and local, were held in 1996, 1997, 1998, and 2000. Bosnia increasingly resembled a huge holding operation, and the foreign mission settled into its role as a Balkan Sisyphus, rolling a rock up the hill of peace implementation only to find—or appear to find—setbacks whenever it looked like progress had been made. This was certainly the impression I had in 1999, having worked in Bosnia for three years as a journalist, analyst, and member of the political department in the OHR. When I left the OHR to set up a think tank with others who had worked in international organizations in Sarajevo, our first report in October 1999 expressed our frustration that the international community in Bosnia was treading water. "Despite its intrusive role [the international community] has failed to achieve breakthroughs on substantive issues which might contribute to a self-sustaining peace process," we concluded.[62] Like most observers we felt that a withdrawal of international support before new institutions were built could bring disastrous consequences. We were then, without recognizing it, partaking in the growing liberal imperialist sentiment, arguing strongly that the international community needed to take a more proactive role in building the institutions of a functioning Bosnian state.

Fast-forward one decade. In 2006, Paddy Ashdown, the longest-serving (May 2002–January 2006) High Representative in postwar Bosnia and as such the leading international official in the country, appeared before the House of Lords in London. He spoke about the transformation in Bosnia, the future of the Balkans, and the achievements of a peace-building mission that had already lasted more than a decade. He placed this description of Bosnia in a wider European context:

> A million refugees returned. That has not happened in 35 years. The refugees I saw driven out of their homes in Belfast [Northern Ireland] when I was a young soldier, marching into the city in 1969 have not returned. There is complete freedom of movement in Bosnia. That has not happened in Cyprus, 25 years after the Cyprus peace conference. Elections are held absolutely peacefully under the aegis of the people of Bosnia and Herzegovina and to the highest international standards. That does not happen in the Basque country of Spain after 25 years of problems there. It is a remarkable success story.[63]

The return of over one million displaced persons and refugees to destroyed villages throughout the whole territory of Bosnia was not the only unexpected achievement of the postwar intervention, however. So was the large-scale restitution of assets (more than two hundred thousand residential properties were restored to displaced persons by 2004), a process without precedent in the history of international peace-building.[64] So was the almost complete demilitarization of postwar Bosnia. As Richard Holbrooke wrote in an article that appeared in April 2008, instead of having three armies controlled by three ethnic groups there was now "a single command structure and a single state army, built along NATO lines."[65] At the end of the war in 1995 Bosnia was one of the most militarized places on earth, with three nearly exclusively mono-ethnic armies and an estimated total of 419,000 men under arms. The number of soldiers has since fallen to less than 10,000 professionals and 5,000 reservists. Conscription was abolished on January 1, 2006. Instead of a country physically divided into hostile states facing each other along a cease-fire line like the two Koreas, Holbrooke wrote, one can today "drive without interference from one end of Bosnia to the other, and the once ubiquitous checkpoints are gone." A local Al Qaeda presence, Holbrooke claimed, had been eliminated. "Without Dayton," Holbrooke noted, "al-Qaeda would probably have planned the September 11 attacks from Bosnia, not Afghanistan." And most strikingly, the primary goal of the U.S. intervention, to end the war once and for all, "has been fully achieved, at a cost of zero American and NATO lives."[66]

In short, ten years after the end of the war Bosnia was no longer a failed state. Its crime rate was significantly lower than in the Baltic states that had joined the European Union in 2004 and comparable to crime rates in West European nations.[67] The average life expectancy was as high as in places like Bulgaria and Romania, which had not experienced war.[68] Taxes were collected; most public services had surpassed prewar levels. Clearly, at *some point something* fundamental changed between 1996 and 2006.

But what was it? Was the change sustainable? And could lessons and experiences from Bosnia be applied more generally to other post-conflict missions? In 1995 some observers and policy-makers might have expected the international deployment in Bosnia to be an exceptional event. It soon became obvious, however, that Bosnia was only the first in a succession of ambitious military interventions and post-conflict missions: in Kosovo and East Timor (1999), then in Afghanistan (2001), and finally in Iraq (2003). It became commonplace to refer to all of these missions as if they were variations on the same theme: sometimes referred to as nation-building, stabilization operations (the preferred term used by the U.S. military), state-building, or post-conflict peace-building. As a new international cadre of nation-builders emerged, moving from one mission to the next, policy-makers asked with ever greater insistence whether there were some universal lessons to be drawn from each and all of these interventions. For those who answered this question in the affirmative, the experience of Bosnia was to frame the debate on every intervention that followed.

THE SECRET OF PEACE-BUILDING

Time and time again, our moral ambitions have been revealed as being far larger than our political, military, or even cognitive means.

DAVID RIEFF, "A NEW AGE OF
LIBERAL IMPERIALISM," 1999[69]

It is useful to distinguish between four different perspectives on the Bosnian state-building experience, all of which have profound implications for the lessons that one might learn from the

Balkans: the planning school, the liberal imperialist school, the futility school, and what I call here principled incrementalism.

The planning school of nation-building argues that the transformation of Bosnia since 1995 was essentially a function of resources, people, and money, which were made available for a sufficiently long period of time. Planners believe that there are universal lessons to be derived from the study of history and from previous cases of nation-building. To the extent that its assumptions are embraced by the U.S. military's counterinsurgency doctrine, the planning school is the most prevalent way of thinking about nation-building among American policy-makers and strategists. For the planners the right fit between means and ends is everything.

A second school of thought, liberal imperialism, focuses on the problem of "spoilers" and warlords. It stresses the need to give an international mission sufficient authority to overcome the efforts of those who seek to obstruct post-conflict peacebuilding. The key to progress, the liberal imperialists posit, is a strong mandate and the charisma of the leading international actor in the field. Under post-conflict conditions it is vital for a determined international authority to establish institutions and to remove obstacles on the path to good governance. For the liberal imperialists, sufficient international authority, backed up by force if needed, is everything.

A third way of thinking about intervention, the "futility" school, is embraced by those who argue that both humanitarian intervention and nation-building are generally bound to fail. The continuing difficulties in Bosnia, political tensions, and challenges to its statehood all highlight the foolishness of outsiders' ambitions to build states or nations in a post-conflict environment. If real and sustainable success proves elusive even in a small European nation of less than four million inhabitants, then it is all the more unrealistic in large and populous societies elsewhere in the world. For members of the futility school, dispelling illusions about the virtues of intervention is the key to avoiding future disasters.

Finally, this essay puts forward a fourth way of interpreting events in Bosnia and elsewhere, which I shall call *principled incrementalism*. It challenges a number of conventional wisdoms about what has and has not worked in postwar Bosnia. It calls into question the notion that there are universal lessons, or that there is even a discipline of "nation-building." Outsiders intervening in complex post-conflict environments usually lack both the knowledge and the authority to prepare a comprehensive plan for social change or to impose decisions by decree and expect these to stick. At the same time, experience shows that interveners can sometimes succeed where they avoid overly rash and risky decisions, focusing instead on emerging opportunities and on finding strong local allies. The key to success is the ability to compromise and broker political deals that can advance the peace agenda. More important even than the number of soldiers is the legitimacy of the intervener in the eyes of the local population. For the incrementalists, context is everything.

A GRAND THEORY OF INTERVENTION— THE PLANNING SCHOOL

What principally distinguishes Germany, Japan, Bosnia and Kosovo from Somalia, Haiti and Afghanistan are not their levels of Western culture, economic development, or

cultural homogeneity. Rather it is the level of effort the
United States and the international community put into
their democratic transformations.

RAND CORPORATION, *AMERICA'S ROLE IN*

NATION-BUILDING, 2003[70]

No institution is as identified with the approach of the planning
school as the RAND Corporation, the United States' biggest
think tank. RAND stands for "Research and Development"
and has been a leading center of military-sponsored scientific
research since its creation in 1948.[71] RAND was set up by the
U.S. Air Force following World War II to provide advice on how
to wage war and win. Its alumni prepared the intellectual ground
for a number of interventions, including Vietnam. The head of
RAND's mathematics division in its earliest years, John Davis
Williams, embodied its institutional ethos, believing "that every
human activity could be understood and explained by numerical
rationality. From the start, one of his pet projects at RAND was
developing a theory of war along the lines of Einstein's grand
unified theory of physics."[72] The ambition of the planning school
is to develop state-building into a science, based on best practices
and on the experiences of previous interventions. To prepare
an intervention—adepts of the planning school believe—requires
using case studies to examine which inputs produced what outputs. Inputs include manpower and money (to pay for soldiers,
police officers, judicial advisers, reconstruction). Outputs are
security, democratic progress, and economic growth.

In recent years RAND's search for a general theory of
nation-building was led by James Dobbins, one of America's
most experienced practitioners in the field who had worked on

the Balkans, Afghanistan, Haiti, and Somalia as a senior official.[73] *The Beginner's Guide to Nation-Building*, published under his watch in 2007, summed up lessons from twenty-four case studies of nation-building efforts led by the United States, European Union, and UN, offering simple prescriptions for policy planners.[74]

Any nation-building effort must start with the question: what does the intervener want to achieve? *The Beginner's Guide* presents the problem of intervention in the form of a decision tree. First, intervening authorities must determine "how extensively to reorder the targeted society." Policy-makers face a choice between "co-option" (under which the intervening authorities try to work within existing institutions) and "deconstruction" (where the intervening authorities "first dismantle an existing state apparatus and then build a new one"). The choice made determines "how large a pool of spoilers the intervention will create," which in turn establishes "how large a commitment of personnel and money will be needed to deter or suppress the resultant resistance."[75] Key to success in all cases is a good plan matching ends with means. Ideally, policy-makers are presented with an intervention menu that shows different options, each carrying a price tag. The job of analysts is to highlight the inevitable trade-offs.[76] In case of a mismatch between inputs and outputs, means and ends, balance can be restored in one of two ways: increasing inputs or lowering aspirations.

As to the question of why Bosnia was more successful than other interventions the planning school has a straightforward answer: it was one of the best-resourced nation-building efforts ever. In Bosnia in 1996 the number of international troops was sixty thousand; there were two thousand international police monitors; and an international donors' conference raised more than five billion dollars for reconstruction, all for a population of less than four million people. This was an extraordinary mobilization of resources. The peak number of soldiers for other peace enforcement missions was 0.1 per one thousand people in El Salvador, two in Cambodia, three in Namibia, three in Sierra Leone, four in Haiti, four in Afghanistan (2010), five in Japan, five in Somalia, seven in Iraq, but nineteen in Bosnia (1996) and twenty in Kosovo (1999)![77]

RAND distinguishes between "heavy peace enforcement" missions (involving a hostile or divided population and a governance vacuum) and "light peacekeeping" operations (where the population is supportive of the occupation and the state in question retains some capacity for governance). *The Beginner's Guide* suggests concrete rules of thumb to quantify the necessary inputs—in terms of financial resource and personnel—in hypothetical nation-building efforts.[78] It begins by taking the average number of soldiers deployed during the first year in eight operations in East Timor, Eastern Slavonia, Japan, Somalia, Haiti, Bosnia, Kosovo, and Iraq. On the basis of this, the experts calculate that for a "heavy" peace enforcement mission, an average of thirteen soldiers per one thousand inhabitants would be needed. For a "light" peacekeeping mission the number would be two soldiers per thousand.[79]

One of the consequences of the planners' approach is an appreciation for more limited missions. *The Beginner's Guide* praises the "small but highly successful missions" in Eastern Slavonia (1996) and East Timor (1999) and concludes that when it comes to post-conflict nation-building, UN-led missions, though "almost always undermanned and under-resourced," have a significantly higher success rate than missions led by the United States. One reason for this is the fact that UN mandates are generally more precise. For instance, the four UN operations in Namibia, Cambodia, El Salvador, and Mozambique were deployed specifically to oversee the implementation of peace accords. UN missions have also remained in place for shorter periods of time than U.S.-led missions.[80] For adepts of the planning school, there is no inherent problem with a light footprint, reflecting limited interests and objectives. If previous experience is to be any indication, far-reaching objectives are very hard to achieve in a large country: "The effort needed to stabilize Bosnia and Kosovo has proved difficult to replicate in Afghanistan or Iraq, nations that are eight to 12 times more populous."[81]

The planning school also notes the importance of thorough debate. A mission for which there is overwhelming domestic support can easily turn sour precisely because strong support cuts short the necessary debate on the required inputs and possible casualties. In 2007, Dobbins recalled that "Congress authorized the invasion [of Iraq in 2003] by an overwhelming bipartisan majority—something that had not occurred for the Gulf War a decade earlier, nor for any of the highly controversial military operations of the Clinton era, in Somalia, Haiti, Bosnia and Kosovo." Given how costly it can be, and how long a commitment might be required, this lack of reflection on what it would really take to succeed was troubling: a "decision to go to war should be difficult, not easy."[82]

At the same time, if a mission goes badly, but success is imperative due to vital national interests, there is always an obvious solution: to readjust the balance between means and ends by increasing the number of inputs; in other words to "surge." While some RAND fellows played a big role in making the case for toppling Saddam Hussein, and others warned already in 2003 that a successful U.S. occupation of Iraq would require an enormous mobilization of resources, both groups shared the conviction that this was ultimately a mission where success was within reach. A root-and-branch overhaul of state and political structures in Iraq would indeed be "tremendously costly and would involve a long period of direct US administration, akin to the early years of British administration of the Iraqi mandate" in the 1920s, a 2003 RAND study noted.[83] And yet, this would also "lay a sounder basis for long-term reform." The problem, in other words, was not that the United States set out to engage in a root-and-branch overhaul of Iraqi institutions, but that it did so without adequate resources in hand. Had there been a proper debate, and had the required resources been made available from the outset, success in Iraq would have been possible. The same was true for Afghanistan. In one of its most striking paragraphs the 2003 RAND report on nation-building compared Kosovo and Afghanistan:

> The United States and its allies have put 25 times more money and 50 times more troops, on a per capita basis, into post-conflict Kosovo than into post-conflict Afghanistan. This higher level of input accounts in significant measure for the higher level of output measured in the development of democratic institutions and economic growth.[84]

This theory holds that there is a clear causal relationship between the amount of assistance provided and the stability that ensues. The supposed correlation between stability and the amount of money spent—a "relative deprivation theory" where unmet economic expectations lead to rebellion—suggests that the solution for problems of disaffected populations and underdevelopment is essentially a question of political will and money. As Ahmed Rashid, one of the best-known commentators on modern Afghanistan, put it in his book *Descent into Chaos*, the solution to the problem of building a nation in Afghanistan was obvious: "Most experts reckoned that Afghanistan, a country the size of Texas, needed about $4 to 5 billion every year for the next ten years to put it on its feet—a small amount in geopolitical donor terms and a pittance compared to what was later spent in Iraq."[85]

The notion that it is within the gift of interveners to bring about rapid economic development, and that investing additional resources would immediately transform the political dynamic in Afghanistan, was also shared by President Obama's national security adviser, General James L. Jones. As White House press secretary Robert Gibbs put it, talking about a military surge in 2009 that was supposed to last for one year, "If we don't get good governance and improvement in governance, if we don't get an increase in development and a change in the economy, I think the president and I think General Jones would agree that no amount of troops are going to leave that country in a situation that is sustainable."[86] Bob Woodward quoted General Jones saying that "the piece of the strategy that has to work *in the next year* [emphasis added] is economic development. If that is not done right, there are not enough troops in the world to succeed."[87] In fact, in Afghanistan substantial amounts of aid did produce high growth rates from the outset, with growth estimated at above 10 percent every year since 2003, much higher than under previous Taliban rule.[88] Massive additional U.S. investment even produced an annual growth in the gross domestic product (GDP) of 41 percent in 2009.[89] And yet the jump in GDP growth in 2009 did not result in greater stability. The International Committee of the Red Cross (ICRC) warned in December 2010 that security was worse than at any time in the last thirty years. In March 2011, there had been further "dramatic deterioration."[90] International estimates of Taliban numbers have been growing—from a few thousand Taliban five years ago to at least thirty-five thousand full-time fighters in 2011. Some scholars have even suggested that "donor programs delivered in an environment of state weakness, war-lordism, racketeering, and rent seeking create conflict and popular disappointment, rather than winning hearts and minds."[91]

The RAND studies argue that "the higher the proportion of stabilizing troops, the lower the number of casualties suffered and inflicted. Indeed, most adequately manned post-conflict operations suffered no casualties whatsoever."[92] The more troops are deployed, the lesser the temptation by hostile forces to resist: this is another lesson that appears to come directly from the Balkans (Bosnia, Kosovo, Eastern Slavonia). Here too the historical precedents are far from clear, however. Experience also suggests that in all post-conflict missions, the environment can some-times change irrespective of the number of troops. In Kosovo, massive riots broke out in March 2004, despite the presence of a significant, albeit unprepared, international peacekeeping force. In Bosnia international leverage *increased* as the total number of troops fell from sixty thousand in 1996 to twelve thousand in 2002. Sometimes an increase in troops can coincide or even con-tribute to an escalation in hostilities. This was apparently the case in southern Afghanistan in 2006. Minna Jarvenpaa helped plan the deployment of British troops in southern Afghanistan's Helmand Province. "When I first traveled to Helmand as part of the British government's planning team in November 2005, there was a 200-strong US contingent in the provincial capital Lashkar Gah," she recalls. "Helmand was by and large quiet, although there had been a small number of incidents attributed to the Taliban. There were some signs that the Taliban were regrouping around Kandahar."[93] The British initially deployed thirty-five hundred troops in April 2006. At the time it was still plausible for British Defence Secretary John Reid to express hope that British troops would accomplish their mission and return home "without a shot being fired." A year later, the *Telegraph* reported that Reid had miscalculated: by then the British had fired four million bullets in Helmand. The United Kingdom gradually increased its troop contribution to more than nine thousand. Five years on, there are nearly thirty thousand American and British troops and some twenty thousand Afghan security forces in Helmand, which has seen some of the worst fighting in all of Afghanistan. In tandem with the deployment of ever greater numbers of troops, the security situation has deteriorated, and in 2011 Helmand is considerably less safe than it was in 2005. Whatever the underlying cause for this deterioration, it is clear that the massive surge failed to prevent it.

There are also serious questions about the methodology of the *Beginner's Guide* and the samples used to arrive at general conclusions. Following the *Guide*'s formula, the number of soldiers deployed in Bosnia would have been more than sufficient for a heavy peace enforcement mission; it is the Bosnia experience that has been used as a reference to establish these numbers. However, in Bosnia the initial approach was to co-opt local elites. International troops arrived on the basis of an agreement signed by all sides. The number of soldiers in Bosnia and Kosovo, where international troops proceeded with great caution to avoid any armed confrontations, is hardly a useful guide for success in places such as Iraq or southern Afghanistan . . . where there is no peace agreement with insurgents and strong local hostility to outside forces. Nor should future missions be based on historical averages when some of the missions in the case studies, such as the operations in Somalia and Haiti, were not deemed successful.

The main message of the planning school is upbeat about interveners' capacity to effect change. The United States in particular knows how to carry out nation-building, the planners argue, and has done so successfully many times in the past decade:

> Iraq was not the first but the seventh society in a little more than a decade that the United States had entered to liberate and rebuild. . . . Six of these seven societies were Muslim. Thus, by the time U.S. troops entered Iraq, no country in the world had more modern experience in nation-building than the United States. No Western military had more extensive recent practice operating within Muslim societies.[94]

The assumption that there exists a quantifiable formula for success was widely shared by the U.S. military. In December 2004 the Pentagon's Defense Science Board's report on troop requirements for "stabilization operations," the military's concept for "nation-building," noted the high ratios needed:

> History indicates that stabilization of societies that are relatively ordered, without ambitious goals, may require 5 troops per 1000 indigenous people; while stabilization of disordered societies, with ambitious goals involving lasting cultural change, may require 20 troops per 1000 indigenous people.[95]

The theory of counterinsurgency embraces the assumption of the planning school that civilians know how to build institutions and bring about good governance and development. The most recent U.S. joint Army/Marine Corps counterinsurgency field manual concluded, based on a study of historical precedents, that in a full counterinsurgency, "between 20–25 counterinsurgents [are required] for every 1,000 residents in an area of operations."[96] This was the ratio in both Bosnia and Kosovo. As the field manual explains over and over again, a counterinsurgency without competent civilian nation-builders "is a moon without a planet to orbit." Success in counterinsurgency relies on "non-kinetic activity"; civilians are a soldier's exit strategy and "some of the best weapons for counterinsurgents do not shoot."[97] As Sarah Sewall, who teaches at the Harvard Kennedy School of Government, explains in her introduction to the manual, counterinsurgency "requires significant, effective, and civilian-led efforts to strengthen economies, local political and administrative institutions, and social infrastructure and services for sustained periods of time."[98] The manual quotes French counterinsurgency expert David Galula, who suggested that "the soldier must then become . . . a social worker, a civil engineer, a school-teacher, a nurse, a boy scout. But only for so long as he cannot be replaced."[99] The optimistic assumption is either that there is a sufficient number of soldiers available who can play this role or that there are civilians available who can replace them.

Given the planners' confidence in the ability of the United States to build other nations, what is remarkable is that the RAND series of case studies excluded the one nation-building effort in which RAND itself had been most heavily involved: Vietnam, the biggest and most expensive nation-building effort before Iraq. It is a striking omission, because Vietnam is the only recent example of U.S.-led "nation building under fire." In Vietnam the United States conducted a surge. By 1968 there were more than six hundred thousand international troops in South Vietnam, which had a population of some nineteen million people. At the time, a bitter debate was dividing RAND's analysts; there was no consensus about the relationship between inputs and outputs. In 1965 the Pentagon commissioned the think tank to study the nature of the Vietnamese insurgency to find out what motivated the South Vietnamese communist insurgents (the Viet Cong). RAND's "Viet Cong Motivation and Morale Study in 1964" found that the insurgents were not fanatical communists nor were they simply interested in obtaining land, but saw themselves as nationalists fighting an anti-imperial war for an independent Vietnam.[100] This research suggested that the ideologically motivated insurgency would be harder to defeat than previously assumed.[101] Other RAND reports from the same era signaled that perhaps more money and troops *would* eventually lead to the defeat of the insurgents, whatever their motivation. One report, "Insurgency and Counterinsurgency: New Myths and Old Realities," was written by the then head of the RAND Economics Department, Charles Wolf. Wolf concluded that "an approach to counterinsurgency that focuses on 'winning popular support' has little chance of success";[102] instead, he argued, it is the control of the food supply that might bring South Vietnamese peasants around to rejecting the insurgents.

Looking back at these debates in the 1960s casts serious doubt on the notion that the United States had learned skills in the 1940s that it could easily apply in the 1990s. Leaving out the Vietnam case study, while including Germany, Japan, Bosnia, and Kosovo, is all the more puzzling given the resemblance between these debates, which divided RAND in the 1960s, and the debate about Afghanistan taking place today. The central claim of the planning school is that missions in Iraq and Afghanistan are feasible *because nation-building has been done before*. In reality, however, leaving aside Vietnam, there are no recent historical examples of U.S.-led "nation building under fire" that could help provide a scientific basis for generalizations about the necessary inputs.[103] A realistic reading of "historical experience" would have to conclude, much more modestly, that neither the United States nor its allies, nor the United Nations or any other international organization, has an understanding of how to "build a generic nation," or how many soldiers it takes to pacify a generic "hostile society," or how much money is needed to buy loyalty or bring about development. Previous missions, in Germany, Bosnia, or Kosovo, contain plenty of food for thought, but none of them can provide a nation-building planner with a quantifiable strategy that applies to the Middle East or Central Asia. A look at various previous missions suggests that some types of interventions—"light interventions" in permissive environments in small nations on the basis of a peace agreement—have an encouraging record. In this respect, the Bosnian example provides useful guidance. As an illustration of what it would take to succeed in "nation building under fire," however, the Bosnian analogy, and any numbers extrapolated from it, is dangerously misleading.

"A WHIP AND SOME CASH"—THE LIBERAL IMPERIALIST SCHOOL

> When the choice is really between any order at all and anarchy, then it is enough just to govern; but more often the task of preserving a state must be seen in terms of governing well.
>
> BERNARD CRICK, *IN DEFENCE OF POLITICS*[104]

At an early meeting of Bosnia's newly elected three-member collective presidency in Sarajevo's National Museum in October 1996, the all-consuming item was the question of seating arrangements. When it became clear that the issue of who sat next to whom could undermine the whole meeting, High Representative Carl Bildt, who acted as a mediator, suggested that the participants walk around the table while they talk. "Even they laughed at this," Bildt recalls, "and eventually agreed to talk while sitting down."[105] The fact that this is what the most senior international civilian official in postwar Bosnia had to do to make Momčilo Krajišnik, the Serb member of the presidency, a close associate of Radovan Karadžić and a soon-to-be sentenced war criminal, sit down, captured the extent of Bildt's powers. Given how difficult it was to even get them seated, it seemed utopian to believe that Bosnia's wartime leaders could be persuaded to dismantle the regimes that they had created and to build strong common institutions.

For liberal imperialists, excessive caution and lack of resolve during the early years in Bosnia were the result of flawed thinking and an impossible mandate. As one of Carl Bildt's successors (from 2002 to 2006), Paddy Ashdown, put it, in these early years "international officials were in the absurd position of having to negotiate even the most minor issues with all three parties to the conflict, often with the very people who had been both the master-minds of the conflict and its profiteers."[106]

Everything—at least according to the liberal imperialist narrative—changed in 1997. An international conference in Germany equipped the OHR with the so-called Bonn powers, which made it possible for the High Representative to sack officials, elected or not, who obstructed the peace implementation process. The Bonn powers also gave the OHR the authority to impose legislation. Now, by the stroke of a pen, politicians, civil servants, even judges could be removed from office and banned from political life forever. There were no checks, no constraints, no institutions to which decisions could be appealed. Armed with the Bonn powers and supported by SFOR, the OHR was finally able to begin removing obstacles, intimidating obstructionists, and reshaping the country. As successive High Representatives became more courageous, dismissing hundreds of officials and imposing hundreds of legal decisions, progress was finally made.

For liberal imperialists, the most important lesson to emerge from postwar Bosnia concerned international authority. It is crucial, they concluded, to challenge warlords and "spoilers" aggressively. In the absence of such determination, attempting to build institutions and a lasting peace is futile. Liberal imperialists are also skeptical about the planners' belief in interveners' capacity to calibrate means and ends. They question the notion that a "light footprint" could ever bring lasting success. For lasting stability to take hold, they posit, certain institutions and social realities have to be in place. What any mission needs is a defined "end-state": a situation where the rule of law, good governance, and a good business climate (so as to ensure sustainable economic development) can take root—and survive the interveners' withdrawal. To withdraw before such an end-state is achieved is to run a big risk. To expect local warlords to build credible institutions, when it is often in their material and personal interest to maintain bad governance, is a sign of dangerous naivete. To achieve progress, they conclude, there is often no alternative but to have outsiders, foreigners, assume direct responsibility, authority, and power.

What made the liberal imperialist narrative that emerged from Bosnia so compelling was the contrast between the period of aggressive international power and the "light footprint" that preceded it. The early years are remembered as a time of wasted effort, when the international community was powerless in the face of brazen obstructionism. In this narrative, Carl Bildt, who arrived in Bosnia with a handful of associates and a bundle of U.S. dollars to head the main international organization, the OHR, found himself deprived of the tools of pressure that the liberal imperialists find indispensable. The OHR had no command over any military or police forces. The limits of economic conditionality became clear when Bosnian Serb leaders, rather than accept any conditions, decided to boycott the international donors' conference in April 1996. Many donors did not want to complicate their work by linking reconstruction to political conditions. Bildt had the prestige of his office. However, as he wrote later, whenever more fundamental problems emerged, "moral authority alone did not cut much ice in the hard political game over the future of Bosnia."[107]

In this narrative it was only once OHR began to enjoy the Bonn powers that progress became possible. First, the international community started to dismiss individual local officials. By 1999, the OHR was in the business of vetting budgets, judges, and appointments to executive positions. The UN police mission, meanwhile, began to get serious about vetting the police forces across the country.[108] Laws, including those creating new institutions, would enter into force the moment they were posted on the OHR's Web site. On a single day in 2002, twenty-five obstructionist officials were dismissed. In the summer of 2004, sixty Serb officials were removed from their positions. Resistance began to crumble.

Searching for the contemporary origins of the liberal imperialist vision, one ends up in an unlikely place: a small provincial town in northwest Bosnia on the river Sava, Brčko. If the Bonn powers were one key theme in the liberal imperialist narrative of what went well in Bosnia, the creation of a district under international governance was another.

Prewar Brčko was a small town in a municipality of seventy thousand, best known for its small river port and for the processing of plums. During the war the town was devastated as Serb, Bosniak, and Croat forces fought for the control of this strategically important town. Carl Bildt, the first head of the OHR in Bosnia, described his shock upon visiting in 1996: The town, he wrote, looked "as if the world [had] come to an end. Snow covered the ruins, which stretched as far as the eyes could see."[109] After the war, Brčko was the only territorial link between the eastern and western halves of the Bosnian Serb entity. During the negotiations in Dayton, the territory was claimed by both the Bosniak-Croat entity and the Bosnian Serb entity, which controlled it at the time. The failure to agree over Brčko almost derailed the Dayton negotiations. In the end, a decision on its future status was postponed.

In 1997 the position of a powerful international supervisor for Brčko was created as a temporary device to buy more time. Then, in 1999, a special Brčko district was set up. It was to be governed for an undetermined period as an internationally administered territory. The internationals in question were U.S. State Department officials, running the district almost independently from the rest of the international mission in Bosnia: *Foggy Bottomia* on the Sava. This political arrangement was without precedent. By 1999 Brčko had become home to nine hundred U.S. soldiers and hundreds of internationals (including those who worked for the supervisor, the UN police mission, the Organization for the Security and Co-operation in Europe, international NGOs, and foreign consultants seconded to the district). Under the decision establishing the district, the

American supervisor was given total control over the fate of the area until such a time that he decided his office was no longer required. As one of his first steps in 1999, the supervisor dissolved the elected assembly. All laws had to be signed by him. All civil servants, the whole local executive, the legislature, and the judiciary were appointed by him. All positions of political power and authority depended on him and could be revoked by him. One former employee, the international lawyer Matthew Parish, captured the spirit of a protectorate, recalling with pride that "international officials brought vision and imagination to Brčko that could not generally be found amongst local politicians and community leaders." It was, for those who participated in it, an amazing experience, and it lasted for more than a decade, overseeing, in the words of Parish, "enormous achievements. Through sheer hard work, a traumatized and fractured society was rebuilt."[110]

After 1999 international administrators set out to turn Brčko into a model district. Henry Lee Clarke, supervisor from 2001 to 2003 (before he joined Paul Bremer's team in Iraq), explained later that it was thanks to his own extraordinary mandate that Brčko could become a "leader in reform in Bosnia-Herzegovina." Clarke listed his achievements: the return of displaced persons; the establishment of a multiethnic police force; the rehiring of a local multiethnic civil service; the setting up of a single multiethnic school district; and, finally, the creation of the most business-friendly climate in all of Bosnia.[111]

The staff of the supervisor's office saw Brčko as a laboratory for reforms. There were practically no constraints to exercising power. The head of the Brčko Law Reform Commission, an Alaskan lawyer, suspended all local judges and prosecutors, rewrote all procedural rules for the district courts, and changed the legal system from an inquisitorial system (as was the tradition in Bosnia and indeed in almost all of Europe) to an adversarial one. The Brčko Law Reform Commission passed no fewer than forty ambitious laws in a year and a half, changing every aspect of political life, from health care to education, the judicial system, and economic regulation.[112]

The main lesson from Brčko, Clarke noted, was the power of international tutelage. When it comes to reforming failed states, he wrote, the international community "must not expect reforms to be self-generating or self-implementing." People in Bosnia and Herzegovina "knew what they needed—jobs, economic growth, less corruption, justice and a responsive government— but not how to get them." If giving people what they truly wanted meant suspending normal democratic processes, so be it. It was a small price to pay for rapid reform. This echoes the confidence of English utilitarian philosopher James Mill, who worked for the British East India Company in the early nineteenth century and was convinced that the remedies to free India from stagnation were both simple and obvious: "Light taxes and good laws, nothing more is wanting for national and individual prosperity all over the globe."[113] Clarke also strongly defended his decision to postpone elections until after the end of his mandate: "I do not regret a single day of the delay. I believe there is a lot more to democracy than holding an election, and in 2002 Brčko was not ready."[114]

Such messages were eagerly received. Brčko had a very good run in the international press. Ahead of Clarke's departure in September 2003, Brčko international administration announced that the small district with seventy thousand people had become the wealthiest place in Bosnia. A 2003 *New York Times* story called Brčko "a remarkable success story . . . and one that offers lessons for the United States as it embarks on its latest effort at nation-building in Iraq." The *New York Times* quoted an analyst of the International Crisis Group summing up the implications of the Brčko model for other parts of the world: "Would-be nation-builders should install a powerful interim administrator, who is unafraid of defying the local political bosses. With a whip and some cash in hand, this proconsul can override ethnic loyalties."[115] All elements of the liberal imperialist creed were summed up in Brčko: distrust of elections, a belief that an international administration knew how to both create jobs and bring justice, and the conviction that with "a whip and some cash" the most amazing reforms were possible in the most unlikely surroundings. Resources were important, but they were nothing without leadership, charisma, will, and a strong mandate. In Brčko all of the essential ingredients for spectacular progress had come together.

Soon the Brčko model became standard procedure everywhere else in Bosnia. As Ashdown told the *New York Times* in 2003, "I looked at Brčko and thought, 'That's what we ought to be doing,' and I used my powers in a similar fashion."[116] On his first day in office, he unveiled what he called "his programme" ("Jobs and Justice") with ten pledges and sixty-nine specific commitments, which he presented to the Bosnian parliament with the promise that "there will always be room for compromise between us if this parliament comes up with sensible and workable solutions."[117] A book about his Bosnian experience, *Swords and Ploughshares*, was to become to liberal imperialism what the RAND *Beginner's Guide to Nation-Building* was to the planning school: a distillation of core assumptions. The central message was simple: nation-building efforts should seek to emulate, on a global scale, what was attempted in Brčko and Sarajevo. Echoing T. E. Lawrence, Ashdown also claimed to have distilled his experience of nation-building into "seven broad principles—the seven pillars of peace-making—that apply more or less universally."[118]

One of Ashdown's principles was the overriding need to establish—as quickly as possible—what he called the rule of law.[119] Elections, he warned, should not be "confused with democracy."[120] Ashdown warned about repeating the Bosnian mistake elsewhere: "We insisted on six elections in six years, with the turn-out falling at each one; but in that time we have barely been able to put six major criminals behind bars." Elections should be held "as late as the intervener can get away with."[121] And, he continued, "I heard it recently said that 'democracy is our (the West's) big idea'. I do not think this is correct . . . Good governance is our big idea; the rule of law is our big idea; a free market-based economy is our big idea."[122] Establishing the rule of law was possible even without elections. The key to any success was "to go in hard from the start" and to establish the rule of law "even if you have to do that quite brutally in the early days by martial law, until your police forces arrive." To be able to do so, Ashdown claimed, required the intervener to enjoy draconian executive powers. It also required an exceptionally close relationship between the military and civilian aspects of peace implementation.

Liberal imperialists differ from advocates of the planning school in another crucial respect: their understanding of planning. In any mission, the success has less to do with matching limited inputs to specific outputs than with sketching a bold vision of what it would take to ensure success. A good plan needs to be holistic—"a state cannot be built sequentially, sector by sector"[123]—and it needs to be comprehensive. As Ashdown put it, "Having a good plan for the army is fine. But one is also needed for reconnecting the water supplies, rebuilding the civil service, re-creating a judicial system, reconstructing the prisons and creating an efficient modern market-based economic system—along with much else."[124] It did not matter that most of these issues were not even mentioned in the Dayton Peace Agreement or in the initial mandate of the OHR: they were now considered vital to the success of the mission. The first "golden hours" are crucial to long-term success. It is "vital to start as quickly as possible on the major structural reforms," from customs to tax administration, from reforming the police and the civil service to restructuring and screening the judiciary. The long-term success of any mission depends on these reforms. Finally, Ashdown noted, it is pointless to give time lines for withdrawal. To be successful, nation-building requires an open-ended commitment. This, Ashdown concluded, was his final lesson and "perhaps the most important: avoid setting deadlines and settle in for the long haul. Peace-keeping needs to be measured *not in months but decades.*"[125]

No other High Representative prepared himself more thoroughly for his job in Bosnia than Paddy Ashdown. The High Representative-in-waiting spent a whole year in briefings with various people, reading voraciously and consulting widely. During this period, I met him a number of times, impressed by his intensity. At one preparatory seminar in Oxford, he told me that if the nationalist parties won Bosnian national elections in 2002, "I will have to be Mister Imposition." His focus was on getting things done: to move quickly from his diagnosis of problems to concrete prescriptions to actions. In Ashdown's view, those who later complained about the absence of due process in the exercise of the Bonn powers—individuals dismissed by OHR had nowhere to appeal or complain—failed to appreciate the urgent need for reforms. When Felix Martin and I published an article in July 2003 describing Bosnia as a European Raj, and arguing that foreigners in Sarajevo were playing the role of "benevolent despots" just as they had in nineteenth-century Calcutta, Ashdown gave an interview to national Bosnian radio. The time was right "for an accelerated transfer of tasks to the Bosnia and Herzegovina authorities," he declared.[126] He also strongly defended his approach, however. "I'm never going to apologise to anyone for moving too fast, for pushing too hard. This country has not got time. It needs people who are impatient," he said. "We have travelled fast. Now, whenever you travel fast, you kick up a lot of dust. But this is dust. It blows away. I want people out there to understand—this journey continues, the pace does not slacken. It cannot."[127] In 2003 the International Crisis Group issued its own report on the political situation in Bosnia and concluded that the High Representative does "need occasionally to ride roughshod over the norms of legality, transparency and democracy."[128] This was a lesson later applied with devastating effect in other missions.

The implications of the liberal imperialist school of thought for post-conflict reconstruction in general are striking. According to its advocates it is only when a peace-building mission is given unlimited powers and significant resources, and only when it is prepared to stay the course for an unlimited period of time, that society can be transformed and a viable state be built. Follow these universal guidelines, Ashdown suggests, and substantial progress is possible anywhere. In 2003, Ashdown wrote to Secretary of Defense Rumsfeld suggesting the postponement of elections in Iraq until the rule of law was established. This, he observed, could take "a decade."[129] Speaking before the House of Lords in the summer of 2006, Ashdown noted the success of a Bosnian judicial reform, which involved—as it had earlier in Brčko—dismissing and rehiring all judges and prosecutors (an approach to reform which the Council of Europe, Europe's oldest human rights watchdog, had described as deeply problematic).[130] This was also the spirit of nineteenth-century British imperialists like John Stuart

Mill, the great liberal philosopher. Mill strongly believed that the "ideally best form of government is representative government." Like his father James, he also worked for many decades for the East India Company, and was thus intimately involved with British imperial rule in India. Imperial rule was acceptable, Mill argued, as long as its long-term goal was the eventual self-government of the people concerned—a goal that distinguishes liberal imperial government from mere despotism. When a population has not attained a sufficiently advanced state of development, "parental despotism" is justified as the optimal means of helping it do so. Writing about British rule in India, Mill argued that "government of leading-strings, seems to be the one required to carry such a people the most rapidly through the next necessary step in social progress. . . . I need scarcely remark that leading-strings are only admissible as a means of gradually training the people to walk alone."[131] An inscription on the wall of the Viceroy's palace in New Delhi, built by British architects in the late nineteenth century, captures the spirit that guided Mill. It reads, "Liberty does not descend to a people. A people must raise themselves to liberty. It is a blessing that must be earned before it can be enjoyed."

During Ashdown's reign in Bosnia, references to imperial experiences became increasingly popular in the United States and in the United Kingdom. Robert Cooper wrote an article about the need for a "new liberal imperialism . . . one acceptable to a world of human rights and cosmopolitan values." But Cooper also warned that "empire is expensive, especially in its postmodern voluntary form. Nation-building is a long and difficult task: it is by no means certain that any of the recent attempts are going to be successful. Great caution is required for anyone contemplating intervention in the pre-modern chaos."[132] For him this was mere common sense: "influencing foreigners is difficult

. . . if securing domestic reform is difficult, the remodeling some-one else's country must be next to impossible." Others did not shares these concerns.

In 2004 British historian Niall Ferguson published a book titled *Empire: How Britain Made the Modern World*. It captured the spirit of an era that saw a succession of seemingly effortless U.S. military victories in Kosovo (1999), Afghanistan (2001), and Iraq (2003). What the British Empire had demonstrated, Ferguson wrote, is that "empire is a form of international government that can work—and not just for the benefit of the ruling power."[133] Ferguson saw a direct continuity between Victorian imperialists who "regarded overthrowing rogue regimes from Abyssinia to Oudh as an entirely legitimate part of the civilizing process" and the present era. "Just as the US Air Force bombed Serbia in 1999 in the name of human rights," Ferguson wrote, "so the Royal Navy conducted raids on the West African coast in the 1840s and even threatened Brazil with war as part of the campaign to end the slave trade."[134] Victorian imperialists dreamed not only of ruling the world but also of redeeming it. And they did so at an acceptable cost: between 1858 and 1947 there were seldom more than one thousand members of the Indian Civil Service ruling over hundreds of millions of subjects.[135]

This was also the philosophy inspiring the fifteen hundred men and women working for the Coalition Provisional Authority in Baghdad's Green Zone following the overthrow of the regime of Saddam Hussein. It was a time of bold decisions, comprehensive and uncompromising reform, the time of Paul Bremer, the head of the Coalition Provisional Authority. Bremer, a Harvard Business School graduate, believed in plans and benchmarks, but he believed even more in the value of bold leadership. In Iraq he certainly did not follow the prescriptions of the planning school: when he found that the means (soldiers and money) that RAND had identified as essential were not actually available, he did *not* moderate his objectives. In May 2003, Bremer sent U.S. Defense Secretary Donald Rumsfeld a copy of a draft of the 2003 RAND report, which estimated that five hundred thousand troops would be needed in Iraq. He later wrote that he did not receive any response.[136] The fact that the number of troops in Iraq was substantially below the ratio recommended by the planning school for an ambitious, "heavy" intervention did not lead Bremer to conclude that he should scale back his ambitions. As he told journalists at the time, the American vision for Iraq needed to be as ambitious as it had been in Germany after World War II.[137] He was already looking forward to restoring basic services, corporatizing and privatizing state-owned companies, and creating the Middle East's first truly free-market economy.

Thus the U.S.-led Coalition Provisional Authority transferred the Brčko approach of international governance from the northern Balkans to Mesopotamia. An occupation government was established under occupation law. In the words of the UN resolution, "all executive, judicial and administrative power [was to rest] with the civilian administrator." Believing that a properly ambitious plan would require time, Bremer initially planned on at least two years of U.S.-led occupation and a presence continuing long beyond the transfer of authority. There was almost nothing that he could not do: from abolishing the army and de-Ba'athification, to firing police chiefs, arresting clerics, and allowing the internment without trial of tens of thousands of Iraqis. Bremer went much further in Iraq than anyone had ever dared in Bosnia. He launched major structural reforms as soon as possible. He rapidly announced the abolition of the army and the privatization of state-owned enterprises. He dissolved trade unions, reformed the university curriculum, and initiated a process to write a new constitution. Economic reform and improving the "business climate" were as much his priorities as they had been the Brčko supervisor's. While the international community never dissolved the SDS, the Bosnian Serb nationalist party, the Coalition Provisional Authority purged the Iraqi administration of former Baath Party members as soon as it took over. In Bosnia it took years of negotiations to transform the militaries. In Iraq it was decided right away. In pursuit of security, the United States went in hard. Although U.S. soldiers stood by in 2003 as looting and anarchy swept through Baghdad following the invasion, a year later they launched a major assault on Fallujah. An arrest warrant was issued for Muqtada al-Sadr, a Shiite political leader with his own militia. His lieutenants were arrested. International provincial administrators were reluctant to compromise even with the non-Sadrist Islamist groups, which were considered too close to Iran. Bremer also worked hard to make sure that his mission was well resourced. The supplemental budget of 2003 provided an additional eighteen billion dollars for reconstruction in Iraq. Although only 2 percent of this money had been spent before the end of his mandate in June 2004, economic growth in Iraq in 2004 was 46 percent.[138] This was, as RAND noted in a later study, "exceeded only by Bosnia" and much higher than in post–World War II Germany and Japan.[139] (Output then fell in 2005 due to the civil war.)[140] If the planning school appeals to reason, numbers, and the experience of the past, the liberal imperialist school appeals to emotions, visions, and the hope of a radiant future. In this, Bremer was as much influenced by the dominant narratives of this time as Niall Ferguson's ode to British imperialism had been by the heady experience of a string of U.S. military victories. These were narratives of heroic nation-builders who had succeeded through sheer will and determination and a strong mandate to transform societies. These were also the narratives of Bosnia's liberal imperialist era: state-building "with a whip and some cash" in action.

There is something missing in the Bosnian story, however, whether it concerns the role of the supervisor in Brčko or the transformation of Bosnia by the Bonn powers. For a narrative that is all about power, there is very little explanation of where the effectiveness of the Bonn powers actually came from. The narrative becomes even more puzzling as one realizes that the OHR or SFOR in Bosnia never had any police or prisons. OHR lacked the tools to enforce its own decisions. There was no Abu Ghraib in postwar Bosnia. When I worked for OHR in 1998 there were numerous instances when individuals who had been dismissed using the Bonn powers quickly resurfaced in different positions; some had to be dismissed more than once.[141] There were also many laws and regulations imposed by the OHR that were simply ignored. Paddy Ashdown could not order the arrests of any of the people he dismissed. By the time he arrived in Sarajevo, there were only twelve thousand SFOR soldiers left in Bosnia (approximately the same ratio as in postwar Iraq). By the end of 2004, U.S. soldiers had left and the NATO mission had been replaced by a few thousand EU troops, soon to be reduced to a mere two thousand, a symbolic presence. And yet impositions continued. One of the reasons was that for many Bosnians (particularly for Bosniaks) the benevolent authoritarian rule of OHR was much preferable to any other political system they had ever experienced, and reminiscent of the relative stability of authoritarian rule under the Yugoslav communist regime. Another was the ability of Ashdown to hint that there might be evidence of war crimes or supporting war criminals implicating (in particular Serb) politicians with a wartime past. Many laws imposed were also first agreed to by all parties, who nonetheless found it more convenient to let OHR assume the responsibility not to have to explain any compromises to their electorates.

Ashdown later told an audience in the summer of 2003 that "the day after Baghdad fell, the telephone lines in Sarajevo were ringing hot. My office lost count of the number of calls wanting to know what pointers Bosnia could offer for the task ahead in Iraq."[142] Strikingly, what Ashdown presented to nation-builders in Iraq in 2003 as the universal principles of the craft (go in hard, avoid early elections, implement drastic reforms in the golden hour, etc.) had not guided the actual transformation of Bosnia in the crucial years after the end of the war. It was a view based on what, in Ashdown's view, should have been done in Bosnia in 1996 but was not. Nor was such an approach ever adapted by the UN mission in Kosovo, which, despite substantial executive powers, never dismissed an elected politician. Nor was it even the approach taken in Brčko in 1997 or 1998, when the first supervisor was still very cautious to avoid provoking any nationalist resistance.[143]

The myth of Bosnia as a liberal imperialist testing ground was much more dramatic than the reality. In the end it was only in Iraq in 2003 that the seven universal principles of state-building were actually put to the test. It was a test they failed.

THE FUTILITY SCHOOL AND INTERVENTION SKEPTICS

After years of heavy-duty international engagement, the country is in far, far better shape than it was when the Dayton agreement was signed. And when one considers

the trauma of that war, it is frankly little short of miraculous how much has been achieved.

HIGH REPRESENTATIVE PADDY ASHDOWN,

JUNE 20, 2003[144]

The need for an international presence with an executive
mandate in Bosnia and Herzegovina is still evident . . .
until the job is completed.

HIGH REPRESENTATIVE VALENTIN INZKO AT THE

UN SECURITY COUNCIL, MAY 9, 2011[145]

In 2008 the Cato Institute, a leading libertarian think tank in
Washington, D.C., published a paper titled "Learning the Right
Lessons from Iraq." It challenged what the authors saw as a
"wrong and dangerous" consensus: the view that success in Iraq
could have been achieved if only there had been more men, more
coordination, and a better counterinsurgency doctrine. "What
Iraq demonstrates is a need for a new national security strategy,
not better tactics and tools to serve the current one," they argued.
"By insisting that Iraq was ours to remake, were it not for the
Bush administration's mismanagement, we ignore the limits on
our power that the war exposes." In reality the failure of Iraq was
not an aberration: state-building missions are "extremely costly,
most of them fail, and most of them corrode American power."[146]

The national security strategy the authors criticized was
one adopted in September 2002, in the wake of 9/11, by the
administration of President George W. Bush. The national
security strategy warned that "America is now threatened less
by conquering states than we are by failing ones."[147] Journalist
Sebastian Mallaby warned in 2002 that "the logic of neoimpe-

rialism is too compelling for the Bush administration to resist. The chaos of the world is too threatening to ignore, and existing methods for dealing with that chaos have been tried and found wanting."[148] Michael Ignatieff wrote one year later that "just beyond the zone of stable democratic states, which took the World Trade Center and the Pentagon as its headquarters, there are the border zones, like Afghanistan, where barbarians rule and from where, thanks to modern technology, they are able to inflict devastating damage on centers of power far away."[149] To be secure, the United States needed to learn how to intervene in zones of premodern anarchy. It needed the tools to confront an "extremely large-scale, transnational globalized insurgency," as David Kilcullen, the Australian counterinsurgency adviser to General David Petraeus in Iraq, later put it.[150] One of these tools was to learn how to build functioning states following interventions or regime change.

For Cato's analysts, such thinking was flawed in every respect: it exaggerated the threats, underestimated the costs, and inflated the capacity of the U.S. (or of any other) government to not recognize the futility of a foreign policy based on such unrealistic premises.[151] Cato reports castigated the "worrisome consensus emerging among humanitarian hawks on the left and neoconservatives on the right" in favor of military intervention.[152] They questioned the analysis of supposed threats that required global state-building efforts. Neither Al Qaeda nor Afghanistan merited American "strategic obsession." Al Qaeda was weaker than it appeared and "not an existential threat to the United States"; even a resurrected Taliban regime in Afghanistan, a worst-case outcome after a U.S. withdrawal, "would not necessarily threaten American security."[153] The notion that failed states constituted major security threats was based on muddled thinking, since "the countries that appear on the various lists of failed states reveal that state failure almost never produces meaningful threats to U.S. national security."[154] Terrorists do not flourish in failed states; many of the people planning the details of 9/11 lived either in Hamburg or in Pakistan. Even Osama bin Laden ultimately felt more secure living in a quiet neighborhood near the Pakistani capital than in the stateless tribal regions on the Pakistani-Afghan border.

Cato's reports stressed the enormous costs of recent and future U.S. interventions. They challenged nostalgia for previous imperial experiences, including the British Empire, which, they noted, "was involved in no fewer than ninety-eight different wars and military campaigns between 1800 and 1906."[155] They warned that an American "strategy of empire" leads to strategic overextension. Taking the formulas of the planning school seriously, they calculated that reaching "ambitious" goals in Afghanistan would require some six hundred thousand troops; that peace enforcement in Yemen would cost roughly seventy-eight billion U.S. dollars in the first year; and that a future peace enforcement operation in Pakistan would require more than two million international soldiers, costing about two hundred thousand dollars each.[156] To transform a "deeply divided, poverty stricken, tribal-based society" in Afghanistan into a "self-sufficient, non-corrupt, stable democracy would require a multi-decade commitment"; and even then "there would be no assurance of success."[157]

Intervention skeptics focused on the limits of U.S. power. These limits were not only about the number of troops available or their cost but even more about limited knowledge and legitimacy. It was not simply a matter of making better plans or improving international coordination. A successful occupation anywhere required, above all, the cooperation of the subject population, something that could not be created through planning.[158] Planning "solves engineering problems . . . the management of foreign societies is another matter altogether."[159] There are limits to what any bureaucracy, civilian or military, is capable of doing. The record of U.S.-led counterinsurgency campaigns to pacify uprisings in poor nations was also abysmal and not easily corrected:

> If you understand the culture, if you avoid counterproductive violence, if you integrate civilians and make reconstruction operations a reward for cooperation, if you train the local forces well, if you pick your allies wisely, if you protect enough civilians and win their loyalty and more, you might succeed. But even avoiding a few of these ifs is too much competence to expect of foreign powers.[160]

The notion that the United States could "turn every soldier into an ethnic-linguistic warrior,"[161] fighters who understood the intricacies of tribal politics in Central Asia, was a fantasy. Nor was the record of civilian nation-building any more reassuring in Cato's view. It was not only the Iraq mission that failed, or Afghanistan that was going badly: there was also Bosnia as a warning, a "nation building fiasco" as one Cato analyst put it in 2011.[162]

Cato authors have long predicted the failure of the international intervention in Bosnia. As Ted Carpenter from the Cato Institute pointed out already in 1992, "The moral case for U.S. military intervention is flimsy, but the argument that America has important interests at stake in the Yugoslavian conflict is still weaker." To justify U.S. interest, proponents therefore exaggerated their case, invoking "vague warnings of instability and a wider war that could (somehow) threaten America's security.

One tactic is to invoke potent memories . . . the more expansive predictions of doom are little more than updated versions of the discredited domino theory of the 1950s and 1960s. Contrary to the alarmist scenarios, local conflicts rarely become continent-wide (much less global) conflagrations."[163] For all of these reasons it was better to recognize publicly the limits of the power of outsiders and more humane to avoid raising hopes among the Bosnians that the world might support the imposition of peace.

Following the end of the war, another Cato paper in 1995 described the Dayton Peace Agreement as "a blueprint for disaster."[164] In 1998 Cato's Gary Dempsey called postwar Bosnia a "Potemkin state, a monumental facade erected and maintained by the international community." To make progress, the international community had to resort to "ill-liberal measures to force Bosnian Croats, Serbs, and Muslims to live under the fiction of one government."[165] In 2011 Ted Carpenter warned that "Bosnia is no closer to being a viable country than it was in 1995. . . . If secession were allowed, the overwhelming majority of Bosnian Serbs would vote to detach their self-governing region (the Republika Srpska). . . . [M]ost of the remaining Croats—who are already deserting the country in droves—would choose to secede and join with Croatia." Carpenter concluded, "Despite a 15-year effort and the expenditure of billions of dollars, the Bosnian nation-building mission is a flop."[166]

What is most remarkable today, however, is less Cato's position, which has not changed, but how much the analysis of many liberal imperialists regarding Bosnia has come to resemble it. In April 2008 Richard Holbrooke had still praised the intervention in Bosnia as a success story. A mere six months later, in October 2008, he and Paddy Ashdown called on the European Union and the United States to take "urgent action," warning that there is a return of the "suspicion and fear that began the war in 1992" and that there was a possibility of a "collapse of the Dayton Peace Agreement." Without an effective international troop presence, things could "get very nasty very quickly."[167] As Paddy Ashdown put it in another article, "After 10 years of progress, which made Bosnia the world's most successful exercise in post-conflict reconstruction, there is a real threat of Bosnia breaking up again."[168] To prevent disaster, OHR must be vigilant and retain its powers. Without the international presence, Bosnia is doomed. As High Representative Valentin Inzko told the UN Security Council on May 9, 2011, "We face the most serious and most direct challenges to the Dayton-Paris Peace Agreement since it was signed over 15 years ago."[169]

The tipping point for the current crisis, Holbrook and Ashdown explained in 2008, was the withdrawal of U.S. forces in 2004, followed by the decline in the influence of the previously powerful OHR following Ashdown's departure and, above all, the actions of a Bosnian Serb politician, Milorad Dodik, the prime minister of the Bosnian Serb entity. Dodik was "aggressively reversing a decade of reform" and preparing for secession of his entity "as soon as the international community leaves or loses interest."[170] What made this remarkable was the fact that for almost a decade Dodik had been the favorite politician of the international community in Bosnia. In 1997 OHR had helped broker the parliamentary majority in the Serb entity that first made Dodik, whose party then had only two members of parliament, its prime minister. Hours after Dodik was elected, NATO troops surrounded key police buildings hosting officers loyal to the hard-line nationalist SDS as a sign of their support to him.[171] When Dodik was sworn in in January 1998, he pledged to implement the Dayton Peace Agreement, to allow refugees to return, and to dismiss all those loyal to Karadžić's SDS from the police. This was celebrated at the time as a "major defeat for hard-line nationalists."[172] The *New York Times* wrote that "the new prime minister, 38, became the first politician in Bosnia to hold high office without links to one of the main nationalist parties."[173] OHR went to great lengths to ensure that Dodik remained prime minister: when a president from another party won elections in the Serb entity in 1998 and tried to replace Dodik as prime minister (constitutionally), he was first warned and then removed from office by OHR. The U.S. ambassador in Sarajevo told me in 2000, pointing to a folder on his desk (allegedly) holding secret files describing corruption, that Dodik was "a crook, but our crook." In 2000 Richard Holbrooke proposed to ban Dodik's main political rivals in the Bosnian Serb entity, the SDS, from participating in elections. In 2003 Holbrooke again attacked the SDS, describing it as "Nazis who should disappear."[174] In 2004 Paddy Ashdown banned from politics almost the entire SDS party leadership, preparing the way for Dodik to return to power, with his party winning by far the most votes in 2006. One reason, Ashdown wrote in 2008, was that Dodik "has been firmly anti-Karadžić. He is not that kind of Serb nationalist."[175]

In recent years some former liberal imperialists have begun to embrace Cato's early skepticism, frustrated with what they saw as insufficient international support for their efforts. Matthew Parish, a former employee in the international supervisor's office in Brčko, praised the international administration in Brčko as the most successful attempt at state-building ever undertaken, "an enormous achievement" and the work of "unsung heroes."[176] He also explained that once the international community allowed a return to local democracy in 2004, Brčko was doomed. Following the 2004 district elections, he wrote, a "deep crisis" ensued immediately: "The quality of district administration plummeted as a result of post-election politicization of the government."[177] Parish predicted the "total disintegration" of multiethnic Brčko: "once the supervisor stepped back from the highly interventionist role, things would unravel."[178] To make a success of Brčko would require that international supervision is "established on an indefinite timescale, without any predetermined exit date that would undermine cooperation by domestic actors."[179] Since there was no appetite for this in Western capitals, both Brčko and Bosnia were doomed, and the best that could be done was to organize its partition. Parish concluded that "if it is difficult to make even Brčko work in the long term, then other state building efforts might by their nature be all the more improbable."[180] International efforts had been futile.

For radical skeptics the recent turn in the debate on Bosnia vindicates their profound doubts about intervention in general. Bosnia has been a protectorate since 1997. Paddy Ashdown was in charge of it for almost four years, with unlimited powers and strong international backing. In no other post-conflict mission was a comparable effort made to bring senior leaders responsible for war crimes to justice. In addition, the region surrounding Bosnia has been transformed since 1999: Franjo Tudjman died, and Croatia joined NATO and is on the verge of joining the European Union; Milošević died, and Serbia applied for European Union accession. To argue that despite enormous efforts in Bosnia and regional changes in the main neighbors the Bosnia's state remains as fragile today as it was in 1995 suggests either a monumental failure or a task that was from the outset impossible. If even a middle-income country of less than four million inhabitants in Europe, in which tens of thousands of foreign troops and thousands of foreign diplomats, experts, and police officers had been active for more than a decade and a half, can so easily find itself back "on the brink," then there would seem to be little hope for state-building efforts anywhere else in the world.

The solution now proposed by worried liberal imperialists to control any threats was to continue with the authoritarian control through OHR. It was no longer assumed that Bosnia was facing a crisis that might pass and temporarily require emergency powers: Bosnia had become a permanent emergency, a state that in OHR's view really could not survive without international tutclage. A similar argument to illustrate the follies and illusions of nation-building in Bosnia had long been made by Cato analysts as well, even if they then drew the opposite conclusions. Already in 1995 Cato had supported an ethnic partition of what it considered an artificial state: "Only a settlement forged by the parties to the conflict, an agreement that reflects battlefield realities and the balance of political and military forces, has any chance of achieving a durable peace."[181] In 1998 another Cato paper quoted the political scientist John Mearsheimer, who warned that "history records no instance where ethnic groups have agreed to share power in a democracy after a large-scale civil war."[182] The red thread that connects the analysis of intervention skeptics and of liberal imperialists is that in both narratives anything that happened in Bosnia since 1995 depended almost exclusively on the international community. Bosnians are passive or motivated by irrational (nationalist) passions. Bosnia's elected politicians are either, at best, irrelevant or, at worst, the source of all problems. According to Parish, most civil servants in Brčko were "mediocre nationalists and crooks," the elected "assembly became a zoo," and politicians in the district were "ogres of the communist age."[183] The citizens of Brčko and Bosnia appear like the townspeople of Hadleyville in the film *High Noon*: they are in the background, not contributing to any progress, while their fate is decided by the heroic character played by Gary Cooper—OHR or the Brčko supervisor's office—who alone confronts the dangerous gang threatening the town. The difference between Cato and the liberal imperialists is that the former do not believe that Gary Cooper should remain in Hadleyville forever, and that before long the hero will either tire of his role or be overwhelmed by much more numerous villains. Much better, then, to leave Hadleyville and its hapless population to itself.

What is remarkable in this account is the extreme and limited choices facing the international community. The option is either partition (with the obvious risks of further displacement and conflict, even renewed fighting) or an eternal international protectorate. One Cato report in 1995 warned that "renewed fighting is highly probable."[184] Another, in 1998, referred to the international community's failure to ensure any returns in the years after the war as the most important evidence of its impotence.[185] In fact, on both accounts the skeptics turned out to be unduly pessimistic. Following 1995 Bosnia never turned into a quagmire. U.S. troops did not have to remain in Bosnia forever. They did not suffer casualties. Bosnians did not prove unable to live together. There has been no renewed fighting for more than fifteen years, nor any serious interethnic violence since the most recent riots in 2001. There has been substantial return of refugees (see the next section). Many areas across Bosnia witnessed the reintegration of minorities into schools and the emergence of a multiethnic police force. In 2010 Bosnia held another round of free and fair national elections, and the Bosnian government met demanding conditions set by the European Union for Bosnian citizens to qualify for visa-free travel. The Bosnian border service is regularly praised by the U.S. State Department for its success in fighting trafficking in human beings. Even now, most commentators note after highlighting the dysfunctional politics, Bosnia's crisis is "unlikely to spill over into violence."

All this raises the question of whether Bosnian citizens, and their elected politicians, are not less irrational and less dependent on international supervision than either adherents of the futility school or liberal imperialists suppose. Having experienced three years of devastating war in the 1990s, and having witnessed the sentencing of most of the leaders of that era for war crimes in an international tribunal, the citizens appear to have no appetite for violence as an instrument of politics. This does not mean an end to profound disagreements about the future, shape, and structure of the Bosnian state, between and among Bosniaks, Croats, and Serbs; but it does suggest that the international intervention did manage to create some conditions whereby intractable issues can now be managed peacefully.

This is certainly what appears to have happened in Brčko. There, seven years after Parish predicted disaster, local politics has continued more or less as before. In fact, a closer look at Brčko, home to less than 2 percent of Bosnia's total population, suggests why both liberal imperialist claims and the defeatism of radical skeptics are misleading. The transformation in Brčko was never as exceptional as presented by the district's international masters, and the stability never as fragile later. The high tide of reforms coincided with a period in which breakthroughs—on refugee return, on integrating minorities into the police, on institution-building—took place across the whole country. It was a period of dramatic change in the wider Balkan region, as Milošević was overthrown in Belgrade in October 2000. Brčko's economic "miracle" was not the result of the imposition of progressive legislation either: Brčko, like Pristina, the capital of Kosovo, benefited above all from the disproportionally high presence of foreigners and benefited from special free-rider provisions that initially allowed the district to retain all customs revenues from its own border crossing with Croatia, rather than sending them to the central government budget. These revenues—the customs revenues for Brčko alone were significantly higher than the total revenues of the much larger Bosnian Serb capital Banja Luka at the time—allowed an impressive growth in public sector salaries. Brčko became the region of Bosnia with the most expensive public administration in the country—the salaries of the mayor and of civil servants were higher than those of any other national official in the country. Ironically, Brčko's politics thus came to resemble the system of Yugoslav socialism, with its ideal of apolitical government, where real elections were dispensed with and all public officials enjoyed material privileges instead. A return to "normal" democratic politics, to local bargaining and coalition-building, does not mark the end of progress, however: it is simply an inevitable step away from a technocratic apolitical interregnum.

In his *Discourses*, renaissance political thinker Nicolo Machiavelli once noted that the authority of an absolute monarch may be appropriate to some circumstances—the conquest of states, or their total revolution—but that in the long run, only republican government can generate security and prosperity: "And if princes are superior to populaces in drawing up laws, codes of civic life, statutes, and new institutions, the populace is so superior in sustaining what has been instituted that it indubitably adds to the glory of those who have instituted them." Machiavelli also argued that a republic draws its strength from political conflicts, and these are even to be encouraged. He cited the example of the ancient Roman Republic:

> To me those who condemn the quarrels between the nobles and the plebs, seem to be cavalling at the very things that were the

primary cause of Rome's retaining her freedom, and that they pay more attention to the noise and clamour resulting from such commotions than to what resulted from them, i.e. to the good effects which they produced . . . all legislation favourable to liberty is brought about by the clash between them.[186]

The key question to ask about Bosnia's current politics today is thus whether the political clashes between different ethnic groups and political families are likely to lead to a renewed cycle of violence, and if such a threat exists, what outsiders might be able to do to prevent it. Political disagreements, difficult coalition negotiations, constitutional crises are all not evidence to argue that nothing has changed since the days when thousands of people were killed in cold blood in 1995. Paddy Ashdown noted in 2003 that "with a few exceptions, the issues we deal with now are not those of conflict, but increasingly the reassuringly familiar challenges of transition, which Hungary and Poland . . . have already overcome."[187] When he took over as High Representative in 2002, he wrote, he realized that "peace and stability was not going to be my problem—that had been basically assured by the time I got there."[188] The most important question is thus how *that* was achieved, a mere six years after the most horrendous conflict in recent European history.

In conclusion, Cato's papers raise many important questions about interventions, nation-building, and counterinsurgency efforts: about their motivation, their costs, and their chances of success. However, to argue that a mission that brought fifteen years of peace with no U.S. casualties falls into the same category of "failure" as Iraq is not a claim based on empirical weighing of the evidence. Cato analysts were wrong in 1992: when the United States *did* intervene in the end it did not stumble into another Vietnam but ended a war without any U.S.

casualties. They were wrong in 1995: Radovan Karadžić did not in the end emerge triumphant, and Bosniaks and Croats did not restart fighting. They were overly pessimistic in 1998: large-scale return of minorities did take place. No intervention achieves all its objectives; perhaps most interventions fail to achieve most; and some might fail across the board. It is the distinctions between these cases, and between policies that make the one outcome more likely than the other, that is the most important question facing policy-makers. To this the futility school offers no answers.

THE CASE FOR PRINCIPLED INCREMENTALISM

All government, indeed every human benefit and enjoyment, every virtue, and every prudent act, is founded on compromise and barter.

EDMUND BURKE, SPEECH ON
CONCILIATION WITH AMERICA[189]

Aziz Ibraković left his village in Doboj municipality on June 16, 1992, soon after the beginning of the war when all of its Bosniak inhabitants were told by the Serb authorities to hand over their weapons. On June 17, Ibraković's village was attacked by artillery. The next day, Serb paramilitaries entered the village. The attackers demolished the mosque and systematically destroyed all of the houses. They killed thirty men in Ibraković's village alone. Doboj municipality had been ethnically mixed before the war, with a Bosniak majority, but during the war all non-Serbs were expelled and all Bosniak and Croat villages destroyed.

Ethnic cleansing had not been an unfortunate by-product of fighting. It was what the war in Bosnia was about all along. In 1992 the term *ethnic cleansing* had entered the international vocabulary with a UN resolution on Bosnia-Herzegovina, defining it as "a purposeful policy designed by one ethnic or religious group to remove by violent and terror-inspiring means the civilian population of another ethnic or religious group from certain geographic areas."[190]

There were good reasons to believe in 1992 that Ibraković would never be able to return to his house, unless his own army would reconquer the territory by force. Early-twentieth-century Europe had seen many instances of ethnic cleansing long before the concept was coined; sometimes peace negotiations justified them post facto; on other occasions there was even a negotiated exchange of people, as in the (in)famous Lausanne treaty that saw Greece and Turkey exchange their minorities in 1922 with the facilitation of the League of Nations. Those to be "exchanged" were not asked: as the Greek prime minister noted at the time, "Both the Greek and the Turkish population involved . . . are protesting against this procedure . . . and display their dissatisfaction by all means at their disposal." It was a way of "solving" minority problems by destroying minority communities.[191]

Ibraković spent the rest of the war in territory held by the army of Bosnia and Herzegovina across the river Bosna. The river marked the frontline, and its banks were heavily mined. Throughout the war, Aziz could see his village from across the water. Like many hundreds of thousands of displaced persons across Bosnia, he never gave up the idea of eventually returning home. When the Dayton Peace Agreement was signed in December 1995, Ibraković immediately contacted other villagers. He began to approach international organizations for help. However, the end of the war did not improve his situation. Following the peace agreement, Doboj turned into a tense frontline town. The border between Bosnia's two entities now followed the old military frontline and had checkpoints manned by U.S. troops. This is what Richard Holbrooke had previously feared: a Cyprus scenario, with "two hostile groups divided for twenty-one years by an ugly wall that cut the island into half."[192]

The dominant party in Doboj was the Bosnian Serb SDS, controlled by associates of indicted war criminal Radovan Karadžić. Special police controlled by hard-liners remained in charge. The international peacekeeping force IFOR was suspicious of the minority return process, which it saw as raising tensions. In 1996, IFOR resisted attempts by civilian organizations to organize assessment visits of displaced persons to view their former homes. Returns by Bosniaks—even to abandoned villages—were seen as posing a security threat. In fact, many visits did meet with organized violence. In November, the United Nations High Commissioner for Refugees (UNHCR) reported that two hundred Bosniak houses had been blown up in Doboj and other places in the Serb entity: "We are seeing systematic destruction of houses to make sure that minorities don't return."[193] Throughout the Bosnian Serb entity, attempts by displaced persons to visit their former homes were met with violence, mobs, arson, and even killings.[194] Nor was the situation any better in the territory controlled by the Bosnian Croat army HVO. Here too houses of potential returnees were burning in 1996. Military mines were used to blow up houses of Serbs interested in returning to Croat-held territory.

The constitution agreed to in Dayton included commitments to the highest human rights standards. It referred specifically to the right to return.[195] Annex 7 of the peace agreement promised the same. However, in 1996 few in the international organizations responsible believed that this was actually implementable. The UNHCR was the main international organization tasked with working on the return of refugees in postwar Bosnia. During the war the UNHCR had had to plead intensively with Serb authorities to be allowed to *evacuate* ethnic minorities from different towns. As a result, as late as 1998 many within the organization considered the notion of any large-scale return into areas not controlled by the same ethnic group utopian. To have to rely on the same authorities that had promoted ethnic cleansing in the first place to help ensure a peaceful return seemed irresponsibly risky to those who put protection first.

The raw numbers when the war came to an end were daunting: at the end of hostilities 1 million people had been displaced inside the country, in addition to 1.3 million refugees abroad. By the time of the Dayton agreement, the wartime project of the Bosnian SDS, the party led by Radovan Karadžić, was substantially complete. In the territory controlled by the Army of Republika Srpska (the Bosnian Serb entity), fewer than 2 percent of the original non-Serb population remained. Almost all mosques, Catholic churches, and other traces of non-Serb culture had been destroyed.

Those who rejected the lukewarm support of international organizations in Bosnia for the right to return included international NGOs such as Human Rights Watch, Amnesty International, and a new NGO that was to become one of the most visible civil society participants in the global debate on intervention: the International Crisis Group. In 1996 it was still in its infancy, with its biggest field office in Sarajevo. In 1997 I joined its Bosnia team. We saw ourselves as champions of a more aggressive approach, providing analysis to shame international actors into taking the promises of the Dayton Peace Agreement, in particular the right to return, more seriously. In 1997 and 1998 we worked on a series of reports examining options to help displaced persons return to their former homes. This turned into a chronicle of an unequal battle between returnees braving the risks, on the one hand, and thugs and paramilitaries with the backing of the wartime nationalist regimes, on the other.[196]

In July 1997, a Croat mob expelled some eight hundred Bosniaks who had returned on their own initiative to their former homes in villages in central Bosnia. British SFOR troops immediately deployed in the area, calming the situation and, following OHR-led negotiations, allowing the refugees to return to their homes within a matter of days. From this incident and others that followed, a number of lessons were drawn. Violence against minorities was rarely, if ever, a product of spontaneous ethnic hostility. It was generally organized by local political figures with higher-level backing. Gathering quality intelligence, in particular on local power structures, could help to identify and suppress patterns of violence. A presence of foreign troops in an area sometimes had an immediate effect on deterring violence.

In August 1997, SFOR gradually asserted its control over special police forces in the Bosnian Serb entity. It required the forces in some parts of the Bosnian Serb entity to disclose the names of officers, as well as the weapons, ammunition, and equipment it held. When one detachment of the Doboj special police refused to comply, SFOR raided its headquarters, confiscating everything it found, and disarming and decertifying all of the officers.

In September 1997, Aziz Ibraković was elected deputy to the Doboj municipal assembly by the votes of displaced Bosniak voters in internationally run local elections. In the same month, Nikola Jorgic, the leader of a paramilitary group, was sentenced by a court in Düsseldorf to life imprisonment for genocide committed in the Doboj region. In January 1998 Milorad Dodik became prime minister of the Bosnian Serb entity with strong backing of the international community. Then, in May 1998, the local head of the UNHCR office in Doboj took Aziz aside and asked him to "set a date for return" to his village. "In the morning we took off. When we reached the heights of our village above the [river] Bosna, we sat down together and just cried. The village was a jungle and we desperately needed help. After one month we began to stay in our village overnight."[197] From there on, things in Doboj began to change. Within a few years more than half of the prewar Bosniak population of Doboj municipality, an estimated eighteen thousand people, returned home. Bosniaks returned to all of the villages in the Doboj region where they had lived before the war. All sixteen destroyed mosques in the municipality were reconstructed. The whole region was demilitarized. Checkpoints and controls were abandoned. Foreign troops left as well. The former SFOR camp near Aziz's village on the Bosna river was vacated. Another nearby garrison, once occupied by SFOR, was handed over to the unified army of Bosnia and Herzegovina. The Doboj mayor, representing the party (SDS) once created by Radovan Karadžić, campaigned on a platform of moderation in 2004 and was elected with the votes of many of the Bosnian Muslim returnees. A Bosniak returnee became president of the municipal assembly in the same year.

The story of Aziz, of postwar Doboj, and indeed of return across the whole country can be told as a story about the efforts of international institutions: their fears, their debates, their cowardice and courage, their coordination, rivalry, wisdom, and ignorance. One can focus on the internal policy debate in the

United States in early 1997 between a secretary of state, Madeleine Albright, pushing for SFOR to support such returnee movements and a reluctant secretary of defense; or among international organizations in Bosnia.[198] There is also a very interesting story of institutional learning in the field, as the international community slowly developed its own methodology, identified groups of displaced persons eager to return, and worked with them. In 1997 OHR helped create a grassroots organization of displaced persons, the Coalition for Return. A new jargon emerged: work was about locating "return axes" or "following the flow" of returnees. Daily work was about brokering deals by which returnees could establish themselves in their former communities, and anticipating problems so as to be able to defuse delicate situations through negotiations.

But telling the story of return in Bosnia as one of international actors is missing the most important point, one also missed by those (few) who argued later that encouraging the return of the displaced and refugees in Bosnia was "foolish."[199] Not only had the right to return been a core principle at Dayton, but also there was a strong constituency willing to push for it to be implemented and prepared to take physical risks. This was the story of hundreds of thousands of displaced Bosnians who felt entitled to their homes and determined to rebuild them. They drove the process. Without the foreign presence there would not have been a return of refugees on anything like the scale Bosnia saw after 2000. And yet there was no great foreign plan. In 1996 most foreigners in Bosnia did not believe return could really happen. There were also serious setbacks later. In Drvar, one month before Aziz and fellow villagers succeeded to return to Doboj, Serb returnees were violently attacked in an orchestrated manner by Croat extremists. In the case of Doboj it looked, in hindsight, as if the timing was right—or could the return have happened even earlier? In the case of Drvar, the timing seemed wrong—but was it really too early? There was no way of telling in advance. In practice every progress was the result of bargaining, endless negotiations in the field, weighing risks, and supporting, wherever possible, domestic initiatives. It was a process of principled incrementalism.

Two migration researchers, Gerard Toal and Carl Dahlman, noted later that "while the goal of recreating the demographic structure of Bosnia 1991 is a utopian one," the real benchmark for the success of the postwar mission should be the situation at the time the war ended. "*Bosnia 1995* was a segregated country with apartheid geography and fetishistic practices of border maintenance. *Bosnia 2004* is not the apartheid state that hardline nationalists would like: the international boundary line is not impermeable, property has been restored to those from whom it was stolen, and returns have reached the one million mark."[200] Bosnia remains a "broken country," they note, scarred by the legacy of the war. It was "neither segregated, nor integrated, neither failed state nor success story."[201]

Returns and the normalization of daily life that it brought about also benefited from wider positive developments. Two aspects stand out: one is the weakening of the wartime regimes of the Bosnian Serbs and Bosnian Croats, who had embraced ethnic cleansing as their major policy goal during the war; the other is the growing importance of the ICTY.

The dismantling of the postwar nationalist power structures of the Bosnian Serb Pale regime, led during the war by Radovan Karadžić, is a story of diplomacy, unintended consequences, conditionality, and luck. Initially Bosnia's warlords and their political masters assumed that they had little to fear from the large number of IFOR troops, which set up checkpoints and military bases throughout the country in 1996. Although the leading Serb party (SDS) was seen as responsible for Srebrenica, there was no move to ban it or prevent it from participating in elections, unlike what happened with the Iraqi Baath Party in 2003. While it succeeded in separating troops, IFOR did not at first disarm special police forces or dissolve the different intelligence services. The biggest challenges for U.S. army doctors in Bosnia looking after some twenty thousand soldiers deployed there were sprained ankles and pulled muscles from sports activities. A *New York Times* article in July 1996 highlighted the fact that U.S. troops stationed in Bosnia were "safer, healthier and less likely to be killed than soldiers in the Army as a whole."[202]

A strategy of avoiding confrontations succeeded in keeping international troops safe (unlike during the preceding war, when a number of UN peacekeepers in Bosnia lost their lives), but the self-limitations of the intervention were infuriating to those—Bosnians and foreigners alike—who had expected peace with some justice. There was no return and no freedom of movement. At the end of the first year, there was also no Bosnian state—no central institution able to exert even limited authority across the whole territory of the country. The first Bosnian elections in 1996 had been won by nationalist parties, including the Bosnian Serb SDS. This looked at the time as if it yielded them solid control. In fact, in hindsight these were Pyrrhic victories, giving wartime leaders a false sense of confidence. Within another year SDS had lost power in the entity it had created.

Different elements came together to put pressure on the Bosnian Serb regime after the end of the war. There was an international reconstruction program, which excluded the Bosnian Serb entity in 1996. There was a U.S. exit strategy to arm the Bosnian Federation entity army. There was a Dayton commitment to hold regular elections, to be organized (at considerable cost) by the Organization for Security and Co-operation in Europe, where displaced persons could vote by absentee ballot. And there was the first High Representative, Carl Bildt, pursuing what he called his Banja Luka strategy.

In 1996, President Bill Clinton unveiled a program whereby a U.S. military consulting firm began to work with the army of the Bosniak-Croat Federation.[203] Ambassador James Pardew, who was responsible for the task force in the State Department, explained the thinking at the time: "This war had an aggressor and it had a victim. The program . . . is to ensure that there will be no future victims and no easy prey for partisans of war."[204] A report commissioned by the Pentagon found that fifty additional tanks for the Federation army would erase any Serb military advantage.[205] This effort, called "train and equip," was controversial at the time. U.S. Senator (and later Vice President) Joe Biden told *Time* magazine in 1996, "We will not be able to leave unless the Bosnian government is armed and prepared to defend itself. That's the ticket home for Americans."[206] A report by the United States Institute of Peace (USIP) stated in September 1997 that "some believe that by mid-1998 the Bosniaks are likely to have a clear advantage and by mid-1999 they will have the ability to inflict a decisive defeat over the Serbs." The USIP report noted that the Bosnian Serbs were also on the verge of economic collapse, which "would make the maintenance of military parity impossible to monitor in the future."[207] All this made some Bosnian Serb leaders extremely nervous.

Carl Bildt was no friend of train and equip. He saw a contradiction between a program of state-building and the strengthening of internal armies. He had his own strategy toward the Bosnian Serbs, however, which he pursued consistently: to convince some among their leadership that the deal they had obtained in Dayton was in their interest and that resisting peace implementation put at risk the very existence of their entity. Bildt was convinced that the Bosnian Serbs were playing with fire: "Sooner or later the policy of isolation and obstruction would mean that the Republika Srpska would go down in flames."[208] Concretely his strategy involved trying to strengthen Serbs who wanted to work with the international community—increasingly based in the largest city of the Bosnian Serb entity, Banja Luka—against the radical wartime leadership of Radovan Karadžić and his associates based in Pale near Sarajevo. By playing Bosnian Serb wartime leaders against each other, Bildt hoped "to bring about a more profound transformation of the political scene in Banja Luka."[209]

The strategy proceeded by trial and error. In 1996, Bildt first encouraged a Bosnian Serb prime minister, Rajko Kasagic, to break with the wartime Bosnian Serb leaders in Pale. In the spring of 1996, Kasagic declared in an interview with *Le Monde* that he wanted to move the entire government from Pale to Banja Luka. In May 1996, a representative office of OHR was opened in Banja Luka. Then indicted war criminal (and still unofficially the Bosnian Serb leader) Karadžić dismissed Kasagic as prime minister, accusing him of "conspiring with the West to hand over the Republika Srpska to the Muslims." At a cabinet meeting in Pale, Bildt later wrote, "Kasagic responded by saying that the policy pursued by Karadžić was resulting in continued isolation, that the Bosnian Serbs would meet the same fate as the Serbs in Krajina [Croatia], and that all of them risked ending up in a refugee camp outside Belgrade."[210] But the first round in this silent wrestling match went to Pale.

Then, in a completely unexpected manner, the Banja Luka strategy was vindicated. Under international pressure, Karadžić appointed his former deputy as new president of the Bosnian Serb entity. Biljana Plavšić was considered at the time as having even more extreme views than Karadžić himself. She had been a member of the supreme command of the armed forces of the Bosnian Serbs. By early 1997, however, she realized the threat that corruption and economic decline posed to the future of the Bosnian Serb entity. While the Bosnian Serbs received neither military nor reconstruction support, she saw their wartime foes building up their strength. As she began to argue for a more pragmatic policy toward the foreign mission, she broke with her former mentor, Radovan Karadžić. This required her to obtain international support: in the summer of 1997 it was British troops in Banja Luka that stopped the paramilitaries sent by Karadžić from entering the city to carry out a coup against her. From then on, Plavšić saw that not only the future of her entity depended on international support, but also her own personal security.

Thus began a new phase in international engagement. In the name of strengthening Plavšić as the elected president of the Bosnian Serbs, and irrespective of her own radical past, international troops began to disarm special police forces in areas around Banja Luka that were not loyal to Plavšić. They carried out the first arrests of indicted war criminals in the western half of the Bosnian Serb entity. At the end of 1997, elections took place in the Bosnian Serb entity. They produced a political earthquake. The SDS of Radovan Karadžić lost, and a new coalition between all those who opposed Karadžić was formed with strong support on the part of international diplomats. This brought together representatives of Bosniak displaced persons and supporters of Plavšić, and it produced the first non-SDS prime minister of the Bosnian Serb entity: a young local politician with no roots in the wartime politics, Milorad Dodik. All of this took place before there even were any Bonn powers and with no shots fired.

From that moment on, Dodik became the main partner for international policy in postwar Bosnia. Dodik moved the government from Pale to Banja Luka. With strong international support he began to govern in half the territory of the Bosnian Serb entity—the other half continued to be controlled by supporters of Karadžić for another two years. The support Dodik received was political, technical, and financial. The implicit deal offered, and which he accepted, was that the international community would help build the institutions of a new, postwar Bosnian Serb entity. SFOR became the praetorian guard for the new leaders in Banja Luka, and international donors provided the new institutions with substantial financial support. This was all part of a bigger bargain acceptable to Serb nationalists like Plavšić. On the eve of elections in 1998, even the U.S. secretary of state, Madeleine Albright, came to Bosnia to campaign on behalf of Dodik and Plavšić.[211]

The strategy worked. What had been a trickle of refugee returns turned into a flood after 2000. Suddenly it became apparent that there were hundreds of thousands of men and women like Aziz throughout the country. In 1997, ghost villages around Prijedor, notorious for the death camps set up by Bosnian Serbs in the spring of 1992 were still "leveled, burned and empty . . . muddy lanes where 6,000 houses once stood."[212] Five years later "more than two thousand [Bosniak] families had come back to live in the villages, the mosque had been rebuilt and the electricity supply restored."[213] More than twelve thousand Bosnian Croats and Muslims had come back to Prijedor municipality by 2002.[214] Something similar happened in central Bosnia, the scene of horrendous fighting during the war between Bosnian Croats and Bosniaks. There, in the village of Ahmići in the early morning of April 16, 1993, some one hundred Bosnian Croat soldiers killed 115 Bosniaks, including thirty-two women and eleven children. The massacre was perpetrated to make coexistence and return impossible. It failed. By 2002, almost all of the displaced Bosniak families had returned to their restored homes in Ahmići and elsewhere across the municipality, where they live to this day alongside their former Croatian neighbors. There is a multiethnic municipal administration in Vitez town, a few miles from Ahmići. The cantonal police is ethnically mixed.

Return of property also took off after 2000, after regional changes in Croatia and Serbia. Although restitution laws were passed in 1998, by the spring of 2000 the rate of implementation of these laws remained so low that completion of the process was thought to take up to forty years. Then two hundred thousand property claims were resolved in four years.[215]

There was one final element, the most important, to explain how Bosnia's local warlords lost power in the end: the International Criminal Tribunal for the Former Yugoslavia. The ICTY had been created by the UN Security Council in May 1993. When international judges arrived in The Hague for the court's first session in November 1993, they had almost no resources. As one judge, Claude Jorda, recalled, "We had no address, no offices, no legal status, no logistics, not even a prosecutor."[216] The ICTY looked more like an alibi than a genuine commitment to bring justice to the Balkans. As the first president of the tribunal, Antonio Cassese, put it, "Our tribunal is like a giant who has no arms and legs. To walk and work he needs artificial limbs. These artificial limbs are the state authorities."[217] For years no intelligence was forthcoming from other states. The ICTY lacked resources, both human and physical. The court clearly failed to constitute a deterrent during the war in Bosnia. Bosnian Serb leaders did not pay it much attention. The cold-blooded genocide in Srebrenica took place two years after the court had been set up. Until late 1995, when the war in Bosnia came to an end, the ICTY had only one indicted person in its jail.

As a result of all this, to most observers it was far from obvious just how important the tribunal was to become after the war ended. From 1997 onward the court began to have a major impact on the situation on the ground in Bosnia. It was a dramatic shift when in Prijedor in the summer of 1997, NATO forces made their first arrest of ICTY suspects. British troops arrested Milan Kovačević, who was under indictment on genocide and other charges. They also shot dead another suspect, Simo Drljaca, when he resisted arrest. Drljaca, the wartime police chief, had earlier given weapons to the local Serb population to resist the return of any refugees. Following this incident, other wartime leaders fled abroad.[218] As Diane Orentlicher wrote in a recent study on ICTY's influence on Bosnia, many people in Bosnia shudder to imagine what their country would be like were it not for the ICTY. Senad Pecanin, a leading journalist in Sarajevo, told her that in a world without ICTY "probably Radovan Karadžić would be a member of Parliament. Ratko Mladic could be chief of staff of the army."[219] Another effect was also important: the existence of an international court allowed institutions in Bosnia to delegate to it issues of war crimes justice. Otherwise, Bosnian local courts would have been seized with war crimes cases, with accusations and charges, making any return of displaced people even harder to achieve.

Finally, and perhaps most important in a region where wars had been fought in the name of ethnic purity, the ICTY trials succeeded in discrediting this agenda: those who had planned it were not heroes but criminals. A judgment summary in a court case against Bosnian Serb leaders (*Prosecutor vs. Momčilo Krajišnik*) argued that the policy in the territory under their control from 1992 onward constituted a "criminal enterprise." Another case against leading Bosnian Croats saw prosecutors make the same claim. In early 2001, ICTY prosecutor Carla del Ponte told journalists about Croatian President Tudjman that "were he not dead he would have been one of The Hague tribunal indictees."[220] In April 2010 the new president of Croatia, Ivo Josipović, came to Bosnia and asked for forgiveness for the crimes in Bosnia supported by his country. As Josipović put it, misguided nations and individuals had "reaped the death and mutilation of hundreds of thousands and the expulsion of millions of people, destroyed economies and families. . . . I am deeply sorry that the Republic of Croatia has contributed to that with its policies in the 1990s."[221] Finally, in April 2011 the Croatian general in charge of the operation that saw two hundred thousand Serbs displaced from Croatia in 1995 was sentenced by the ICTY to twenty-four years in prison for war crimes.

Throughout this period the ICTY played an invaluable role in winning the wider battle of ideas and norms. All these changes were supported by a wider regional change, the end of the Tudjman regime in Croatia after his death in 1999, and the overthrow of Milošević in Serbia by his own people in October 2000. This opened the door to a flood of arrests and trials, as the United States and the European Union put pressure on all Balkan states to hand over suspects.

The story of the ICTY's impact on Bosnia illustrates how long it took for the international community to come to recognize even the usefulness of its own instruments. It clearly would have been preferable to have a strong court with credible powers and sufficient resources from the outset. When the ICTY was formed in 1993, it had an annual budget of $276,000.[222] By 1994 this had risen to $10 million. By the end of 2011, by its own account the ICTY will have cost almost $1.9 billion. This allowed the

court to grow to an institution with twenty-eight judges and at
its peak more than eleven hundred staff, overtaking the tribunal
in Nuremberg. As of the end of March 2011, ICTY had indicted
161 people and sentenced sixty-four. Gareth Evans wrote later
about the ICTY and the Rwanda tribunal that "their expense
and uneven record makes it not especially likely that any of
them will be replicated elsewhere."[223] If somebody would have
spelled out in 1993 that the plan was to create a court that would
be active for almost two decades and would cost nearly two billion dollars, it might never have been created. This would have
been a tragic mistake. The truth is simple: proper justice is both
very important and (if provided by an international court) very
expensive. As David Wippman, professor of law at Cornell University, points out, at the level of basic administrative costs, the
U.S. justice system and ICTY are roughly comparable, while a
major U.S. criminal trial involving numerous victims costs far
more than any trial in The Hague. The sum spent prosecut-
ing the Oklahoma City bombers Timothy McVeigh and Terry
Nichols was $82.5 million, not counting the costs of appeal.[224]
The Saville inquiry report, an investigation into the deaths of
thirteen people on Bloody Sunday commissioned by the British
government, cost £195 million and lasted twelve years.[225] The
ICTY was a huge investment, but perhaps the most important
one the international community undertook in postwar Bosnia.

If the international community would have closed the OHR
in 2004—when SFOR left and all wartime property that had
been claimed was restituted—few would have questioned that
this was a successful intervention. But OHR stayed on, and
overreached. It started to impose ever more institutions without
the bargaining and political compromises that had been central
to its earlier successes. As Gary Bass noted in his history of
nineteenth-century humanitarian interventions, "Humanitar-

ian interventions are emergency steps; one should be suspicious of a permanent emergency."[226]

In reality, interveners are never in a good position to understand what objectives are actually achievable or how to achieve them before a mission starts. It is by trial and error—by learning from failure as well as success—that a mission understands gradually what it might be able to achieve. This is an argument for prudence, not recklessness. When an intervention takes place it is also wise to act carefully when a mission's ignorance of the possible consequences of its actions is greatest. The myth of a golden hour, an early moment in a mission when a post-conflict society is like a hot iron, ready to be shaped and formed by strong strokes, is a dangerous one: it usually tells us more about the initial ignorance of the intervener, unaware of any of the constraints that exist, than about any inherent features of society. Revolution is a treacherous method of social change.

The values and principles underlying any intervention are also crucial to its success; they define what success looks like beyond preventing a return to war. This is why having a peace agreement—and in the case of the Balkans, the ICTY—made such a difference. It provided a focus. It helped guard against open-ended utopian social engineering. It also set up the norms that were to provide the north star for the mission. Incrementalism, unless guided by principles, degenerates easily into mere opportunism. Principled incrementalism is about muddling through with a sense of purpose.

INTERVENTION AND RESTRAINT

We can now give an unambiguous and reassuring answer to the question this book asks: Can intervention work? Yes, it can, because it did. In the case studied in detail in this essay, the killing fields of Bosnia were transformed in the course of one decade in an unexpected and encouraging manner. It was within the gift of outsiders not only to bring this war to a temporary end, but also to then build a peace that has since lasted for more than fifteen years.

One lesson the international community learned in the early 1990s is that there is a high price, in human, moral, and strategic terms, of not attempting to intervene when this seems within our power in the face of mass atrocities. People are still haunted by the ghosts of Rwanda and Srebrenica. In 1999 Kofi Annan evoked the trauma of Rwanda as a concrete illustration of the horrors of non-intervention, actions for which he—as head of UN peacekeeping—was also responsible at the time:

> The experience of Rwanda in 1994 [was] a terrible demonstration of what can happen when there is *no* intervention, or at least none in the crucial early weeks of a crisis. General Dallaire, the commander of the UN mission, has indicated that with a force of even modest size and means he could have prevented much of the killing. Indeed he has said that 5,000 peacekeepers could have saved 500,000 lives.[227]

Another lesson learned in the Balkans is that for humanitarian interventions to be undertaken, "pseudo-universalist" arguments need to be set aside. In the 1990s skeptics of intervention held that any serious military intervention in Bosnia would necessarily lead to a new wave of costly wars in the name of stopping human suffering. UK Foreign Minister Douglas Hurd defended a conservative anti-imperialism, against "benevolent international interventionism," and told the European Parliament in 1992, "We must not exaggerate our power to remove those agonies." He noted that Britain could not "sort out every manmade disaster in the world."[228] To get involved in Bosnia today, he and others implied, would create irresistible pressures to send foreign troops to Georgia, Tajikistan, and Azerbaijan tomorrow. For British historian Brendan Simms, all of this added up to a "particularly disabling form of conservative pessimism" combined with a "disabling pseudo-universalism" which held that if the United States and Britain considered intervening in Bosnia, they ought to also intervene everywhere else: "This was a domino theory in reverse: Britain should not resist aggression and ethnic cleansing in one part of the world—even in an area which obviously fell within Britain's sphere of influence on the UN Security Council—because that would somehow commit her to doing the same in all parts of the globe."[229] The report of the International Commission on Intervention and State Sovereignty, published in December 2001, also warned against the trap of pseudo-universalism: "The reality that interventions may not be able to be mounted in every case where there is justification for doing so is no reason for them not to be mounted in any case."[230]

This point remains relevant. In a recent speech justifying U.S. air strikes to try to prevent mass atrocities in Libya, President Obama stated that in some cases humanitarian interests may justify U.S. military action, but that such a decision needs to be made on a case-by-case basis: "Given the costs and risks of intervention, we must always measure our interests against the need for action." In response, some critics warned that this was "without punch and power," "maybe to save lives, but not change regimes."[231] Charles Krauthammer argued that "if you go to take Vienna, take Vienna. If you're not prepared to do so better then to stay home and do nothing."[232] But these were the choices that had led to three years of watching Bosnia burn. It is precisely in cases where more limited interventions are possible that humanitarian intervention will be considered. In this sense Obama's speech in the spring of 2011 was a return to the 1995 speech by President Clinton explaining why the United States was sending troops to Bosnia. To assert that we sometimes should intervene in some cases of mass atrocities does not mean that we always can; nor does it require that such interventions are always followed by multiannual nation-building missions.

The third lesson from the past decades is how much any success depends on the local and regional context. In the case of the Balkans, one of the most powerful sources of soft power for the international interveners was the attraction of European Union membership as a goal for elites and populations in all Balkan countries. It was this promise of joining a community of prosperous and stable democracies as equal members that gave reformers in all countries powerful arguments to leave behind the nationalist visions of the previous decade. It was the actual accession of some former communist countries to NATO in 1999 and to the European Union in 2004 that made such a promise credible to ordinary Bosnians, Croats, and Serbs. If soft power is the ability to get others to "want what you want," then being a gatekeeper to a community that is seen as attractive is a unique asset, just as becoming part of another prosperous community of affluent democracies—the non-communist "West" after World War II—helped make the U.S.-led occupations of Germany, Italy, and Austria successful. In reality it makes little sense to consider the interventions in Somalia, Bosnia, Kosovo, Iraq, and Afghanistan as parts of a single phenomenon. Interventions to help implement a peace agreement are radically different from those that follow regime change; nation-building under fire poses radically different challenges from those facing the principled incrementalist approach to institution-building that the international community (mostly) followed in Bosnia. There is no evidence that even the most powerful countries, such as the United States, have found a way to make "nation building under fire" successful. There is encouraging evidence that limited missions in support of peace agreements and with sufficient resources can produce a good result. If the Bosnia intervention is judged by whether it led to the successful implementation of the provisions of the Dayton Peace Agreement, and not by the criteria of liberal imperialist open-ended state-building, it certainly qualifies as a success. When missions end, politics, political conflicts, will continue. To pretend that this can be prevented by outsiders forever, irrespective of the wisdom of local actors, is to make the case for empire, not humanitarian interventions.

Changing other countries is extremely difficult. Historically occupations have rarely ended with an outcome that was satisfactory to the occupier. But supporting certain norms and values and opposing others has led to some astonishing successes in recent years. There are other less comfortable lessons from Bosnia. To end mass atrocities, it may be necessary to deal with evil, accept limited goals, and bide our time. Not all good things go together. It is always true in interventions that the perfect will be the enemy of the good. So can intervention work? The answer from the last two decades is that where we believe that any price is worth paying, and that failure is not an option, we are likely to fail. Where we tread carefully, and fear the consequences of our mistakes, there is a chance.

ACKNOWLEDGMENTS

This book emerged from my time as the Ryan Professor and director of the Carr Center on Human Rights Policy. I am immensely grateful to the Harvard Kennedy School for making this project possible and for the understanding they showed when I was elected to Parliament. I learned an enormous amount from the school, the center, colleagues, and students. This book would not have been possible without them. In particular, I would like to thank Vin Ryan, Charlie Clements, and the fellows and staff of the Carr Center; and David Elwood, Mary-Jo Bane, and the Kennedy School faculty for their wisdom, understanding, and support, both professional and personal.

—Rory Stewart

*   *   *

Many of the ideas in this book emerged from joint work with my colleagues at the European Stability Initiative (ESI), the best team I have ever come across when it comes to developing new ideas. I want to thank all of them for their inspiration—in particular, Piotr Zalewski for his help as editor; Kristof Bender

193

and Minna Jarvenpaa for detailed feedback to many drafts; and Marcus Cox, Kristof Gosztonyi, Eggert Hardten, Verena Knaus, Felix Martin, Alex Stiglmayer, and Besa Shahini for many intense debates on all the issues discussed here.

The actual writing took place during my time with the Harvard Kennedy School, first as a visiting and then as an associate fellow at the Carr Center on Human Rights Policy. I am grateful to the school, the center, colleagues, other fellows, and all of our impressive students. It was a privilege to work alongside all of them. Special thanks to Charlie Clements, and of course to Rory, for persuading me to come to the United States, agreeing to take up the challenge of a joint book, and then finding time to work long nights—in Istanbul, Scotland, Cumbria, and London—despite the demands of a political career. I am also grateful for the enormous patience and encouragement of everyone at W. W. Norton, Jake Schindel, Brendan Curry, and Roby Harrington.

Very special thanks to Katharina, who commented on drafts as a colleague while supporting the whole project as head of our family; and to my daughters Fanny, Amelie, and Melek, for their inspiration and patience.

—Gerald Knaus

NOTES

Introduction

1 You could be in the very middle (*amid*); or in a gathering of many (*among*); or in relation to only two (the English *between*). You could be apart from the things, or integrated with, separating, or linking them (see the use of words such as *interlayer, interloop, interregnum,* or *intermarriage*).

2 So too when we *come into* something, or something *comes over* us: again there is a sense of something unexpected befalling us.

3 If we said we interfered (from the Latin root for *to strike*), we would imply we were meddling, without having the right to do so; and if we said interloped (from the Old English for *to run*), we would be intruding into (literally cutting into) someone else's domain. An interloper is unauthorized.

4 Even neutral related words like *entertain* or *enterprise* (*enter-* is a version of *inter-*) have a sense of active volition or grip of holding something or taking something in hand. But *intervene* benefits from connotations that are relatively neutral, constructive, and passive. This is not inevitable. Some "compounds," particularly those using the English (as opposed to the Latin) *to come,* include more aggressive and negative possibilities: see the idea of an *in-comer* as an invader or an intruder: the word *incoming* as the cry used for a missile landing; or even *to come down* upon someone, and *to come on* at someone in

the old sense of attacking. And *coming to* somewhere—an ad*vent*—denotes an important or even miraculous arrival (not to mention an adventure).

5 Michael Walzer, "The Argument about Humanitarian Intervention," *Dissent*, Winter 2002, 29–37. Accessed at http://them.polylog .org/5/awm-en.htm.

6 William Jefferson Clinton, "U.S. Support for Implementing the Bosnian Peace Agreement," address to the nation, November 27, 1995. Accessed at http://dosfan.lib.uic.edu/ERC/briefing/dispatch/1995/html/ Dispatchv6no48.html.

7 The two of us come from very different cultures and backgrounds. One of us is a Central European, growing up in the Vienna of the late Cold War and ending up in Istanbul; the other is a Scotsman from a colonial family born in Hong Kong and brought up in Malaysia. One has been working for various international organizations in the Balkans and run an independent think tank; the other was (very briefly) a soldier, then a diplomat, and now a politician. But we have come to very similar conclusions about the events of the last twenty years.

8 St. Augustine and St. Thomas Aquinas both include in their just-war theory (alongside self-defense, minimal harm, etc.) the condition that the war should be winnable.

9 Bernard Williams, "Moral Luck," in *Moral Luck* (Cambridge, UK: Cambridge University Press, 1982).

10 This worldview, developed on the most exacting rational foundations in the universities, is echoed (in an intuitive, nonphilosophical form) today by politicians and human rights activists. Such actors may not be fully aware of the stern and ascetic implications of the philosophy they purport to endorse. But they have no other developed ethical system to put in its place. They generally lack a coherent theory on how circumstance, nationality, resources, success, and luck connect to moral principles. And they, therefore, rarely mention the two things in the same breath, lurching instead in our interventions between Machiavellian horse-trading and the most vacuous idealism. Ought may imply can, but rarely in policy on intervention.

11 International missions were in the dark about the most fundamental features of postwar Balkan societies even years after their arrival: whether economies were in fact growing; what the extent of serious crime and public order issues was (see the ESI report titled "The Worst in Class. How the International Protectorate Hurts the Euro-

pean Future of Bosnia and Herzegovina" (2007); and even how many people there were. One ESI report, "Post-industrial Society and the Authoritarian Temptation" (2004), noted how little was known about basic demographic facts in Bosnia; "Utopian Visions. Governance Failures in Kosovo's Capital" (2006) argued that the population of Kosovo's capital was less than half the size assumed by international organizations, something since confirmed by a census; "The Lausanne Principle: Multiethnicity, Territory and the Future of Kosovo's Serbs" (2004) showed that the most basic assumptions about Kosovo Serbs—where they were, how many there were, and how many had left—were wrong. All reports can be found at www.esiweb .org.

12 Gerald Knaus and Felix Martin, "Travails of the European Raj," *Journal of Democracy*, vol. 14, no. 3 (July 2003), http://www.journal ofdemocracy.org/articles/gratis/KnausandMartin.pdf. For the wider debate and reactions that followed, see http://www.esiweb.org/index .php?lang=en&id=225.

13 Albert O. Hirschman, *The Rhetoric of Reaction: Perversity, Futility, Jeopardy* (Cambridge, Mass.: Belknap Press of Harvard University Press, 1991).

14 Conor Cruise O'Brien, "Bosnia: Hands Off," *Atlantic*, November 1992, http://www.theatlantic.com/magazine/archive/1992/11/bosnia-hands-off/5341/.

15 Here are the insights, formalized in their common application to Afghanistan: In 2002, (1a) to prevent a Taliban insurgency, it was necessary to stop the Afghan people from turning against the Karzai government; (1b) to stop the Afghan people from turning against the government, it was necessary to establish security, economic development, and decent government; (1c) to establish security, sustainable economic development, and decent government, it was necessary to have a large number of international troops on the ground and large amounts of international aid. (2) But the international community put in few troops and little aid ("a light footprint"). Therefore, (3a) it was impossible to establish security, sustainable economic development, or decent government; (3b) therefore it was impossible to stop the Afghan people turning against the government; and (3c) therefore there was a Taliban insurgency.

16 See Sean Rayment, "General Sir David Richards: 'We Can't Afford to Lose the War in Afghanistan,' " *Telegraph* (UK), October 4, 2009, http://www.telegraph.co.uk/news/worldnews/asia/afghanistan/625

8025/General-Sir-David-Richards-We-cant-afford-to-lose-the-war-in-Afghanistan.html. This was also the view of General Stanley McChrystal, for example, who remained very confident that his policy (a U.S.-led full-spectrum counterinsurgency strategy) could bring success despite the extreme and apparently intractable problems with the Karzai government. The principles of state-building and counterinsurgency were almost a magic talisman—a guarantee of success, almost regardless of the context. But these truths—like Buddha's four noble truths—were not regarded simply as articles of faith, but logical conclusions, capable of proof and analysis.

17 Iraqis in 2003 hardly knew what was going on in Iraq. This was not only because it was so dangerous that even Iraqis hesitated to cross Baghdad. Nor was it only because of the accelerating complexity of a country where most of the new politicians had been in exile or operating in secret Iranian revolutionary cells, and where fifty-four new political parties had emerged in the single small province of Maysan alone. Iraqis might have been able to sketch possible outcomes (for example, another Stalingrad, flowers for the coalition forces, chemical weapons exploding, a prolonged war, or invasions by Iran, Syria, or Turkey). But they would have found it impossible to assign probabilities to those larger outcomes, let alone predict how twenty-five million others would collectively feel, plan, and act in a situation when a head of state is toppled and a nation is turned on its head.

18 Interveners are generally members of one of three institutions: the military, the foreign service, or the development agencies. Soldiers are recruited and trained to fight battles and do not like politicians at home, still less politicians in a conflict zone. Senior diplomats are more accustomed to drafting resolutions in the United Nations in New York than sitting in a dusty provincial office. Development workers think their task is to alleviate poverty and wonder whether their presence is contributing to that goal. None of them were equipped to deal hour after hour with men who say, "My name is Sheikh Saad bin Abdul Wahid bin Falih bin Majid bin Khalife, my ancestor was in a boat with Wilfred Thesiger in 1952, please build a clinic in my area," or to stand like Gordon of Khartoum on the residency steps confronting a thousand demonstrators. The job of an administrator, which Rory had on the ground in Iraq in 2003, was not the job of a diplomat, a development worker, or a soldier: it was the job of a 1920s Chicago ward politician.

19 For one striking illustration of this, look at ESI's report on Mount

Olympus and the experience of the UN International Police Mission in Bosnia: "On Mount Olympus: How the UN Violated Human Rights in Bosnia and Herzegovina, and Why Nothing Has Been Done to Correct It," February 10, 2007, http://www.esiweb.org/index.php?lang=en&id=156&document_ID=84.

20 George Packer, "The Last Mission," *The New Yorker*, September 28, 2009, http://www.newyorker.com/reporting/2009/09/28/090928fa_fact_packer.

21 For more on the soft power of the European Union in the Balkans, see Elizabeth Ponds's *Endgame in the Balkans: Regime Change, European Style* (Washington, DC: Brookings Institution, 2006). Gerald wrote about "member state building" as the post-1999 international strategy in the Balkans. See Gerald Knaus and Marcus Cox, "The 'Helsinki Moment' in Southeastern Europe," *Journal of Democracy*, January 2005, http://muse.jhu.edu/login?uri=/journals/journal_of_democracy/v016/16.1knaus.html.

22 James Dobbins et al., *The Beginner's Guide to Nation-Building* (Santa Monica, Calif.: RAND Corporation, 2007), 256.

The Plane to Kabul

1 See, for example, Ahmed Rashid: "I think Simon missed out one very important part of the mission in 2001 and that was nation-building. Both George Bush and Tony Blair promised that they would change the lives of the Afghans. The truth is that that has not happened to the degree that the Afghans expected. Why? Because of Iraq. There was an enormous diversion from Iraq and resources, troops, manpower, money, everything was diverted to Iraq." "Should Britain Withdraw Troops from Afghanistan?" BBC "In Afghanistan" Series—BBC Radio 4 Recording, November 5, 2008, Chatham House. Transcript available at http://www.chathamhouse.org.uk/events/view/-/id/936/.

2 Pia Karlsson and Amir Mansory, *An Afghan Dilemma: Education, Gender and Globalisation in an Islamic Context* (Stockholm: Pedagogiska Institutionen, 2007), frontispiece.

3 Robert S. McNamara with Brian VanDeMark, *In Retrospect: The Tragedy and Lessons of Vietnam* (New York: Times Books, 1995), 322.

4 Even exceptional figures working for the UN or NGOs rarely served longer than four years.

5 As late as the 1950s, during the Malayan Emergency, my father drove down roads on which colleagues and predecessors had been killed with no more protection than a pistol placed on the dashboard.

6 In 2000, even before the Afghan intervention, I was told by a British official that "no development program in Afghanistan was worth losing a British life." Shortly after deciding that Yemen was one of the central international priorities for the British government, in 2010 the Foreign Office considered closing the entire embassy on the grounds that it was too unsafe for staff (it was finally left open).

7 And these attitudes spread into the Afghan government. In October 2010, the governor of Helmand told me he "hoped" his subdistrict governors would soon be able to drive between towns in Helmand rather than being flown by the coalition military.

8 Good practice in personnel management and in following approved accounting procedures was no longer an optional skill but a sine qua non for promotion. Thus, in the formal statement to Parliament on the British Foreign and Commonwealth Office's performance and finance in 2010, the head of the Foreign Office acknowledged the importance of "diplomacy, policy, international activity, languages and negotiation, but not at the expense of people's ability to be responsible stewards of public funds and good leaders of their teams. In recent years the Foreign Office has made some pretty impressive strides in improving its management and its leadership. . . . Of course, you have very senior diplomatic responsibilities, but you also have senior management and leadership responsibilities, including the management of money and of people." Simon Fraser CMG, Testimony to UK Foreign Affairs Committee, December 16, 2010. This was in part in response to pressure from the "treasury" to allow the Foreign Office to be assessed in almost exactly the same terms as any home civil service department. So second nature has the emphasis on "management" (as opposed to the old emphasis of spending time with the citizens of the country) become that Sir Michael Jay, who introduced the reforms, denied that this increased emphasis was in any way at the cost of the old emphasis on policy: "The idea that there is a management and that there is a policy and that the two are somehow separate is misguided. It is as misguided in government as it is in business or anywhere else." Testimony to UK Foreign Affairs Committee, December 8, 2010. Compare with: "It demonstrates a point I made before: top government officials need specialists— experts—at their elbows when they make decisions on matters out-

side their own experience. If we had had more Asia experts around us, perhaps we would not have been so simpleminded about China and Vietnam. We had that expertise available during the Cuban Missile Crisis; in general, we had it available when we dealt with Soviet affairs; but we lacked it when dealing with Southeast Asia." McNamara, *In Retrospect*, 117. The new head of the Foreign Office explicitly rejected pressure to change the promotion system back: "I don't believe that it is necessary to [change the promotion system to favor country experts], because promotions within the Foreign Office are done in a transparent and merit-based way." Simon Fraser CMG, Testimony to UK Foreign Affairs Committee, November 24, 2010.

9　"The UK's Foreign Policy Approach to Afghanistan and Pakistan," Foreign Affairs Committee, No. 9, "Overarching Issues of Concern: Who's Driving British Policy on Afghanistan?," section 230, http://www.publications.parliament.uk/pa/cm201011/cmselect/cmfaff/514/51414.htm#n374.

10　Promotion in the UK Foreign Office around the world no longer had anything to do with linguistic or area expertise. The post of deputy ambassador in Iran, which previously might have been the reserve of a Farsi-speaking specialist, was occupied by a young generalist originally from the Cabinet Office. Many of the more scholarly linguists or area experts now felt disadvantaged in promotion. And no alternative stream has been created to offer them the prestige or reward that they were now denied through promotions. By the beginning of 2011, only two British ambassadors in the Middle East had the current "extensive" Arabic language skills to be able to conduct their working business in Arabic.

11　Much of British diplomatic time, worldwide, was spent in responding to the demands of other government departments in London and tracking new global initiatives from ministers.

12　As recently as 1999, by contrast, the second political secretary in the British embassy in Jakarta visited (on thirty trips) all but one of the provinces of Indonesia—one of the very largest geographical areas in the world.

13　But the Foreign Office was still in a better position than most of its "bilateral and multilateral peers." The latest U.S. State Department quadrennial review calls for even more emphasis on importing staff from domestic departments and ever more emphasis not on traditional diplomatic skills but on "global skill sets." More and more people were being promoted for moving fluidly through the abstractions of an imagined "global" context. See "The First Quadrennial Diplomacy and Development Review: Leading through Civilian Power," U.S. Department of State, http://www.state.gov/s/dmr/qddr/.

14 These new bureaucratic expectations and structures reflect a worldview that could not simply be shifted through introducing new language courses or longer tour lengths. In fact, such remedies, without a fundamental shift of culture, may simply be a distraction. Real expertise in language is very difficult to achieve. Even colleagues with two years of language training often hesitated to conduct really serious government business except through a professional interpreter. There was too much risk around precise technical terms and political nuances for even a fair degree of fluency to give much more than an ability to conduct informal relationships. There also rarely seemed, in my experience, to be a clear correlation between speaking a local language well and being well-informed, intelligent, and energetic officers.

15 Some of their/our limits can be hinted at but not articulated, since to describe them would involve getting beyond the limits and seeing them from the other side. They will be limited by language and cultural assumptions in ways that a future generation might observe but we cannot. They may also have a distinct psychological makeup, which would be almost impossible to capture. I have focused on more public and obvious structures such as university courses and promotion mechanisms, while being aware that they are as much the result as the cause of the surrounding culture.

16 Take my friends as examples. Matt was the leading policy voice for Oxfam; Lindy was the head of the massively funded office for the Department for International Development and then Britain's senior civilian representative in southern Afghanistan; Rachel ran Human Rights Watch and John, the United States Institute of Peace; Minna ran the monitoring board for the Afghan National Development Strategy; Tom and James were journalists; Ali ran the Aga Khan Development Network, which spent almost three hundred million dollars in seven years doing everything from building the mobile phone network, to restoring the old cities of Herat and Kabul and building the country's first five-star hotel. Chris was the Canadian ambassador and then the deputy representative of the secretary-general of the United Nations.

17 Mountstuart Elphinstone, *Account of the Kingdom of Cabul and Its*

Dependencies in Persia, Tartary and India (London: Longman, 1815), 253.

18 Commandant Haji Mohsin Khan and Rais Salam Khan were brothers-in-law.

19 Department for International Development (UK), "Political Participation Fund Iraq," mission criteria, 2005.

20 Or in the words of the 1911 *Encyclopaedia Britannica*, in the entry on John Lawrence, "The adventurous and warlike spirits, Sikh and Mahommedan, found a career in the new force of irregulars directed by the chief commissioner himself [Lawrence]."

21 At the end of the Carter administration, Holbrooke moved to Lehman Brothers and intermittently worked on presidential campaigns. He remained on Wall Street for twelve years before becoming ambassador to Germany for a year and then becoming assistant secretary for European and Canadian affairs, during which time he drove through the Dayton peace negotiations. He returned to Wall Street in 1996 and worked at Credit Suisse Boston for three years before becoming U.S. ambassador to the United Nations for a year. He was then again in finance with AIG and a consulting firm for the next nine years, while taking a very active role in charity, before becoming Special Representative for Afghanistan and Pakistan in 2009, a position he held until his death in late 2010.

22 Michael Kelly, "The Negotiator," *The New Yorker*, March 6, 1995, 81.

23 John Beames, *Memoirs of a Bengal Civilian* (London: Chatto and Windus, 1961).

24 Packer, "Last Mission."

25 Some Americans argued that Holbrooke's day-to-day activities were "so frantic . . . that he couldn't possibly keep track of everything he was doing." Ibid.

26 "USAID-financed road costs vary considerably depending on road type, terrain, security costs and other factors. However, a rough average for USAID asphalt roads is $548,000 per kilometer, while gravel roads cost an average $180,000 per kilometer. USAID's most expensive road, the 4-lane Kabul Airport road, was $1.6 million per kilometer." USAID Afghanistan, "Frequently Asked Questions," http://afghanistan.usaid.gov/en/about/frequently_asked_questions.

27 Mohammed Atef, the military commander, was killed in Kabul in 2001; Abu Farraj al-Libbi, who ran external operations, was captured in Pakistan in 2005; Abu Zubaydah, who was responsible for much of the logistics, was captured in Pakistan in 2002; Abdul Hadi al-

Iraqi was captured in Iraq in 2007. Of the best-known senior figures in Al Qaeda, only Ayman al-Zawahiri remained uncaptured by the spring of 2011.

28 "Remarks by the President on a New Strategy for Afghanistan and Pakistan," March 27, 2009, http://www.whitehouse.gov/the_press_office/Remarks-by-the-President-on-a-New-Strategy-for-Afghanistan-and-Pakistan/.

29 Ibid.

30 Writers have emphasized Afghanistan's isolation for millennia. Aristotle considered the Paropamisus range in Afghanistan to be the very end of the world. Early Muslim writers mocked its central highlands as a last savage redoubt of paganism. Sir John Mandeville, the medieval traveler, described its environs as a country of darkness. It is not just the ancient Buddhist site at Bamiyan that is dramatically concealed by mountains: you approach Kabul from the plains of the Punjab, through the drama of the Khyber Pass, the narrow Sarobi gorges, and dizzying switchback roads until you arrive at six thousand feet, surrounded by snow-capped peaks. By 1978, the country had been at peace for decades. It was not a developed country. The few upper-class women in miniskirts in tree-lined Kabul comprised a tiny anomaly in a nation where the World Bank estimated 95 percent of women were unable to read or write and communist and Islamist movements were already forming and would eventually topple governments. But there was no sign of anarchy, still less of civil war. Foreigners traveled freely through most of the country; hippies packed the cafes of Kabul; upper-class Kabulis lived a liberal "Western" existence.

31 The price at the farm gate was then about $250 a kilo, and it seemed from the struggle with the packs in the mud that each weighed at least twenty kilos.

32 "Supplementary Written Evidence from Sir Sherard Cowper-Coles KCMG LVO," December 23, 2010, http://www.publications.parliament.uk/pa/cm201011/cmselect/cmfaff/514/514we10.htm.

33 Ashraf not only deployed behind this ambition a prodigious amount of erudition, highly educated staff, and energy but also captured an astonishing amount of support—financial and intellectual—in the West for his strategy. Of his brilliant proposals, the most impressive and successful was his National Solidarity Program, in which hundreds of millions of dollars would be given directly to elected village councils to spend as they wished.

34 Sean Rayment, "General Sir David Richards: 'We Can't Afford to Lose the War in Afghanistan,' " *Telegraph* (UK), October 4, 2009, http://www.telegraph.co.uk/news/worldnews/asia/afghanistan/6258025/General-Sir-David-Richards-We-cant-afford-to-lose-the-war-in-Afghanistan.html.

35 The conference and, indeed, most of the development strategy of the next few years were organized around a document presided over by Ashraf, known as "Securing Afghanistan's Future." The strategy, backed by $8.2 billion of aid, was one of state-building. It became the cornerstone of the Afghan National Development Strategy and exemplified the high theory of state-building through intervention. And his views influenced the fundamental assumptions of a whole generation of policymakers. "Securing Afghanistan's Future: Accomplishments and the Strategic Path Forward," March 17, 2004, http://www.scribd.com/doc/49142816/Securing-Afghanistans-Future.

36 Afghan President Hamid Karzai said in 2004 in the preface to Ashraf's new document that our goal is a "stable, democratic, financially sustainable State that is committed to the goal of poverty elimination."

37 "Remarks by the President on a New Strategy for Afghanistan and Pakistan," March 27, 2009; "White Paper of the Interagency Policy Group's Report on U.S. Policy toward Afghanistan and Pakistan," http://www.whitehouse.gov/assets/documents/Afghanistan-Pakistan_White_Paper.pdf; "NATO's 60th Anniversary Summit," Congressional Research Service, March 20, 2009, http://fpc.state.gov/documents/organization/121913.pdf.

38 Prime Minister Gordon Brown said that "just as the Afghans need to take control of their own security, they need to build legitimate governance." "PM Gordon Brown's Speech about the Strategy on Afghanistan and Pakistan," Speech to the House of Commons, April 30, 2009, http://ukinindia.fco.gov.uk/en/news/?view=PressS&id=17123756.

39 What was this governance that Afghans (or we) needed to build, and that could also be transparent, stable, regulated, competent, representative? Did all nations intrinsically have governance? Was all governance good governance? Did it bring new benefits or was it simply a cure for something like corruption? Was governance an object or a process? Doubtless there were some academics who could have answered these questions; policy-makers generally could not. They sometimes made it a duo, "governance and the rule of law," and sometimes a triad, "security, economic development, and gov-

ernance," to be addressed through a comprehensive approach to the three Ds, "defense, development, and diplomacy"—which suggested "governance" was something to do with a foreign service.

40 This was not supposed to be simply a theoretical path but rather a practical proposal, to enable you to achieve success, provided other conditions were favorable. Some emphasized that what mattered was planning. High Representative Paddy Ashdown emphasized precepts (both military and spiritual) such as avoiding cowardice, poor discipline, indecisiveness, dissension, and impatience. Ashraf Ghani, Clare Lockhart, and Michael Carnahan, "Closing the Sovereignty Gap: An Approach to State-Building," Overseas Development Institute, September 2005, 6, http://www.odi.org.uk/resources/down load/1819.pdf.

41 Ibid., 13. This was in essence a project management theory. It said that one needed support, money, a plan, leadership, and to check what one was doing occasionally. But the same was true, not just for building a state, but for building a garden shed.

42 See "Securing Afghanistan's Future" document, presented in Berlin, 2004. There was no weight given in the analysis to ethnicity, religion, history, or politics. No space had been given for autonomy or consent by local communities, nor to traditional Afghan structures. See the version on http://www.scribd.com/doc/49142816/ Securing-Afghanistans-Future.

43 HM Government, "UK Policy in Afghanistan and Pakistan: The Way Forward," April 2009, 14, http://www.humansecuritygateway .com/documents/UKGOV_UKPolicy_Afghanistan_Pakistan_The WayForward.pdf.

44 The language enshrined the crudest moral slogans of tabloid newspapers in recondite bureaucratic formula. It is multipurpose and perhaps will be applied as easily to Yemen or Libya.

45 Larissa MacFarquhar, "The Conciliator," *The New Yorker,* May 7, 2007, http://www.newyorker.com/reporting/2007/05/07/070507fa_fact_ macfarquhar?currentPage=all.

46 Julie Henry, "Gordon Brown Warns of 'Chain of Terror' as He Pays Tribute to Dead Marines," *Telegraph* (UK), December 13, 2008, http://www.telegraph.co.uk/news/worldnews/asia/afghanistan/374 1784/Gordon-Brown-warns-of-chain-of-terror-as-he-pays-tribute-to-dead-Marines.html.

47 MacFarquhar, "Conciliator."

48 Personal communication to author.

49 MacFarquhar, "Conciliator."

50 Afghanistan was at various points under the same empire as Iran, Turkmenistan, Uzbekistan, Tajikistan, or Pakistan. There were Persian, Turkmen, Uzbek, and Tajik populations in Afghanistan, and the Afghan Pushtun were only arbitrarily divided by the Durand Line from their Pakistani kinsmen. The economies were linked, and millions of Afghans have studied and worked in Iran or Pakistan. There were, therefore, many more reasons for Afghanistan to develop into a country like one of its neighbors than for it to collapse into Somalian-like civil war or solidify into Malaysian democracy.

51 Some Afghan cabinet ministers told me Afghanistan was not suited to democracy; others wanted to restore the monarchy. If it was to be a democracy—as presumably the internationals intended—was it to be a parliamentary or presidential system? Would there be elections for provincial governors? What would be the role of Islam in the Islamic Republic of Afghanistan?

52 Others raised the specter (suggested by the example of Pakistan) that this would lead to a military coup.

53 "PM Gordon's Speech about the Strategy on Afghanistan and Pakistan," April 30, 2009, as reported by the UK government: http://ukinindia.fco.gov.uk/en/news/?view=PressS&id=17123756. See similar sentiments from the Lord President of the Council, House of Lords Main Chamber Debates, April 29, 2009, vol. 710, part no. 67, http://services.parliament.uk/hansard/Lords/ByDate/20090429/maincham berdebates/part008.html.

54 Or for that matter "decentralization," and "subdistrict government."

55 Compared, for example, to Nepal, where every village presented me with a shopping list of demands for international assistance.

56 Anglea Merkel in a July 24, 2007, press conference, http://www.bundes regierung.de/Content/DE/Archiv16/Pressekonferenzen/2007/07/2007 -07-24-merkel-koenigs.html. For the Italian conference, see http://www .rolafghanistan.esteri.it/ConferenceRol. For Sarkozy's letter, November 2, 2009, see http://ambafrance-uk.org/Lettre-de-felicitations-du,16272. html. For Brown's comments in Parliament, July 13, 2009, see http://uki nindia.fco.gov.uk/en/news/?view=PressR&id=20560927. For Obama's speech in Kabul on March 28, 2010, see "President Obama Lands in Kabul for Surprise Afghanistan Visit," *Times* (UK), March 29, 2010, http://www.timesonline.co.uk/tol/news/world/us_and_americas/arti cle7079353.ece.

57 There are certainly no thoughts given to whether it meant the same in every European language, let alone in Dari or Pashto.

58 World Bank, *World Development Indicators 2007* (Washington, D.C.: World Bank, 2007), 262.

59 Joseph Raz, "The Rule of Law and Its Virtue," *Law Quarterly Review*, vol. 93, 1977, 195.

60 "About the World Justice Project," http://www.worldjusticeproject .org/about/ (accessed May 2011).

61 Ibid.

62 Freedom House concluded that by 2007, "limited progress has been made on . . . strengthening judicial and law enforcement service" and lamented "a prevailing atmosphere of weak rule of law and impunity." "Afghanistan (2007)," Freedom House, http://www.freedomhouse.org/ modules/mod_call_dsp_country-fiw.cfm?year=2007&country=7119.

63 See Chris Johnson, William Maley, Alexander Thier, and Ali Wardok, "Afghanistan's Political and Constitutional Development," Overseas Development Institute, January 2003, http://www.odi.org .uk/resources/download/4810.pdf.

64 Fareed Zakaria, "The Stakes in Afghanistan," *Washington Post*, August 3, 2004, http://www.washingtonpost.com/wp-dyn/articles/ A35556-2004Aug2.html.

65 "Press Briefing by Manoel de Almeida e Silva Spokesman for the Special Representative of the Secretary-General and by UN Agencies," UN News Centre, August 1, 2004, http://www.un.org/apps/ news/infocusnews.asp?NewsID=778&sID=1.

66 "U.S. in First Clash over Afghan Disarmament," Reuters, July 31, 2004.

67 It was disguised in phrases such as "realistic expectations," "not trying to create Hampshire in Helmand," "reasonable level of security and government," and even "Afghan good enough."

68 James Dao, "History by Army Lays Out Missteps in Afghanistan," *New York Times*, December 31, 2009.

69 Ahmed Rashid, "American Commander Alters Military Strategy in Afghanistan," *Foreign Policy in Focus*, January 17, 2003, http://www .fpif.org/articles/american_commander_alters_military_strategy_ in_afghanistan#.

70 After extensive consultation, General McNeill reconfigured military plans and formed Joint Regional Teams.

71 "The United States might be able to begin drawing down some of its troops in 2004." Kenneth Katzman, "Afghanistan: Current Issues

and U.S. Policy," CRS Report for Congress, Congressional Research Service, August 27, 2003, http://fpc.state.gov/documents/organization/24047.pdf.

72 Associated Press, "25th ID Takes Over Lead Role in Afghanistan," *Army Times*, April 15, 2004, http://www.armytimes.com/legacy/new/1-292925-2825204.php.

73 Dao, "Army History Finds Early Missteps in Afghanistan."

74 Eric Schmitt, "U.S. General Maps New Tactic to Pursue Taliban and Qaeda," Militaryphotos.net, March 3, 2004, http://www.militaryphotos.net/forums/showthread.php?7433-U.S.-General-Maps-New-Tactic-to-Pursue-Taliban-and-Qaeda and http://www.khilafah.com/index.php/news-watch/south-asia/8422-army-history-finds-early-missteps-in-afghanistan.

75 Gerry J. Gilmore, "Abizaid: 2005 'Can Be a Decisive Year' against Extremism," American Forces Press Service, U.S. Department of Defense, March 2005, http://osd.dtic.mil/news/Mar2005/20050302_68.html.

76 General Karl Eikenberry, in testimony to the Senate Armed Services Committee, said, "Our current operation in Southern Afghanistan, Operation Mountain Thrust, seeks to deny the enemy safe havens, interdict his movement routes, and, most importantly, extend the authority of the central government. The combat phase of this operation is only the precursor to our longer-term goal of strengthening good governance, the rule of law, reconstruction and humanitarian assistance, and economic development. This emphasis on governance and development is indicative of our overall approach to the Afghan campaign." Gerry J. Gilmore, "Progress in Afghanistan Is 'Truly Significant,' General Says," American Forces Press Service, U.S. Department of Defense, June 28, 2006, http://www.defense.gov/news/newsarticle.aspx?id=15931.

77 "The situation will improve by the end of this year." "News Briefing with Lt. Gen. Eikenberry from the Pentagon," News Transcript, U.S. Department of Defense, May 10, 2006, http://www.defense.gov/transcripts/transcript.aspx?transcriptid=238.

78 Richard Norton Taylor, "Afghanistan Close to Anarchy, Warns General," *Guardian* (UK), July 21, 2006, http://www.guardian.co.uk/world/2006/jul/21/afghanistan.richardnortontaylor.

79 General Richards also was hoping to win the support of local people by creating secure zones where development can take place. See Embassy of Afghanistan in Ottawa, "Afghan News 07/29-30/2006—Bulletin

#1449," http://www.afghanemb-canada.net/public-affairs-afghanistan-embassy-canada-ottawa/daily-news-bulletin-afghanistan-embassy-canada-ottawa/2006/news_articles/july/0729-302006.html. According to an *Economist* interview, Richards coined a five-letter strategy: " 'R, D, G, P and S,' standing, respectively, for reconstruction, development, governance, Pakistan, and security." It's hardly catchy, but it does the job of summarizing his strategy against the Taliban, which, he says, depends for its success on making progress in all five dimensions "synergistically." Much of the interview, though, is more personal. He defends his record in overseeing NATO's violent deployment to southern Afghanistan last year, distances himself from tactics of static defense adopted by the British in Helmand the previous summer, justifies a decision to strike a deal to extricate British forces from the town of Musa Qala, and warns the Americans against poppy eradication. "From Canada to Kandahar," *The Economist*, February 16, 2007, http://www.economist.com/research/articlesBySubject/PrinterFriendly.cfm?story_id=8691739.

80 Alex Morales, "Afghanistan Car Bomb Kills 5 after 200 Rebels Die," *Bloomberg*, September 4, 2006, http://www.bloomberg.com/apps/news?pid=newsarchive&sid=ag0AhMjnlLTo&refer=germany.

81 Terry Friel, "U.S. General in Afghanistan Seen Tough on Taliban," Reuters, February 5, 2007, http://www.reuters.com/article/2007/02/05/us-afghan-general-idUSSP16017620070205?pageNumber=2. At the end of 2006, General Richards felt that his successor's situation would be improved with more troops. "I have every confidence that my successor, with a big injection recently of additional, highly experienced combat troops . . . will . . . not only contain the insurgency but actually improve on it." He seemed content with the troop numbers, saying in a September interview with the BBC, "I'm very confident . . . that we do have enough to make a real difference here this autumn, setting conditions for a much better 2007." "NATO Hails Afghan Mission Success," BBC News, September 17, 2006, http://news.bbc.co.uk/2/hi/europe/5354208.stm. UK Foreign Office Minister Kim Howells said in an interview, "I would certainly like to see many more troops and resources coming from NATO members." Morales, "Afghanistan Car Bomb Kills 5 after 200 Rebels Die."

82 General Dan McNeill, commander of International Security Assistance Force (ISAF), Afghanistan, set the stage with a review of the efforts of ISAF to build governance and capacity where none previously existed. McNeill stated that he found the expression "winning

the hearts and minds" to be misleading, and suggested that a better approach would be trying "to avail oneself of the will of the people." To succeed in this effort, he identified three conditions: (1) The elite of the country must be enthusiastic in supporting change. (2) The public must be willing to accept the change. (3) The international community must accept the redefined state.

83 "DoD News Briefing with Gen. Dan McNeil via Videoconference from Afghanistan at the Pentagon," News Transcript, U.S. Department of Defense, June 5, 2007, http://www.defense.gov/transcripts/transcript.aspx?transcriptid=3980.

84 "US Embassy Cables: Nato Commander Criticises British Anti-drug Strategy," *Guardian* (UK), December 2, 2010, http://www.guardian.co.uk/world/us-embassy-cables-documents/103541.

85 B. F. Griffard, "Common Security and the Global War on Terror," issue paper, Center for Strategic Leadership, U.S. Army War College, May 2007, vol. 3-07, http://www.csl.army.mil/usacsl/publications/IP03-07.pdf. See also Ahmed Rashid, "Taliban Takeover of Town Could Mark Start of Military Offensive," Eurasianet.org, February 4, 2007, http://www.eurasianet.org/departments/insight/articles/eav020507.shtml: NATO forces are to embrace a more aggressive stance under McNeill, who is believed to oppose the type of local peace arrangements that Richards promoted.

86 In June 2007, McNeill was beginning to argue that he still had insufficient resources: "The things that we're short that have the most effect on us: first, our maneuver forces, three-and-a-half to four battalions short; secondly, helicopters that would include medium-and heavy-lift helicopters and attack helicopters; and then thirdly, the OMLTs, the Operation Mentor Liaison Teams. Any of those resources, and especially all of them, would be helpful for us to prosecute our operational context." "DoD News Briefing with Gen. Dan McNeil," June 5, 2007. At the end of the year, he requested five thousand more troops. See John Kerry, "A Winning Strategy in Afghanistan," speech delivered at Johns Hopkins University Paul H. Nitze School of Advanced International Studies, December 5, 2007, http://www.johnkerry.com/blog/entry/kerry_a_winning_strategy_in_afghanistan/.

87 Espen Barth Eide, "Why Is Norway in Afghanistan? How Can We Best Complete Our Mission?" opening address at the 42nd Leangkollen Conference, May 2, 2007, http://www.regjeringen.no/en/dep/fd/aktuelt/taler_artikler/politisk_ledelse/statssekretaer_

espen_barth_eide/2007/why-is-norway-in-afghanistan-how-can-we-.html?id=456378.

88 "Interview with NATO's Afghanistan Commander, 'A Counter-Insurgency Takes a Long Time, Longer Than We Thought,' " *Der Spiegel*, August 11, 2008, http://www.spiegel.de/international/world/0,1518,571345,00.html.

89 McKiernan curtailed aerial bombardments and through that the number of civilian deaths. (The number of civilian deaths fell by 40 percent compared to the average when he took over.) He began cautiously to form militia groups. See Steve Bowman and Catherine Dale, "War in Afghanistan: Strategy, Military Operations, and Issues for Congress," CRS Report for Congress, Congressional Research Service, December 3, 2009, http://www.fas.org/sgp/crs/row/R40156.pdf.

90 General David McKiernan, Atlantic Council, Washington, D.C., November 18, 2008, transcript available at http://www.acus.org/event_blog/general-david-d-mckiernan-speaks-councils-commanders-series/transcript. He also took a new approach to airpower in a directive that emphasized "proportionality, restraint, and utmost discrimination in the use of firepower." It provided specific conditions for the use of air-to-ground munitions and underscored the need to minimize the risk to civilians. 105 ISAF slide, "Tactical Directive," October 2, 2008.

91 "Pentagon Reviews Afghanistan Strategy for Upcoming NATO Summit," *Foreign Policy Bulletin: The Documentary Record of United States Foreign Policy*, vol. 18, no. 2, 2008, 224–245, http://journals.cambridge.org/action/displayAbstract?fromPage=online&aid=1912408.

92 The deputy commander for security for the NATO-led ISAF said the Taliban's leadership was in "disarray" and had not been able to carry out the attacks it had hoped to this year and would be even weaker next year. "This has been a shaping year," he said. See David Rohde, "Afghan Police Suffer Setbacks as Taliban Adapt," *New York Times*, September 2, 2007, http://www.nytimes.com/2007/09/02/world/asia/02taliban.html.

93 Yochi J. Dreazan and Peter Spiegel, "U.S. Fires Afghan War Chief," *Wall Street Journal*, May 12, 2009, http://online.wsj.com/article/SB124206036635107351.html.

94 Michael J. Carden, "Gates Recommends McChrystal for Top Command in Afghanistan," American Forces Press Service, U.S. Depart-

ment of Defense, May 11, 2009, http://www.defense.gov/news/newsarticle.aspx?id=54289.

95 "COMISAF Initial Assessment," August 30, 2009, http://www.washingtonpost.com/wp-dyn/content/article/2009/09/21/AR2009092100110.html. McChrystal's commander's assessment of 2009 was leaked to the *Washington Post* that fall.

96 Embassy of Afghanistan in Ottawa, "Afghan News 2/31/2008–Bulletin #2271," http://www.afghanemb-canada.net/public-affairs-afghanistan-embassy-canada-ottawa/daily-news-bulletin-afghanistan-embassy-canada-ottawa/2008/news_articles/december/12312008.html.

97 Reflecting on 2009, General David Petraeus told the Senate Armed Services Committee, "We've spent much of the past year working to get the inputs right in Afghanistan. . . . We've worked to get the structures right, put the best leaders in charge, develop the right concepts and provide the authorities and resources needed for unity of effort. And with those inputs now in place we're starting to see the outputs." Lisa Daniel, "Success in Afghanistan Achievable, Petraeus Says," American Forces Press Service, U.S. Department of Defense, March 16, 2010, http://www.defense.gov/news/newsarticle.aspx?id=58353. "Petraeus: Afghan War Under-resourced," Press TV, August 31, 2010, http://www.presstv.ir/detail/140789.html.

98 Michael Hastings, "The Runaway General," *Rolling Stone,* June 22, 2010, http://www.rollingstone.com/politics/news/the-runaway-general-20100622?page=5.

99 Rajiv Chandrasekaran, "Gen. David Petraeus Says Afghanistan War Strategy 'Fundamentally Sound,' " *Washington Post,* August 16, 2010, http://www.washingtonpost.com/wp-dyn/content/article/2010/08/15/AR2010081501514.html.

100 David Ignatius, "Petraeus Rewrites the Playbook in Afghanistan," *Washington Post,* October 19, 2010, http://www.washingtonpost.com/wp-dyn/content/article/2010/10/18/AR2010101803596.html.

101 "NATO Secretary General: 2010 Will Be a Decisive Year in Afghanistan," NATO News, February 1, 2010, http://www.nato.int/cps/en/SID-25280172-B1A32623/natolive/news_61156.htm. "Miliband—2010, a Decisive Year for Afghanistan," Government News (UK), February 2, 2010, http://www.government-news.co.uk/ministry-defence/201002/miliband-2010-a-decisive-year-for-afghanistan.asp.

102 As Sherard Cowper-Coles, the British ambassador to Afghanistan, observed in 2007, "The millenarianism that propelled interventions

214 NOTES TO PAGES 56–59

only a few years ago has gone right out of fashion. So no one . . . is saying that the problems which confront Afghanistan after decades of war, centuries of underdevelopment and millennia of isolation need anything other than a long-term approach. Our watchwords are indeed modesty and realism." Within two years the total number of international troops in Afghanistan had doubled. Rory Stewart and Sherard Cowper-Coles, "Are We Failing in Afghanistan?" *Prospect*, January 20, 2008, http://www.prospectmagazine.co.uk/2008/01/arewefailinginafghanistan/.

103 "COMISAF Initial Assessment."

104 "Obama's Remarks on the Strategy in Afghanistan," *New York Times*, December 16, 2010, http://www.nytimes.com/2010/12/17/world/asia/17afghan-text.html?pagewanted=all.

105 "Press Briefing by Press Secretary Robert Gibbs, Secretary of State Clinton, Secretary of Defense Gates, and General Cartwright," White House, Office of the Press Secretary, December 16, 2010, http://www.whitehouse.gov/the-press-office/2010/12/16/press-briefing-press-secretary-robert-gibbs-secretary-state-clinton-secr (emphasis added).

106 See text released by the White House, reprinted in "Obama's Remarks on the Strategy in Afghanistan" (emphasis added). Such language was almost universal among senior NATO commanders. In January 2010, Britain's chief of the General Staff said the mission in Afghanistan had been "under-resourced" for years. The deputy commander of ISAF told me in October 2010 it was at last "properly resourced."

107 "2011 'Decisive' for Afghanistan—German FM," January 2, 2011, http://english.ruvr.ru/2011/01/02/38605083.html. "And Westerwelle-ruft-Jahr-der-Entscheidung," http://www.nachrichten.de/politik/Afghanistan-Westerwelle-ruft-Jahr-der-Entscheidung-aus-aid_67898623 4850498315.html.

108 Memorandum to Komer, December 1, 1966, FRC 77-0775, Secret—copy sent to author.

109 McNamara, *In Retrospect*, 322–333.

110 McNamara also espoused liberal and democratic principles such as the value of public debate and of international consensus, in a way that former vice president Richard Cheney might not. McNamara said, "We failed to draw Congress and the American people into a full and frank discussion and debate of the pros and cons of a large-scale US military involvement in Southeast Asia before we initiated the action. We did not hold to the principle that US military action—other than in response to direct threats to our own security—

should be carried out only in conjunction with multinational forces supported fully (and not merely cosmetically) by the international community." Ibid., 322.

111 This is a political problem—but not in the narrowest sense of money and votes.

112 McNamara, *In Retrospect*, 352. But the conclusion McNamara reached on this level is not unique: "We failed to analyze and debate our actions in Southeast Asia—our objectives, the risks, and costs of alternative ways of dealing with them, and the necessity of changing course when failure was clear—with the intensity and thoroughness that characterized the debates of the Executive Committee during the Cuban Missile Crisis." Ibid. Identical criticisms of policy process can be found in almost any book on the Iraq intervention of 2003 under the guise of "dodgy dossiers," sound-bite propaganda, lack of UN support, ignorance of the region, and an absence of postwar planning.

113 Ibid., 353.

114 Ibid.

115 The Soviet Union lost more troops after they decided to withdraw from Afghanistan than in the entire previous span of their occupation.

116 Ronald Reagan, "A Time for Choosing (The Speech—October 27, 1964)," http://www.reagan.utexas.edu/archives/reference/timechoosing.html.

117 As quoted by Thomas Friedman on CBS's *Face the Nation*, March 14, 2004, http://www.cbsnews.com/htdocs/pdf/face_031404.pdf, 5.

118 "Remarks by the President on a New Strategy for Afghanistan and Pakistan," March 27, 2009.

119 In the nineteenth-century "Great Game," we were afraid of Russia.

120 Robert Cooper, "The New Liberal Imperialism," *Guardian* (UK), April 7, 2002, http://www.guardian.co.uk/world/2002/apr/07/1. "It is not going too far to view the West's response to Afghanistan in this light."

121 *Hansard* (House of Commons), 6th series, vol. 390, col. 3, September 24, 2002, http://www.parliament.the-stationery-office.co.uk/pa/cm200102/cmhansrd/vo020924/debtext/20924-01.htm#20924-01_spmin0.

122 Lyndon B. Johnson, President's News Conference, July 28, 1965, American Project, http://www.presidency.ucsb.edu/ws/index.php?pid=27116#axzz1KpAcFjNV.

123 "Gordon Brown: UK Is Safer Thanks to British Troops in Afghani-

stan," *Defence News*, December 15, 2008, http://webarchive.nationalar
chives.gov.uk/+/http://www.mod.uk/DefenceInternet/DefenceNews/
MilitaryOperations/GordonBrownUkIsSaferThanksToBritish
TroopsInAfghanistan.htm. The other great fear of Afghanistan was,
of course, around its heroin production—it was believed to produce
"93 per cent of the world's heroin." Where such accurate figures
came from with an illegal crop is a mystery.

124 Lyndon B. Johnson, President's News Conference, July 28, 1965: "It
is guided by North Vietnam and it is spurred by Communist China
. . . to extend the Asiatic domination of Communism."

125 "Speech by the Rt. Hon. Paddy Ashdown, High Representative in
Bosnia and Herzegovina, to the International Rescue Committee,"
Office of the High Representative, Press Office, June 20, 2003, http://
www.ohr.int/print/?content_id=30130.

126 In the nineteenth century the equivalent fear was that the Russians
would base themselves in Afghanistan.

127 John Bolton, in the *Wall Street Journal*, for example, drew clear links
between Afghanistan policy ("decisively defeat[ing] militants on
both sides of the border") and the future of Pakistan in which "there
is a tangible risk that several weapons could slip out of military control. Such weapons could then find their way to al Qaeda or other
terrorists, with obvious global implications." Or "a well-organized,
tightly disciplined group to seize control of the entire Pakistani government . . . , a radical Islamicist regime in Pakistan would control a substantial nuclear weapons capacity." John R. Bolton, "The
Taliban's Atomic Threat," *Wall Street Journal*, May 2, 2009, http://
online.wsj.com/article/SB124121967978578985.html. Or (from *Forbes
India*): "When Americans depart in two years, the Taliban who are
now very strong will take over in a very short time," says Raphael
Israeli, an Islamic affairs expert and a fellow of Jerusalem Center for
Public Affairs. "If Afghanistan falls, the Taliban in Pakistan—they
exported the Taliban to Afghanistan—might follow suit in the long
run. India will find itself straight on the boundary of terror." Shloka
Nath and K.P. Narayana Kumar, "Seven Security Nightmares India
Must Prepare For," *Forbes India*, August 27, 2010, http://business
.in.com/printcontent/16512. This is echoed by Joe Klein: "No one in
the Administration who follows Afghanistan closely believes we can
simply 'get out,' as critics propose. The U.S. has significant national-
security interests in the region. The first, oft stated, is to prevent
al-Qaeda from returning to a Taliban-controlled Afghanistan and

using it as a safe haven. But that isn't nearly as important as the problem next door in Pakistan, with a wobbly civilian government that has more than 80 nuclear weapons and a history of military coups, some of which have been led by Islamists." Joe Klein, "What It Will Take to Finish the Job in Afghanistan," *Time*, January 6, 2011, http://www.time.com/time/world/article/0,8599,2040968-2,00 .html#ixzz1KvdWQe00.

128 Paul Wolfowitz's remarks to the Department of Defense, on October 16, 2002: "I believe there is actually an opportunity here . . . with positive effects throughout the Middle East and indeed throughout the world's two billion Muslims." Available at http://www.iraqwatch .org/government/US/Pentagon/dod-wolfowitz-101602.htm.

129 Dwight D. Eisenhower, President's News Conference, April 7, 1954, American Project, http://www.presidency.ucsb.edu/ws/index .php?pid=10202#axzz1LtANy6i8.

130 Christopher Alexander, as quoted in "Should Britain Withdraw Troops from Afghanistan?" BBC "In Afghanistan" Series–BBC Radio 4 Recording.

131 Stewart and Cowper-Coles, "Are We Failing in Afghanistan?"

132 On the circumstances of American withdrawal, Henry Kissinger said, *"Many in the U.S. and other countries might simply construe our actions as abandoning South Vietnam."* This, Kissinger continued, "would erode the credibility of U.S. commitments, and could encourage increased subversion in Asia." ("Memorandum, September 11, 1969.") In his October 1969 meeting with the British counterinsurgency adviser Sir Robert Thompson, Nixon returned to the themes: " 'What was at stake now,' the President added, 'is not only the future peace of the Pacific and the chances for independence in the region, but the survival of the United States as a world power with the will to use this power.' " Cited in Benjamin S. Bodurian, "Credibility and Nixon Administration Strategy in Ending the Vietnam War, 1969–1973," Williams College, 165, 164, 168, http://www.thepresidency.org/stor age/documents/Fellows2009/Part_III.pdf.

133 "Transcript: Bush Discusses War on Terrorism," *Washington Post*, October 6, 2005, http://www.washingtonpost.com/wp-srv/politics/ administration/bushtext_100605.html.

134 Ahmed Rashid, "Should Britain Withdraw Troops from Afghanistan?" BBC "In Afghanistan" Series–BBC Radio 4 Recording.

135 Laura Rozen, "Obama Announcement on Afghanistan and Pakistan Policy," *Foreign Policy*, March 27, 2009, http://thecable.foreignpolicy

.com/posts/2009/03/27/obama_announcement_on_afghanistan_
and_pakistan_policy (emphasis added).

136 Stewart and Cowper-Coles, "Are We Failing in Afghanistan?"
(emphasis added).

137 Packer, "Last Mission."

138 Ibid.

139 Quote by Rodric Braithwaite in his excellent book, *Afgantsy: The
Russians in Afghanistan, 1979–89* (London: Profile, 2011), 7.

140 Karl E. Meyer and Shareen Blair Brysac, *Tournament of Shadows:
The Great Game and the Race for Empire in Central Asia* (New York:
Basic Books, 2006), 157. If Lawrence called his ideal policy as viceroy "masterly inactivity," if he was much less inclined to intervention
than his predecessors, it was in part because he had spent far longer
than them on the ground. Conversely, if Holbrooke could see Vietnam was not a threat but believed Afghanistan was, this was at least
in part because he had much more contact with the reality of rural
Vietnam and little with Afghanistan.

141 There was one contractor who had served in Afghanistan. Almost
none of the members of either the U.S. Senate Committee on Foreign
Relations or the House of Commons Select Committee on Foreign
Affairs had worked or lived for extended periods abroad.

142 Archibald Forbes, *The Afghan Wars, 1839–42 and 1879–80* (London:
Seeley, 1892), 187.

143 Gertrude Bell Archive, Newcastle University Library, Letters
from August 23, 1920 (http://www.gerty.ncl.ac.uk/letter_details
.php?letter_id=412), September 5, 1920 (http://www.gerty.ncl.ac.uk/
letter_details.php?letter_id=416), and November 1, 1920 (http://
www.gerty.ncl.ac.uk/letter_details.php?letter_id=431).

144 See, for example, Sir Henry Rawlinson, a celebrated and experienced
member of the Council of India, concerning the threat of a Russian
presence in Afghanistan in 1868: "In the interests, then, of peace;
in the interests of commerce; in the interests of moral and material
improvement, it may be asserted that interference in Afghanistan
has now become a duty, and that any moderate outlay or responsibility we may incur in restoring order at Kabul will prove in the sequel
to be true economy." Meyer and Brysac, *Tournament of Shadows*, 155.

145 Forbes, *Afghan Wars*, 324–325.

146 Sixty-five meetings or events; twenty-three lectures and academic
events or classroom talks at societies, public lectures, a U.S. military
base, and universities (speaking not just in Oxford but in three dif-

ferent parts of Scotland and three different parts of Alaska); and sixteen meetings and interviews for magazines, books, radio, television, and film on Afghanistan. This was relatively typical of the whole year. I was lucky enough to rehearse my arguments, not only in meetings with senators, prime ministers, and all of the generals and ambassadors in Kabul, but also in op-eds for the *New York Times*, for cover stories for *Time* magazine, and in a BBC documentary about intervention.

147 In general, students responded to highly articulate, well-organized teachers whose courses had clear lessons (or "takeaways"), guides for action, and relevance. The emphasis was on universal, transferable, and, accordingly, relatively abstract skills, and many students left with an optimistic sense that they could apply the skills they learned at Harvard anywhere in the world.

148 "Mountain Advice," Mountain Rescue England and Wales, http://www.mountain.rescue.org.uk/mountain-advice.

149 I also feared the same old questions, beginning with the instant solutions: "Why don't you just spray the crop?" "Why don't you just buy the crop?" or "Why don't you use it for medicinal purposes?" Certainly little more than some interesting observations on credit and seed arrangements, or discussion of the problems of apricots becoming bruised during transport, or stories about police chiefs in narcotics areas buying their jobs for more than a hundred thousand dollars. But little more.

150 Tomas Ruttig, Martine Biljert, and Jolyon Leslie. Paul Fishstein has worked in Afghanistan since 1978 and therefore has a total of thirty-two years of experience in Afghanistan and Pakistan. He has worked on health sector development, public administration reform, refugees and migration, education, and agricultural economics. He was the director of the foremost think tank in Afghanistan. Michael Semple has worked in Afghanistan since 1989 and has interacted with leading figures in the succession of Afghan regimes, and the different armed movements that have campaigned against them. His experiences as development worker, political officer, and conflict negotiator give him an unparalleled network into most elements of Afghan and Pakistani society. Michael has a deep interest both in Afghan political history and in current Afghan political strategies. Andrew Wilder was born and raised in Pakistan and has studied and worked on issues relating to Pakistan and Afghanistan for the past twenty-five years. He wrote his Ph.D. dissertation on

electoral politics in Pakistan, and his research during the first round of elections in post-9/11 Afghanistan foretold many of the current problems facing policy-makers. From 2002 to 2005 Andrew established and directed the Afghanistan Research and Evaluation Unit, Afghanistan's first independent policy research organization.

151 In Lashkar Gah, waiting for a military plane, two years later, an educational adviser explained precisely and convincingly why more girls were in school in Helmand than in 2008. The number was lower than the government boasted but much more than I suspected, and it had little to do with the Taliban one way or the other.

152 Memorandum to Komer, December 1, 1966.

153 Ibid.

154 If this is compatible with skills at internal management and the jargon of multilateral global issues, so much the better. But it is the practical understanding of the country and the relationships with its people that are the priorities.

155 Much of their work will, of course, be involved with commerce, multilateral, and human rights issues, and only some of it with more extreme measures such as intervention.

156 Secretary Clinton remarked, on March 29, 2011, in a press conference, "We do not have any information about specific individuals from any organization that are part of this. But of course, we are still getting to know the people leading the Transitional National Council." See http://www6.lexisnexis.com/publisher/EndUser?Action =UserDisplayFullDocument&orgId=574&topicId=138360025&docId =1:1413637577&isRss=true.

157 Such reforms began after Warren Hastings and were continued by Sir Charles Trevelyan and finalized in the creation of the Indian Civil Service, following the "mutiny" of 1857.

The Rise and Fall of Liberal Imperialism

1 Gareth Evans, *The Responsibility to Protect: Ending Mass Atrocity Crimes Once and for All* (Washington, D.C.: Brookings Institution, 2008).

2 Frances Fukuyama, "Nation-Building 101," *Atlantic Monthly*, January/February 2004, http://www.theatlantic.com/past/docs/issues/2004/ 01/fukuyama.htm. Fukuyama wrote a book that appeared in 2004: *State Building—Governance and World Order in the Twenty-First Century* (Ithaca, N.Y.: Cornell University Press, 2004). A good case

can be made that "nation-building" and "state-building" are different concepts: In Europe "nation-building" usually refers to the process of constructing a national identity. However, in the current, U.S.-dominated debate, the use of these terms almost makes them interchangeable. Fukuyama defines state-building as "the creation of new government institutions and the strengthening of existing ones." He also explains, "Critics of nation-building point out that outsiders can never build nations, if that means creating or repairing all the cultural, social, and historical ties that bind people together as a nation. What we are really talking about is state-building—that is, creating or strengthening such government institutions as armies, police forces, judiciaries, central banks, tax-collection agencies, health and education systems, and the like." This is also how RAND uses "nation-building" in its publications.

3 Robert Cooper, "The New Liberal Imperialism," *Observer* (UK), April 2002.

4 One of the first to write about "a new age of liberal imperialism" in 1999, following the Kosovo war, was David Rieff, in "A New Age of Liberal Imperialism," *World Policy Journal*, vol. 16., no. 2, Summer 1999. This was followed by many more publications in 2002 and 2003. Sebastian Mallaby, a *Washington Post* editorial writer, wrote "The Reluctant Imperialist: Terrorism, Failed States, and the Case for American Empire," *Foreign Affairs*, March/April 2002, arguing that in the past, imperialism had provided the answer to the threat posed by failed states. Niall Ferguson wrote in 2003 in *Foreign Affairs* that "it is fast becoming conventional wisdom that the power of the United States today closely resembles that of the United Kingdom roughly a century ago" (*Empire: How Britain Made the Modern World* [London: Penguin Books, 2003]). Max Boot wrote in late 2003 that "compared with the grasping old imperialism of the past, America's 'liberal imperialism' pursues far different, and more ambitious, goals. It aims to instill democracy in lands that have known tyranny, in the hope that doing so will short-circuit terrorism, military aggression, and weapons proliferation." Boot, "Neither New nor Nefarious: The Liberal Empire Strikes Back," *Current History*, vol. 102, no. 667, November 2003. In June 2004 Mallaby published an addendum in *Foreign Affairs* to his earlier article, regretting having used the "imperial" label in the context of this debate. David Rieff published a book in 2005 (*At the Point of a Gun: Democratic Dreams and Armed Intervention* [New York: Simon and Schuster, 2005]) expressing second

thoughts about humanitarian intervention in the wake of the Iraq invasion.

5 James Dobbins et al., *The Beginner's Guide to Nation-Building* (Santa Monica, Calif.: RAND Corporation, 2007), xx–xxi, http://www.gees .org/documentos/Documen-02155.pdf.

6 Kofi Annan, "Intervention," Ditchley Foundation Lecture 35, June 26, 1998, http://www.ditchley.co.uk/page/173/lecture-xxxv.htm.

7 As Karin von Hipple pointed out, the intervention in Somalia did produce some positive outcomes: "It did put a stop to the famine—an estimated 100,000 lives were saved by the intervention (President Clinton claimed one million)—yet the human cost was one hundred fifty-six peacekeepers and several thousand Somali civilians." Karin von Hippel, *Democracy by Force: U.S. Military Intervention in the Post-Cold War World* (Cambridge: Cambridge University Press, 2000), 61.

8 Roméo Dallaire, *Shake Hands with the Devil: The Failure of Humanity in Rwanda*, (Cambridge, Mass.: Da Capo Press, 2004), 514.

9 UN Rwanda Report, December 1999. Iqbal Riza, a former deputy head of the UN peacekeeping division, later told a journalist that he had "not shaken his sense of personal responsibility for Rwanda." James Traub, *The Best Intentions: Kofi Annan and the UN in the Era of American World Power* (New York: Picador, 2007), 59.

10 "Report of the Secretary-General pursuant to General Assembly Resolution 53/35–The Fall of Srebrenica," UN General Assembly, November 15, 1999, 108, http://www.un.org/peace/srebrenica.pdf.

11 David Rieff, *Slaughterhouse: Bosnia and the Failure of the West* (New York: Touchstone, 1995), 22.

12 Colin Powell quoted in "Why Generals Get Nervous," *New York Times*, October 8, 1993.

13 Michael Dewar, "Intervention in Bosnia–The Case Against," *World Today*, February 1993.

14 Ibid.

15 Ibid.

16 Quoted in "Ethnic Cleansing," *Newsweek*, August 17, 1992.

17 John Keegan, "A Primitive, Tribal Conflict Only Anthropologists Can Understand," *Telegraph* (UK), April 15, 1993.

18 Helsinki Watch–Human Rights Watch, "War Crimes in Bosnia-Hercegovina," August 1992.

19 Gary Bass, *Stay the Hand of Vengeance: The Politics of War Crimes Tribunals* (Princeton, N.J.: Princeton University Press, 2000), 213.

20 Samantha Power, "Why Can't We?" Commencement Address, Uni-

versity of Santa Clara Law School, Calif., May 20, 2006, 5, http:// www.scu.edu/news/upload/santa%20clara%20final%20may%20 20%202006_samantha%20power.pdf.

21 Samantha Power, "*A Problem from Hell*": *America and the Age of Genocide* (New York: Harper Perennial, 2003), 13.

22 Ibid., 508.

23 Ibid., 504.

24 Douglas Jehl, "U.S. Looks Away as Iran Arms Bosnia," *New York Times*, April 15, 1995, http://query.nytimes.com/gst/fullpage.html?res =990CE0D9173BF936A25757C0A963958260. See also Ivo Daalder, *Getting to Dayton: The Making of America's Bosnia Policy* (Washington, D.C.: Brookings Institution, 2000).

25 Quoted in Daalder, *Getting to Dayton*, 14.

26 Richard Holbrooke, *To End a War* (New York: Random House, 1999), 66.

27 Ibid., 219.

28 Ibid., 218.

29 Carl Bildt, *Peace Journey: The Struggle for Peace in Bosnia* (London: Weidenfeld and Nicolson, 1998), 135.

30 Holbrooke, *To End a War*, 307.

31 Look at the ICTY judgment on Croatian general Ante Gotovina and others (April 15, 2011): http://www.icty.org/x/cases/gotovina/ tjug/en/110415_summary.pdf.

32 Mark Danner, "Endgame in Kosovo," *New York Review of Books*, May 6, 1999, http://www.markdanner.com/articles/show/48.

33 Brendan Simms, *Unfinest Hour: Britain and the Destruction of Bosnia* (London: Penguin Global, 2002), 342.

34 David Owen, *Balkan Odyssey* (New York: Harcourt Brace, 1995), 353, as quoted in John Ashbrook and Spencer D. Bakich, "Storming to Partition: Croatia, the United States, and Krajina in the Yugoslav War," *Small Wars and Insurgencies*, vol. 21, no. 4, 2010, 537.

35 Samuel Huntington, "The Clash of Civilisations," *Foreign Affairs*, Summer 1993.

36 Bildt, *Peace Journey*, 86. When the war erupted in Bosnia, Croatia lent direct and active support to Bosnian Croat hard-liners who sought an understanding with Bosnian Serb extremists on how to divide the country between them. In 1993 Bosnian Croat forces launched a war within a war against Bosniak (Muslim) civilians, expelling them from territory they saw as belonging to a future Greater Croatia.

37 Holbrooke, *To End a War*, 147.

38 James O'Brien, who was at Dayton as a State Department lawyer and worked on U.S. Balkan policy until 2001, later wrote that U.S. leverage was about "money, guns and indictments": Milošević was eager to see sanctions lifted; Croatia's offensive and further fighting in Bosnia changed the military balance; and ICTY indictments further increased the leverage of negotiators. See James O'Brien, "The Dayton Agreement in Bosnia: Durable Cease-Fire, Permanent Negotiation," in *Peace versus Justice: Negotiating Forward- and Backward-Looking Outcomes*, edited by William Zartman and Viktor Aleksandrovich Kremenyuk (Lanham, Md.: Rowman and Littlefield, 2005).

39 The responsibilities of the Bosnian state included only foreign policy, foreign trade policy, and customs policy; monetary policy; immigration, refugee, and asylum policy and regulation; international and inter-entity criminal law enforcement; establishment and operation of common and international communications facilities; regulation of inter-entity transportation; and air traffic control. See Annex 4 of the General Framework Agreement at the official Web site of the OHR, http://www.ohr.int/dpa/default.asp?content_id=372.

40 Holbrooke, *To End a War*, 276.

41 Ibid., 277.

42 "Transcript of President Clinton's Speech on Bosnia," CNN, November 27, 1995, http://www.cnn.com/US/9511/bosnia_speech/speech.html.

43 Daalder, *Getting to Dayton*, 144.

44 "Transcript of President Clinton's Speech on Bosnia."

45 Daalder, *Getting to Dayton*, 148.

46 Anthony Lake, Speech at George Washington University, March 1996.

47 Power, *"A Problem from Hell,"* 82.

48 Ibid., 141.

49 Ibid., 380.

50 Danner, "Endgame in Kosovo."

51 Power, *"A Problem from Hell,"* 507.

52 Ashraf Ghani, "Islam and State-Building in a Tribal Society—Afghanistan 1880–1901," *Modern Asian Studies*, vol. 12, no. 2, 1978. Ghani also set up an Institute for State Effectiveness: http://www.effectivestates.org/about.htm.

53 For a good overview of different experiences, see Richard Caplan, *International Governance of War-Torn Territories: Rule and Reconstruction* (Oxford: Oxford University Press, 2005). Eastern Slavonia

represented only the second time in the UN's history that the organization had been given a mandate to administer a disputed territory, the first one having been West New Guinea in the 1960s.

54 James Dobbins et al., *America's Role in Nation-Building—From Germany to Iraq* (Santa Monica, Calif.: RAND Corporation, 2003), 83.

55 Joint Chiefs of Staff Directive 1067, April 1945.

56 In its review of the German case, the RAND report notes as one lesson: "Dismembered and divided countries can be difficult to put back together." Dobbins et al., *America's Role in Nation-Building*, 20.

57 David M. Edelstein, *Occupational Hazards: Success and Failure in Military Occupation* (Ithaca, N.Y.: Cornell University Press, 2008), 2.

58 Ibid., 1.

59 The occupation of France after Waterloo (1815–18); the occupations of Italy, western Austria, western Germany, Japan, and the Japanese Ryukyu Islands after World War II; and the Soviet occupation of North Korea. Edelstein defines occupation as "the temporary control of a territory by a state (or group of allied states) that makes no claim to permanent sovereignty over that territory." Ibid., 3.

60 Ibid., 23.

61 After World War II, U.S. leaders did not believe that South Korea was ready for self-rule, but they did not want it to fall to communism either. There was a lot of resistance to the occupation motivated by Korean nationalism. "Koreans did not understand why they were not given complete independence soon after the arrival of American troops," the U.S. adviser at the time wrote. In 1946 there was an uprising where some twelve hundred people were killed. All U.S. troops finally withdrew in 1949. In the last year there were guerrilla uprisings throughout Korea, with an estimated eight thousand insurgents. Tens of thousands were killed. The Korean War broke out one year after the United States left. Ibid., 62–70.

62 ESI Report, "Reshaping International Priorities in Bosnia and Herzegovina—Part I—Bosnian Power Structures," October 14, 1999, http://www.esiweb.org/index.php?lang=en&id=156&document_ID=4.

63 "The Further Enlargement of the EU: Threat or Opportunity?" House of Lords EU Committee, 53rd Report of Session 2005–06, November 23, 2006, 17, http://www.publications.parliament.uk/pa/ld200506/ldselect/ldeucom/273/273.pdf.

64 Rhodri C. Williams, "Post Conflict Property Restitution and Refugee Return in Bosnia and Herzegovina: Implications for International Standard Setting and Practice," *NYU Journal of International*

Law and Politics, vol. 37, 2005, 442, 543, http://www.law.nyu.edu/ ecm_dlv3/groups/public/@nyu_law_website__journals__journal_ of_international_law_and_politics/documents/documents/ecm_ pro_059622.pdf.

65 Richard Holbrooke, "Lessons from Dayton for Iraq," *Washington Post,* April 23, 2008, http://www.washingtonpost.com/wp-dyn/con tent/article/2008/04/22/AR2008042202522.html.

66 Ibid.

67 In 2004 there were fewer murders in Bosnia than in many EU member states: 77, or 2.02 per 100,000 inhabitants, compared to 2.22 in the Czech Republic, 2.75 in Sweden, and 9.38 in Lithuania. In that year the perpetrators were identified in 91 percent of the cases in the Federation, and 96 percent of the cases in Republika Srpska. For more on Bosnian crime rates, see ESI Discussion Paper, "The Worst in Class. How the International Protectorate Hurts the European Future of Bosnia and Herzegovina," November 8, 2007, Berlin, http:// www.esiweb.org/index.php?lang=en&id=156&document_ID=98.

68 The average life expectancy in Bosnia is 72.2 years, compared to 79 in Switzerland, 72.3 in Croatia, 69.5 in Bulgaria, and 59 in Russia. Another indicator of public health are infant mortality rates. Bosnia (12 deaths per 1,000 life births) is far behind Sweden (3.2 deaths per 1,000 life births) and Austria (4.4) but close to Bulgaria (11.8) and ahead of Romania (14.9) and Turkey (27.5). See article on Rumeli Observer Blog: http://www.esiweb.org/rumeliobserver/2010/03/12/ what-is-really-wrong-with-bosnia/.

69 Rieff, *At the Point of a Gun*, 41.

70 Dobbins et al., *America's Role in Nation-Building*, xix.

71 Alex Abella, *Soldiers of Reason: The RAND Corporation and the Rise of American Empire* (New York: Mariner Books, 2009), 3. Abella refers to RAND as "the essential establishment organization."

72 RAND analysts were nothing if not ambitious. John Davis Williams teamed up with one of the most renowned mathematicians of the era, John von Neumann, to help him develop a general theory of war. Ibid., 21.

73 James Dobbins's career personified the rise of the new liberal interventionism. He has been assistant secretary of state for Europe, special adviser to the president and secretary of state for the Balkans, and special envoy for Afghanistan, Kosovo, Bosnia, Haiti, and Somalia.

74 Dobbins et al., *Beginner's Guide to Nation-Building*.

75 Ibid., 5.

76 Ibid., xxvi.

77 Ibid., 39–40.

78 Based on previous experiences, RAND calculates what a generic nation-building effort would require in a typical small and poor nation with a population of five million people and a per capita income of $500. For a light effort, it would require some 8,000 international troops, 1,000 international police, and total costs of $1.5 billion per year to succeed. A heavy operation in the same country would have to involve many times more resources, requiring at least 65,000 foreign military and 8,000 police. It would cost $15 billion per year. Consequently, "peace enforcement is appropriately a last rather than first resort, to be employed only if the stakes are great." Ibid., 102.

79 Ibid., 41.

80 James Dobbins et al., *The UN's Role in Nation-Building: From the Congo to Iraq* (Santa Monica, Calif.: RAND Corporation, 2005), 226.

81 Dobbins et al., *Beginner's Guide to Nation-Building*, 258.

82 James Dobbins, "Who Lost Iraq—Lessons from the Debacle," *Foreign Affairs*, September/October 2007.

83 Dobbins et al., *America's Role in Nation-Building*, 205.

84 Ibid., executive summary, xix.

85 Ahmed Rashid, *Descent into Chaos: The US and the Disaster in Pakistan, Afghanistan, and Central Asia* (London: Penguin Books, 2009), lv.

86 Quoted in Bob Woodward, *Obama's Wars* (New York: Simon and Schuster, 2010), 142.

87 Ibid., 143.

88 As Ahmed Rashid wrote, when the Taliban had arrived in power, they "had no interest in rebuilding the country nor the money to do so." *Descent into Chaos*, 171.

89 World Bank online data bank.

90 "Red Cross Says Afghan Conditions Worst in 30 Years," Reuters, December 15, 2010; "Security Deteriorating in Afghanistan, Life 'Untenable,' " Reuters, March 16, 2011.

91 "Winning 'Hearts and Minds' in Afghanistan: Assessing the Effectiveness of Development Aid in COIN Operations," Report on Wilton Park Conference 1022, March 11–14, 2010; Andrew Wilder, "Hearing on U.S. Aid to Pakistan: Planning and Accountability, Testimony to House Committee on Oversight and Government

Reform," Subcommittee on National Security and Foreign Affairs, December 9, 2009.

92 Dobbins et al., *America's Role in Nation-Building*, xxv.

93 Personal interview with Minna Jarvenpaa, January 2011.

94 Dobbins et al., *Beginner's Guide to Nation Building*, xviii.

95 "Defense Science Board 2004 Summer Study on Transition to and from Hostilities," U.S. Department of Defense, December 2004, viii.

96 The U.S. Army/Marine Corps, *Counterinsurgency Field Manual* (Chicago: University of Chicago Press, 2007), 23.

97 All quotes from ibid.

98 Sarah Sewall, Introduction to the University of Chicago Press Edition, in ibid., xxxii.

99 Ibid., 68.

100 John C. Donnell and others, "Viet Cong Motivation and Morale in 1964: A Preliminary Report," RAND Corporation, Santa Monica, Calif., March 1965, http://www.rand.org/pubs/research_memoranda/2006/RM4507.3.pdf.

101 In fact, RAND analysts soon divided into anti- and pro-war factions. Today, looking back at U.S. experiences in nation-building, RAND ignored the Vietnam experience altogether in its case studies.

102 Charles Wolf, "Insurgency and Counterinsurgency: New Myths and Old Realities," RAND Corporation, Santa Monica, Calif., July 1965, 9, http://www.rand.org/pubs/papers/2005/P3132-1.pdf.

103 The writer Max Boot refers to examples of what he calls "progressive US imperialism in the Caribbean, Central America, and the Pacific" as case studies of the American liberal empire in action. He considers the Philippines the "greatest success" of this period of U.S.-led nation-building. Boot, "Neither New nor Nefarious."

104 Bernard Crick, *In Defence of Politics* (London: Continuum International, 2000), 114.

105 Bildt, *Peace Journey*, 294.

106 Paddy Ashdown, "Broken Communities, Shattered Lives: Winning the Savage War of Peace," Speech to the International Rescue Committee (IRC), London, June 20, 2003, http://www.ohr.int/ohr-dept/presso/presssp/default.asp?content_id=30130.

107 Bildt, *Peace Journey*, 203.

108 For more on the UN vetting process, see ESI Report, "On Mount Olympus: How the UN Violated Human Rights in Bosnia and Herzegovina, and Why Nothing Has Been Done to Correct It," February 10,

2007, http://www.esiweb.org/index.php?lang=en&id=156&document_ID=84.

109 Bildt, *Peace Journey*, 6.

110 Matthew Parish, *A Free City in the Balkans: Reconstructing a Divided Society in Bosnia* (London: I. B. Tauris, 2009), 198.

111 Henry L. Clarke, "Brčko District: An Example of Progress in the Basic Reforms in Bosnia and Herzegovina," Meeting Report 293 at the Wilson Center, noon discussion on February 4, 2004.

112 Michael Karnavas, "Creating the Legal Framework of the Brčko District of Bosnia and Herzegovina: A Model for the Region and Other Postconflict Countries,"*American Journal of International Law*, vol. 97, no. 1, January 2003.

113 James Mill is quoted in Gerald Knaus and Felix Martin, "Travails of the European Raj," *Journal of Democracy*, vol. 14, no. 3, July 2003, http://www.journalofdemocracy.org/articles/gratis/KnausandMartin.pdf.

114 Clarke, "Brčko District."

115 Mark Landler, "Rare Bosnia Success Story, Thanks to U.S. Viceroy," *New York Times*, June 17, 2003, http://www.nytimes.com/2003/06/17/international/europe/17BOSN.html.

116 Ibid.

117 As Ashdown put it, "We would grab the initiative for our state-building programme at the start." Paddy Ashdown, *Swords and Ploughshares: Bringing Peace to the 21st Century* (London: Weidenfeld and Nicolson, 2007), 226.

118 Ashdown, "Broken Communities, Shattered Lives."

119 Thomas Carothers writes that normally "the rule of law can be defined as a system in which the laws are public knowledge, are clear in meaning, and apply equally to everyone" and where "anyone accused of a crime has the right to a fair, prompt hearing." This was not the case in an international protectorate where all decisions by either the supervisor in Brčko or the High Representative in Sarajevo could not be appealed, and where foreigners with diplomatic immunity held ultimate authority. See Thomas Carothers, ed., *Promoting the Rule of Law Abroad: In Search of Knowledge* (Washington, D.C.: Carnegie Endowment for International Peace, 2006), 4.

120 Ashdown, *Swords and Ploughshares*, 88.

121 Ibid., 87.

122 Ibid., 134.

123 Ibid., 78.

124 Ibid., 146.

125 Ashdown, "Broken Communities, Shattered Lives" (emphasis added).

126 Nick Hawton, "Raj Claims Hit Home," Institute for War and Peace Reporting, Balkan Crisis Report 447, 2003, http://h-net.msu.edu/cgi-bin/logbrowse.pl?trx=vx&list=h-genocide&month=0307&week=d&msg=3AFglTzC2TOTuomzwXsoEg&user=&pw=. For the article, see Knaus and Martin, "Travails of the European Raj."

127 Ashdown made this statement in response to an open letter that Marcus Cox and I sent him on July 16, 2003, "After the Bonn Powers." For his full response, see Hawton, "Raj Claims Hit Home."

128 Nick Hawton, "High Representative Insists He Will Use His Powers to See the Job Through," Institute of War and Peace Reporting, September 2005, http://groups.yahoo.com/group/balkanhr/message/5764.

129 L. Paul Bremer, "Facts for Feith," *National Review Online*, March 19, 2008.

130 The Council of Europe had noted already in March 2002, discussing OHR plans for judicial reforms in Bosnia, that it was inappropriate "to remove from office judges already enjoying life tenure although no professional misconduct of the individual judge can be established." It continued, "If the international community is not willing to abide by its own principles when faced by major difficulties, what can we expect from local politicians?" Quoted in Knaus and Martin, "Travails of the European Raj."

131 John Stuart Mill, *Considerations on Representative Government*, 1861, http://www.constitution.org/jsm/rep_gov.htm.

132 Robert Cooper, *The Breaking of Nations: Order and Chaos in the Twenty-First Century* (London: Atlantic Books, 2003), 73.

133 Ferguson, *Empire*, 371.

134 Ibid., 375.

135 Ibid., 184.

136 Paul Bremer, *My Year in Iraq: The Struggle to Build a Future of Hope* (New York: Threshold Editions, 2006).

137 Rajiv Chandrasekaran, *Imperial Life in the Emerald City: Inside Baghdad's Green Zone* (London: Bloomsbury, 2008), 68–69.

138 Ibid., 321.

139 James Dobbins et al., *Occupying Iraq: A History of the Coalition Provisional Authority* (Santa Monica, Calif.: RAND Corporation, 2009), xxxi–xxxii.

140 Ibid., xxxiii.

141 The first use of the dismissal powers by OHR targeted individuals in the Croat parts of the country in 1998. Nowhere did it lead to real improvements. One hard-line mayor of Stolac was dismissed in the spring of 1998; in November 1999 his successor was dismissed as well, owing to lack of progress. A Croat deputy mayor in Drvar, Drago Tokmakcija, was dismissed in the spring of 1998, again in February 1999 (from his HDZ party post), and a third time in November 1999 (from his post in the cantonal privatization agency); throughout this period he remained the local strongman in his area. What changed things in hard-line areas of Herzegovina was not the use of the Bonn powers but the suspension of political and financial support from neighoring Croatia, following the death of Croatian President Franjo Tudjman in late 1999.

142 Ashdown, "Broken Communities, Shattered Lives."

143 Serbs started construction of an orthodox church in a Bosniak area of Brčko (Meraje) in 1997 as a provocation. An order issued by the supervisor to stop this was ignored, and the church was completed in violation of his order. Supervisor Farrand "judged that had he used the US army to prevent the church's construction, the resulting civil unrest would have set back the broader project of supervision." Parish, *Free City in the Balkans*, 85. In August 1997 there were also violent riots in Brčko town.

144 Ashdown, "Broken Communities, Shattered Lives."

145 "Speech by High Representative Valentin Inzko to the UN Security Council," Office of the High Representative and EU Special Representative, May 9, 2011, http://www.ohr.int/ohr-dept/presso/presssp/default.asp?content_id=46014.

146 Benjamin H. Friedman, Harvey M. Sapolsky, and Christopher Preble, "Learning the Right Lessons from Iraq," Cato Institute, Policy Analysis no. 610, February 13, 2008, 2.

147 "The National Security Strategy of the United States of America," September 2002, http://www.au.af.mil/au/awc/awcgate/nss/nss_sep2002.pdf.

148 Sebastian Mallaby, "The Reluctant Imperialist: Terrorism, Failed States, and the Case for American Empire," *Foreign Affairs*, vol. 81, no. 2, March–April 2002, 6.

149 Ignatieff, *Empire Lite*, 3.

150 David Kilcullen, *The Accidental Guerilla: Fighting Small Wars in the Midst of a Big One* (Oxford: Oxford University Press, 2009), 12.

151 Justin Logan and Christopher Preble, "Washington's Newest Bogey-

man: Debunking the Fear of Failed States," *Strategic Studies Quarterly*, Summer 2010. See also Justin Logan and Christopher Preble, "Failed States and Flawed Logic: The Case against a Standing Nation-Building Office," Cato Institute, Policy Analysis no. 560, January 11, 2006.

152 Ivan Eland, "The Empire Strikes Out: The 'New Imperialism' and Its Fatal Flaws," Cato Institute, Policy Analysis no. 459, November 26, 2002, 19.

153 Malou Innocent and Ted Galen Carpenter, "Escaping the 'Graveyard of Empires': A Strategy to Exit Afghanistan," Cato Institute, White Paper, September 14, 2009, 6.

154 Logan and Preble, "Washington's Newest Bogeyman."

155 Eland, "Empire Strikes Out," 11.

156 Logan and Preble, "Washington's Newest Bogeyman."

157 Innocent and Carpenter, "Escaping the 'Graveyard of Empires,' " 3.

158 Friedman et al., "Learning the Right Lessons from Iraq," 9.

159 Ibid., 8.

160 Ibid., 11.

161 Thomas Johnson, "Tribal Politics: Why We Must Understand the Human Terrain," *Vanguard*, 2008, http://www.vanguardcanada.com /AfghanTribalPoliticsJohnson.

162 Ted Galen Carpenter, "Learning from Our Mistakes: Nation-Building Follies and Afghanistan," *Big Peace*, July 10, 2010.

163 Ted Galen Carpenter, "Cato Institute Foreign Policy Briefing No. 19: Foreign Policy Masochism: The Campaign for U.S. Intervention in Yugoslavia," Cato Institute, Foreign Policy Briefing, July 1, 1992, http://www.cato.org/pubs/fpbriefs/fpb019.pdf.

164 Ted Galen Carpenter, "Holbrooke Horror: The U.S. Peace Plan for Bosnia," Cato Institute, Foreign Policy Briefing no. 36, October 27, 1995, http://www.cato.org/pub_display.php?pub_id=1562.

165 Gary Dempsey, "Rethinking the Dayton Agreement: Bosnia Three Years Later," Cato Institute, Policy Analysis no. 327, December 14, 1998, http://www.cato.org/pubs/pas/pa327.pdf, quoting John Mearsheimer, "The Only Exit from Bosnia," *New York Times*, October 7, 1997.

166 Carpenter, "Learning from Our Mistakes."

167 Paddy Ashdown and Richard Holbrooke, "A Bosnian Powder Keg," *Guardian* (UK), October 22, 2008, http://www.guardian.co.uk/ commentisfree/2008/oct/22/ashdown-holbrooke-bosnia-balkan-day ton/print. Soon other articles appeared with a similar message. The "nationalist passions that brought war to the Balkan state in 1992

are reemerging" (see http://www.guardian.co.uk/world/2009/may/03/bosnia-war-nationalism-poor-economy); "the country now stands on the brink of collapse" (Patrice C. McMahon and Jon Western, "The Death of Dayton: How to Stop Bosnia from Falling Apart," *Foreign Affairs*, September/October 2009); an ongoing crisis "could unravel the United States-brokered Dayton accords of 1995" (Dan Bilefsky, "Tensions Rise in Fragile Bosnia as Country's Serbs Threaten to Seek Independence," *New York Times*, February 26, 2009).

168 Richard Holbrooke, "Lessons from Dayton for Iraq," *Washington Post*, April 23, 2008, http://www.washingtonpost.com/wp-dyn/content/article/2008/04/22/AR2008042202522.html.

169 "Speech by High Representative Valentin Inzko to the UN Security Council."

170 Paddy Ashdown, "Europe Needs a Wake-up Call: Bosnia Is on the Edge Again," *Guardian* (UK), July 27, 2008, http://www.guardian.co.uk/commentisfree/2008/jul/27/serbia.balkans.

171 "World News Briefs; NATO Troops Shore Up New Bosnia Premier," *New York Times*, July 19, 1998, http://www.nytimes.com/1998/01/19/world/world-news-briefs-nato-troops-shore-up-new-bosnia-premier.html?src=pm.

172 "World News Briefs; Bosnian Serb Deputies Elect a Moderate," *New York Times*, January 18, 1998, http://www.nytimes.com/1998/01/18/world/world-news-briefs-bosnian-serb-deputies-elect-a-moderate.html?src=pm.

173 Ibid.

174 "Richard Holbrooke Brands Bosnian Serb Nationalist Party 'Nazis' and Praises Former Democractic Pres. Izetbegovic," October 8, 2003, http://www.oocities.com/famous_bosniaks/english/nazis.html.

175 Ashdown, "Europe Needs a Wake-up Call."

176 Parish, *Free City in the Balkans*, xiii–1.

177 Ibid., 159.

178 Ibid., 134.

179 Ibid., 221.

180 Ibid., 1.

181 Carpenter, "Holbrooke Horror."

182 Dempsey, "Rethinking the Dayton Agreement," quoting Mearsheimer.

183 Parish, *Free City in the Balkans*, 162–63.

184 Carpenter, "Holbrooke Horror."

185 Dempsey, "Rethinking the Dayton Agreement."

186 Nicolo Machiavelli, *Discourses*, Sect. 1.4.

187 Ashdown, "Broken Communities, Shattered Lives."

188 Ashdown, *Swords and Ploughshares*, 220.

189 "Burke's Speech on Conciliation with America," http://burke.clas sic-authors.net/ConciliationAmerica/.

190 United Nations General Assembly, UN Resolution on "Ethnic Cleansing" and Racial Hatred, A/RES/47/80, 89th Plenary Meeting, December 16, 1992, http://www.un.org/documents/ga/res/47/a47r080.htm.

191 ESI Report, "The Lausanne Principle," June 7, 2004, http://unpan1.un.org/intradoc/groups/public/documents/UNTC/UNPAN016678.pdf.

192 Holbrooke, *To End a War*, 133.

193 ESI Report, "A Bosnian Fortress," December 19, 2007, 6, http://www.esiweb.org/index.php?lang=en&id=156&document_ID=100.

194 In the municipality of Zvornik, some Bosniak returnees managed to secretly return to their homes in remote villages on territory belonging to the Bosnian Serb entity in 1996. When they were discovered, not only were they attacked and their houses burned down (again) by a Serb mob, but IFOR troops insisted on escorting them back to the Federation, while keeping the main road from the Bosniak-Croat entity to the abandoned villages in Zvornik closed for the next three years. Carl Dahlman and Gerard Toal, "Broken Bosnia: The Localized Geopolitics of Displacement and Return in Two Bosnian Places," *Annals of the Association of American Geographers*, 2005. Here the two look at return to Jajce and Zvornik.

195 "All refugees and displaced persons," the constitution reads, "have the right freely to return to their homes of origin . . . to have restored to them property of which they were deprived in the course of hostilities since 1991 and to be compensated for any such property that cannot be restored to them." Bosnian Constitution Article II: Human Rights and Fundamental Freedoms, paragraph 5, http://www.ccbh.ba/public/down/USTAV_BOSNE_I_HERCE GOVINE_engl.pdf.

196 See especially International Crisis Group, "Minority Return or Mass Relocation," Europe Report no. 33, May 14, 1998.

197 ESI, "Bosnian Fortress," 7.

198 Steven Erlanger, "How Bosnia Policy Set Stage for Albright-Cohen Conflict," *New York Times*, June 12, 1997.

199 Parish, *Free City in the Balkans*, 17.

200 Dahlman and Toal, "Broken Bosnia," 456.

201 Ibid.

202 Mike O'Connor, "For US Troops, Bosnia Seems to Be Healthy Place," *New York Times*, July 3, 1996.

203 Colin Woodard, "Backup Plan in Bosnia: US Equip and Train," *Christian Science Monitor*, September 18, 1996.

204 Ibid.

205 Pentagon Report from 1996, analyzing Bosnian military needs, is quoted in Mark Thompson, "Bosnia: Generals for Hire," *Time*, June 15, 1996, http://www.time.com/time/magazine/article/0,9171,983949,00.html.

206 Thompson, "Bosnia: Generals for Hire."

207 Lauren Van Metre and Burcu Akan, "Special Report, Dayton Implementation: The Train and Equip Program," U.S. Institute of Peace, September 1997.

208 Bildt, *Peace Journey*, 219.

209 Ibid., 239.

210 Ibid., 217.

211 Steven Erlanger, "Albright in Bosnia Urging More Reconcilation Efforts," *New York Times*, August 31, 1998, http://www.nytimes.com/1998/08/31/world/albright-in-bosnia-urging-more-reconcilation-efforts.html?pagewanted=all&src=pm.

212 Isabelle Wesselingh and Arnaud Vaulerin, *Raw Memory: Prijedor, Laboratory of Ethnic Cleansing* (London: Saqi Books, 2005), 91.

213 Ibid., 91.

214 Ibid., 99.

215 Williams, "Post Conflict Property Restitution and Refugee Return in Bosnia and Herzegovina."

216 Wesselingh and Vaulerin, *Raw Memory*, 115.

217 Power, *"A Problem from Hell,"* 492.

218 In a 2004 article in the *New York Review of Books*, Tim Judah wrote about the changes he saw in Kozarac, a town near Prijedor that had been thoroughly "cleansed" of all non-Serbs in 1992. By 2004, Judah wrote, "half the original population [had] returned." Tim Judah, "The Fog of Justice," *New York Review of Books*, January 15, 2004, http://www.nybooks.com/articles/archives/2004/jan/15/the-fog-of-justice/.

219 Diana Orentlicher, *That Someone Guilty Be Punished: The Impact of the ICTY in Bosnia* (New York: Open Society Institute, International Center for Transitional Justice, 2010), 87.

220 Paul Hockenos, *Homeland Calling* (Ithaca, N.Y.: Cornell University Press, 2003), 19.

221 Sabina Arslanagic, "Josipovic Delivers Unprecedented Apology to

Bosnia," *BalkanInsight*, April 14, 2010, http://www.balkaninsight
.com/en/article/josipovic-delivers-unprecedented-apology-to-bosnia.

222 "The Cost of Justice," UN ICTY, http://www.icty.org/sid/325.

223 Evans, *Responsibility to Protect*, 100.

224 David Wippman, "The Costs of International Justice," *American Journal of International Law*, vol. 100, 2006, 862. Wippman compares the average cost of the International Criminal Tribunal for the Former Yugoslavia (ICTY) and that of federal trials on a per-day basis.

225 James Clarke, "Was the Bloody Sunday Report Value for Money?" BBC, June 14, 2010, http://www.bbc.co.uk/news/10292828.

226 Gary J. Bass, *Freedom's Battle: The Origins of Humanitarian Intervention* (New York: Vintage Books, 2009), 365.

227 Annan, "Intervention."

228 Simms, *Unfinest Hour*, 7.

229 Ibid., 23.

230 Evans, *Responsibility to Protect*, 63.

231 Josef Joffe, "Ending American Exceptionalism," *New York Times*, March 30, 2011.

232 Charles Krauthammer, "Professor Obama Goes to War: President's Deep Discomfort with U.S. Power Hurts Our Chances in Libya," *New York Daily News*, March 25, 2011.